FRAME OF GOVERNMENT

A Book of Documents

Frame of

HENRY WILKINSON BRAGDON

SAMUEL P. MC CUTCHEN

STUART GERRY BROWN

Government

The Macmillan Company, New York

Macmillan New York, London

To the Reader

The body of this book contains four different kinds of text:

1. Introductory sections giving the historical background.

2. The texts, sometimes abbreviated, of major documents, printed on left-hand pages.

3. General explanations of the leading ideas and developments, on the top right-hand pages facing the texts.

4. Explanatory notes, giving information about details, on the lower right-hand pages facing the texts.

One way to read this book systematically is as follows:

1. Read the introductory material to a document.

2. Read right through the document, rather rapidly, simply to get the over-all sense of what it is about.

3. Read, section by section, the general discussion on the top right-hand pages, referring back constantly to the document itself.

4. Read the explanatory notes, again referring to the actual texts on the left-hand pages.

5. Go through the document again, thinking of what each section means, referring again, if necessary, to the explanatory material.

No book of this size can give all the answers. The annotated bibliography at the back of the book should prove helpful to those who want to find out more.

© The Macmillan Company 1962

The Macmillan Company, New York
Collier-Macmillan Canada, Ltd., Galt, Ontario
Divisions of The Crowell-Collier Publishing Company

PRINTED IN THE UNITED STATES OF AMERICA

Foreword

The reexamination of those documents which set forth the rules and express the purposes of our democratic republic is an exercise often advocated by pundits but, alas, I fear not often taken up by us the citizens—or, perhaps, by the pundits! How many of us have ever reread a Supreme Court opinion of John Marshall? Or the Northwest Ordinance? The Communists have their sacred texts—the writings of Marx, Engels, Lenin—upon which they bring up their children, modern revelation, so they believe, which prophesies the inevitable course of history. Study these writings, the Communists tell each other, and you will know the truth. If experience clashes with expectation, so much the worse for experience. There may be some comfort in such dogmatism. But it is a comfort free men must and do deny themselves. We Americans do indeed revere some of the expressions of our Founding Fathers, but there are no sacred texts of democracy. By its nature free government is dynamic and follows no prescribed and inevitable course. There are, nevertheless, landmarks of democracy, and there are controlling principles written down in public papers. These documents form a kind of frame of government within which the substance of our policy and of our politics lives and moves and has its being. I salute the editors of this book for their efforts—highly successful, it seems to me—to bring these documents conveniently together, to display them in their original context, and to show in a lucid and arresting manner how their meaning has been altered by the years, and how they have altered the meaning of the years. I hope my fellow citizens will be reminded by these pages, as I have been reminded, both of the ways in which we Americans keep our freedoms viable and the immense privilege it is to enjoy them.

June, 1962   ADLAI E. STEVENSON

Introduction

WE ARE accustomed to thinking of the United States as a young nation. Surely it has no such long history as France or Great Britain, China or India. It is not yet two hundred years—less than three normal lifetimes—since the outbreak of the Revolutionary War.

Yet the United States of America may be regarded as the oldest modern nation. By this is meant that the United States was the first great country to try to put into practice the ideas that government exists for the people and is based on the people's consent. Today all the major countries in the world attempt to practice these principles or at least pay lip service to them—even the Communist dictatorships profess to be "people's democracies."

While the basic notions of government by and for the people are universally attractive, democracy is in fact a difficult form of government. It demands from those who try to practice it the virtues of unselfishness, tolerance, self-restraint, and loyalty. Loyalty to what? To a leader? No. To a party, to the state? Only partly. To the country, to the flag? Yes, certainly, but that is not enough. Successful democracy demands devotion to and understanding of certain principles and methods of conducting human relationships. It was lack of this devotion and understanding that made it possible for the enemy to brainwash some American prisoners in the Korean War. It is lack of this devotion and understanding that accounts for many of the present ills of our society. If we are serious about winning the Cold War, we must devote as serious study to our political system and the philosophy behind it as the Communists devote to the works of Marx and Lenin, because the Cold War is a struggle for the minds of men.

Most of the basic ideas as well as the structure of American government are set forth in documents written in the eighteenth century and applied and interpreted by later Supreme Court opinions. An understanding of these basic documents and of their later interpretations is of the greatest importance to all American citizens. Indeed, it is as important for an American citizen to know these texts as for a Muslim to know the Koran, or for a Christian to know the Bible. But they are not easy reading. No one but a scholar would have the Northwest Ordinance or a collection of legal decisions on his bedside table. Few people even know how to take hold of these documents when they try. It is the purpose of this little book to provide handles. We have called it *Frame of Government* because we have selected only those basic documents which empower, guide, and limit our government today.

The authors have given all the documents headings and subheadings to reveal their structure and to lead the reader into them. Some texts have been cut down or excerpted. The meanings of terms and larger concepts are explained on facing pages. Above all, this book reveals that these great texts are not remote abstractions. They originated, all of them, in human needs and human struggles. They were hammered out, all of them, in the white heat of political controversy. Our daily lives are conditioned by them more than we realize. Our future happiness and safety, our future dignity and worth as individuals, our future greatness as a nation and an influence in the world are all in some degree dependent upon how well Americans understand their great political heritage.

What Jefferson said at the close of his First Inaugural Address is as true today as in 1801:

These principles form the bright constellation which has gone before us and guided our steps through an age of revolution and reformation. The wisdom of our sages and the blood of our heroes have been devoted to their attainment. They should be the creed of our political faith, the text of civic instruction, the touchstone by which to try the services of those we trust; and should we wander from them in moments of error or of alarm, let us hasten to retrace our steps and to regain the road which alone leads to peace, liberty, and safety.

The authors desire to express their gratitude to Mr. Colin Irving, of the Phillips Exeter Academy, who read the entire manuscript with care and imagination; and to Hon. Francis T. P. Plimpton, Deputy United States Representative to the United Nations, who read the Appendix on the U.N. Charter and made valuable suggestions.

Contents

[DOCUMENTS APPEAR ON EVEN NUMBERED PAGES]

Maps

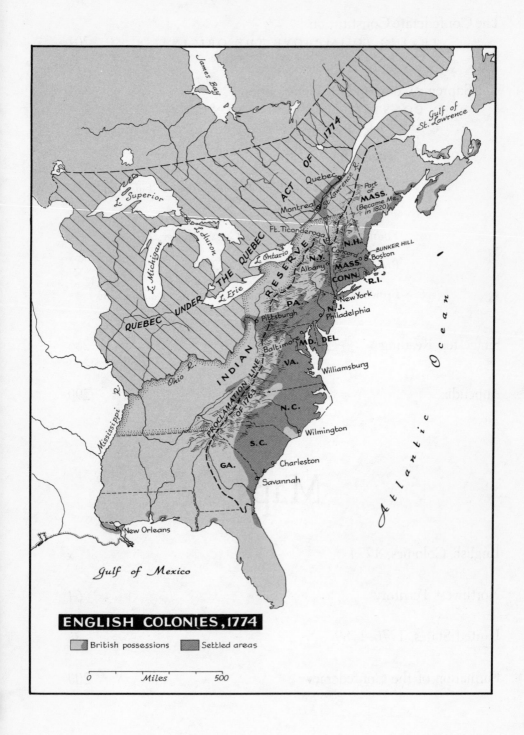

James Bay

Gulf of
St. Lawrence

ACT OF 1774

L. Superior

Quebec

Montreal

St. Lawrence R.

Port
of
MASS.
(Became Me.
in 1820)

L. Michigan

L. Huron

Ft. Ticonderoga

N.H.

L. Ontario

RESERVE

Concord

BUNKER HILL

Boston

QUEBEC UNDER THE

Albany

N.Y.

MASS.

L. Erie

CONN.

R.I.

QUEBEC

PA.

New York

Pittsburgh

N.J.

Ohio R.

Philadelphia

INDIAN

Baltimore

MD. DEL.

VA.

Mississippi R.

Williamsburg

PROCLAMATION LINE OF 1763

N.C.

Wilmington

S.C.

GA.

Charleston

Savannah

New Orleans

Gulf of Mexico

Atlantic Ocean

ENGLISH COLONIES, 1774

British possessions   Settled areas

0   Miles   500

The Declaration
of Independence

THE NATURAL RIGHTS OF MAN

WHEN THE embattled farmers at Concord Bridge fired the shot heard around the world, they had no idea of independence from Great Britain. Although arrayed against British redcoats in the king's service, they regarded themselves as loyal and loving subjects of His Britannic Majesty, George III. They were simply defending their rights as Englishmen, and blamed recent invasions of these rights on Parliament, not on the monarch.

Even after the skirmishes at Lexington and Concord proved to be but a prelude to full scale warfare, American patriots continued to profess loyalty to the crown, and for a time the chaplains in the Continental Army led the troops in daily prayer for the king's health. In July, 1775, the Continental Congress petitioned George III for reconciliation in reverential terms. In August a Maryland clergyman wrote to a friend in England, "The King has not more affectionate and loyal subjects in any part of his dominions than the Americans." In November the Pennsylvania Assembly instructed its representatives in Congress: "We strictly enjoin you, that you in behalf of this Colony, dissent from, and utterly reject, any propositions, should such be made, that may cause or lead to a separation from our Mother Country. . . ."

But the war with Britain became increasingly bitter, and it became apparent that George III was personally committed to crushing the rebellion. He refused even to receive the conciliatory "Olive Branch Petition" that the Congress had addressed to him. Instead, he issued a proclamation denouncing the rebellion in violent terms and threatening "condign punishment" for the "wicked and desperate persons" who had led the Americans into treason. Even so, loyalty to George III died hard. The colonists had been brought up from infancy to love and respect their king as they loved and respected their parents. The monarch was as much a symbol to be revered as the stars and stripes today. A subject of King George would no more speak ill of him than a loyal American would today use the flag as a dish towel.

Then in January, 1776, appeared the pamphlet *Common Sense*, written by a disaffected Englishman, Tom Paine, recently come to America. Paine rang changes on the theme, " 'Tis time to part." He painted in glowing terms the future of an *independent* America as an asylum of liberty, a beacon of progress. He argued that Americans had nothing to gain, and a lot to lose, by continuing the connection with Britain. He was perhaps most persuasive when he attacked monarchy in general and George III in particular. Only by means of "history stuffed with fables" had gullible people come to believe in the institution of monarchy. A king was apt to be "the principal ruffian of some restless gang," and George III, "the sullen tempered Pharaoh of England," was one of the worst of his breed. Paine's vigorous pamphlet had an astonishing circulation and undoubtedly convinced many Americans that the time had come to break away. His denunciation of "the royal brute of Great Britain" sounded all the more persuasive when it was learned that George III had placed the colonies entirely outside his protection and was hiring thousands of German mercenaries to crush the Americans. Meanwhile his agents in this country were enlisting Indian allies to harass the frontier, and the royal governor of Virginia was calling on slaves to rise against their masters. Such actions were surely not those of a benevolent father of his people, but those of an implacable foe.

In addition to the radical change in feeling against the monarch, there were strong practical arguments for independence. American trade with Britain had entirely ceased, and there was a desperate need for new markets and sources of supply. To fight England the Americans needed foreign aid. Only as independent states could they arrange trade agreements, and only when representing an independent America could the Congress make alliances with Britain's rivals, France and Spain. Finally, government had broken down in the colonies because British officials were no longer obeyed. The theoretical basis of government and law had also broken down. All colonial governments were legally based on grants of power by the British crown; all law supposedly represented the royal will; all officials were the king's agents. Once the Americans realized they were actually fighting the British crown and not merely Parliament, it was necessary to set up government on a new principle. On May 15, 1776, the Continental Congress resolved that "the exercise of every kind of authority under the said Crown should be totally suppressed, and all the powers of government exerted, under the authority of the people of the colonies. . . ." And on June 7 Richard Henry Lee, head of the Virginia delegation, rose in Congress to propose that the colonies ought to be "free and equal states."

Four days after Lee's resolution was presented, a committee of five, with Thomas Jefferson of Virginia as chairman, was appointed to draw up a statement justifying such action. There matters stood for three weeks because leaders of the middle colonies—New York, New Jersey, Pennsylvania, Delaware and Maryland—were not ready to burn their bridges, but still hoped for some sort of reconciliation.

Events were moving fast, however. Throughout the middle colonies the "Patriots" who demanded independence were more active and better organized than the "Loyalists" who remained true to the king. Late in June the Patriots were able either to get new assemblies elected in the middle colonies or to persuade the existing assemblies to withdraw their opposition to a clean break with England. Then at the end of June an immense British fleet appeared at the mouth of New York Harbor and started to land 30,000 troops under the command of General William Howe. Instead of frightening the Americans, General Howe's force stiffened their will to resist and pushed some last waverers toward the idea that only an independent America could summon the resources to defeat Britain's armies. On July 2, therefore, the Continental Congress approved Lee's resolution and voted to declare independence, only New York abstaining.

Meanwhile Jefferson had been at work. His assignment was not considered of vital importance in a body of men working night and day at the great task of directing a war, and two members of his committee never appeared. The two others, John Adams and Benjamin Franklin, were quite willing to leave to Jefferson the task of explaining America's case.

In composing the Declaration Jefferson did not write anything especially new. He simply pieced together and put into his own words a brief statement of the theoretical right of revolution, a long list of colonial grievances, and the substance of Lee's resolution. It was designed to give Americans a new resolve to fight for their liberties, to weaken Britain by creating sympathy for the American cause, and to arouse enthusiasm in Europe for the Revolution. Franklin and Adams made a few verbal changes, and Congress made several more before voting to accept it on July 4, 1776.

The Declaration appears to have been successful in its immediate purposes. Printed copies were issued the very night of July 4, and fast-riding messengers immediately carried them the length and breadth of the thirteen states. As soon as the electrifying news arrived, the Patriots organized celebrations. To the accompaniment of fife and drum, salutes of musketry and cannon, bonfires, peals of church bells, and processions, the Declaration was read to cheering crowds. Many of the celebrations lasted well into the evening, with the drinking of toasts to the states, to the new union, to the Congress, to the Continental Army, to George Washington, along with damnation for George III, and for Tories a perpetual itching without the satisfaction of scratching.

Everywhere the king's picture was ripped down and often committed to the flames. In Savannah, Georgia, a solemn funeral procession attended by "a greater number of people than ever appeared on any occasion before in this Province" carried an effigy of George III to a public place and buried it. In New York City an equestrian statue of the king, erected by grateful subjects in 1770, was pulled down and melted into musket balls.

Although when it was written it may have seemed a revolutionary manifesto, as ephemeral as a party platform or a campaign speech, the Declaration has turned out to be one of the two or three most enduring and influential documents of modern times. Ever since it was published it has been a force for democracy, freedom, and individual rights both in this country and abroad. When Lafayette went back to France after the Revolutionary War, he hung a copy of the Declaration in a niche in his dining room, with an empty niche alongside awaiting a similar French declaration of human rights. When the Spanish-American colonies revolted in the nineteenth century, they drew up declarations of independence often modeled on ours. In America itself the Declaration has kept men constantly aware of the idea of equal rights and equal opportunities. It has operated at various times in our history toward ending Negro slavery, enlarging the number of voters, equalizing job opportunities, and extending educational opportunity. Abraham Lincoln once said that he never had a political idea that did not spring from it.

To the Reader ∽

In studying the following pages on the Declaration of Independence the reader should note:

1. *The various divisions of the document* as well as the *headings, subheadings, and numbering of grievances* have been inserted by the authors of this book; they are to help the reader grasp the structure and contents of the document.

2. *Analysis of general features* of the Declaration is placed at the top of the right-hand pages.

3. *Explanatory notes on particular passages or features* are printed in the lower part of right-hand pages.

*The Declaration
of Independence*

❧

IN CONGRESS, JULY 4, 1776

The Unanimous Declaration of the
Thirteen United States of America.

PURPOSE

WHEN, in the course of human events, it
becomes necessary for one people to dissolve the political bands which have connected
them with another, and to assume, among the
powers of the earth, the separate and equal station to which the laws of nature and of nature's
God entitle them, a decent respect to the opinions of mankind requires that they should declare
the causes which impel them to the separation.

Purpose

This opening paragraph makes clear that the purpose of the Declaration of Independence was to sway public opinion on both sides of the Atlantic. It was frankly and openly a piece of propaganda, written to justify an action already taken and to win support for it.

The Declaration forced American citizens to stand up and be counted. A time of indecision was over. Patriot leaders no longer had an avenue of retreat. "We must all hang together now," said Benjamin Franklin, "or most assuredly we shall all hang separately." Either you were for independence and loyal to the Congress and the new state governments, or you were opposed.

The Declaration also had an impact in Europe. It was published in several British newspapers and bitterly attacked. It also found defenders, especially since the action of George III in hiring Hessian troops was widely unpopular and his attempt to crush America was feared because it might establish a precedent for upsetting English liberties at home. In France and throughout Western Europe generally, the Declaration was especially admired by the educated middle class and by all who wanted to make government less arbitrary and more responsive to the people's will.

Ever since it was composed, the Declaration of Independence has continued to appeal to the beliefs of mankind. Abroad, it has inspired all who have wanted to throw off the yoke of colonial rulers, whether the Latin American republics early in the nineteenth century or India in the twentieth. At home, it has been a constant stimulus toward greater equality, greater liberty, and wider participation in government. "The history of American democracy," it has been said, "is a gradual realization, too slow for some, and too rapid for others, of the implications of the Declaration of Independence."

Explanatory Notes

"The Unanimous Declaration of the Thirteen United States of America." As of July 4, support for the Declaration was not unanimous, since the New York delegation was still awaiting instructions from home and therefore did not join the other states in voting for independence until July 9.

". . . one people. . . ." Jefferson originally wrote "a people." The adjective "one" is stronger, since it suggests that the colonists are united in support of their cause. "One people" also suggests that although the different states were separate sovereignties, they were also a nation. Although Jefferson referred to Virginia as "my country," he was equally devoted to the union, and, like his fellow Virginian George Washington, "rejoiced in the greater name of American."

BASIC PRINCIPLES

We hold these truths to be self-evident:—That all men are created equal; that they are endowed by their Creator with certain unalienable rights; that among these are life, liberty, and the pursuit of happiness. That, to secure these rights, governments are instituted among men, deriving their just powers from the consent of the governed; that, whenever any form of government becomes destructive of these ends, it is the right of the people to alter or to abolish it, and to institute a new government, laying its foundation on such principles, and organizing its powers in such form, as to them shall seem most likely to effect their safety and happiness. Prudence, indeed, will dictate, that governments long established should not be changed for light and transient causes; and accordingly all experience hath shown that mankind are more disposed to suffer while evils are sufferable, than to right themselves by abolishing the forms to which they are accustomed.

Basic Principles

This portion of the Declaration of Independence is the heart of the document. It is universal in its application. The Americans are no longer asserting their peculiar rights as Englishmen, since they had ceased to be Englishmen, but their universal rights as human beings.

The main argument in this passage is taken directly from John Locke's *Second Treatise of Civil Government* (1690), written to defend the English in their "glorious revolution" of 1688 against James II. Locke argued that laws of nature gave people a right to rebel against an unjust king. He based this on a belief that such laws are as universal and as "scientific" as the laws of motion recently discovered by his friend Isaac Newton.

Many of Locke's ideas were not original with him. The conception of God-given natural rights was first stated by the Stoic philosophers of ancient Greece and was later developed by jurists of the late Roman Empire, as well as by medieval theologians, such as Thomas Aquinas. The theory of government as a contract between ruler and subject had been the basis for the relationship between lord and vassal under the feudal system.

Locke's writings were popularized in France by Voltaire, Montesquieu, Rousseau, and others; they provided the theoretical basis for the early phases of the French Revolution. In America his ideas were so universally accepted that Jefferson presented them as self-evident truths.

The Declaration rests on two axioms: that God has made all men equal, and that He has endowed them with certain rights. But can we accept these? Is there anything more obvious than that men are in fact

(Continued on p. 11)

Explanatory

Notes "... the pursuit of happiness." According to John Locke and his followers the three basic rights of man were life, liberty, and property. Locke thought, in fact, that protection of property was the chief business of the state. But Locke also maintained that men as rational beings go through life avoiding pain and seeking pleasure—in other words, pursuing happiness. In emphasizing the pursuit of happiness, Jefferson made the American cause appear more unselfish than if he had emphasized defense of property. It has been argued that when he made this change in emphasis, he ultimately affected the American outlook on life, that only Americans think of happiness as a right and expect children to be happy in school, working people to be happy in their jobs, and happiness to be the principal aim of marriage.

9

But when a long train of abuses and usurpations, pursuing invariably the same object, evinces a design to reduce them under absolute despotism, it is their right, it is their duty, to throw off such government, and to provide new guards for their future security. Such has been the patient sufferance of these colonies; and such is now the necessity which constrains them to alter their former systems of government.

*un*equal—in stature, in health, in talents, in opportunity? And to bring the issue close to home, what right to liberty was enjoyed by the slaves owned by the author of the Declaration?

Jefferson's answer to those who argue for natural inequality would be that all men are *equal in rights*; they may not have equal talents, but they have an equal right to develop what talents they have. As to slavery, Jefferson thought it a moral wrong, but it was beyond his political skill to bring about its early abolition.

The Declaration goes on to argue that governments are established for the sole purpose of protecting individual rights. Government thus becomes a *contract* between the people and their rulers. By its terms the people give up as much of their rights as may be necessary to enable government to protect the rest. For instance, the people give up some property in the form of taxation so that the government may hire firemen and policemen. Thus government rests on "consent," upon the willingness of the people—or at least a majority of them—to be taxed. These arguments also bristle with difficulties. Most existing governments in the eighteenth century were originally based on conquest, not on any solemn contract, and no government needs popular support if it can command power. The answer to these objections is that the *rightful* basis of government is consent; a government may seize power, but its just powers come only from the people.

Finally, Jefferson argues a right of revolution. If a government destroys those rights it was set up to protect, the contract is broken, and the people have a right to seek new agents and write a new contract. But does such a right actually exist aside from power? If the rebels do not have sufficient force to overthrow the government, they ultimately land in jail, exile, or before a firing squad. And if the rebellion succeeds, do the *people* actually set up a new government, or does one gang of rulers replace another gang? Here again, Jefferson is writing about what should be, not what necessarily occurs.

Awareness of objections to the "glittering generalities" of the Declaration of Independence must not obscure their tremendous power. Jefferson here stated a case for the dignity of the individual, for government as the servant not the master of the people, and for the right of people to choose their rulers. He did this in such few words, in such simple yet eloquent prose, and in such important circumstances that the Declaration of Independence is as pertinent to the twentieth century as it was to the year 1776.

Explanatory

Notes "... it is their right, it is their duty, to throw off such government, ..." Note the word "duty." Your rights are given to you by God, and you have a moral obligation to defend them.

GRIEVANCES

The history of the present King of Great Britain is a history of repeated injuries and usurpations, all having in direct object the establishment of an absolute tyranny over these states. To prove this, let facts be submitted to a candid world.

INTERFERENCE WITH COLONIAL LEGISLATURES

1. He has refused his assent to laws the most wholesome and necessary for the public good.

2. He has forbidden his governors to pass laws of immediate and pressing importance, unless suspended in their operation till his assent should be obtained; and when so suspended, he has utterly neglected to attend to them.

3. He has refused to pass other laws for the accommodation of large districts of people, unless those people would relinquish the right of representation in the legislature—a right inestimable to them, and formidable to tyrants only.

4. He has called together legislative bodies at places unusual, uncomfortable, and distant from the depository of their public records, for the sole purpose of fatiguing them into compliance with his measure.

5. He has dissolved representative houses repeatedly, for opposing, with manly firmness, his invasions on the rights of the people.

6. He has refused, for a long time after such dissolutions, to cause others to be elected, whereby the legislative powers, incapable of annihilation, have returned to the people at large for their exercise; the State remaining, in the mean time, exposed to all the dangers of invasions from without, and convulsions within.

7. He has endeavored to prevent the population of these States; for that purpose obstructing the naturalization of foreigners; refusing to pass others to encourage their migration hither, and raising the conditions of new appropriations of lands.

Grievances

Having established a right of revolution, it was now Jefferson's task to show that Britain had, in fact, broken the contract, not only by failing to protect American rights, but by attempting to subject the Americans to "absolute despotism." The greater part of the Declaration is therefore devoted to a statement of grievances against "the present King of Great Britain." Relentlessly Jefferson piles wrong on wrong, every one of them blamed personally on George III. Note the effectiveness of the monotonous, dirge-like repetition: "He has refused. . . . He has forbidden. . . . He has utterly neglected. . . . He has obstructed. . . . He has plundered. . . . He has. . . . He has. . . . He has. . . ." *(Continued on p. 15)*

Explanatory

Notes Grievances 1–7. This first set of grievances concerns the conflict between colonial legislatures and the British crown. The struggle began long before the Revolution. All the colonies, except Rhode Island, Connecticut, and Maryland, had to submit laws to the crown for approval or disapproval. Royal judgment of laws might be expressed through the colonial governors, who enjoyed the right to veto bills, or by the British Privy Council. In the year 1706, for example, the Privy Council disapproved of 52 out of 105 laws submitted by the Pennsylvania legislature. Colonial laws that appeared to conflict with British interests got especially severe treatment. Witness the fate of legislation about immigration. The Privy Council forbade the efforts of colonies to attract settlers through remission of taxes, cheap land, or promise of quick naturalization. The English thought, mistakenly, that their population was declining. If Englishmen were encouraged to go to America, so they thought, factories would lie idle and the land would go untilled. Colonial laws forbidding the immigration of criminals were also vetoed; it was cheaper for England to use the colonies as a dumping ground for "Rogues, Villains, and Sturdy Beggars" than to keep them in jail.

Another area of conflict involved royal prerogative, the exclusive power of the crown. Did a colonial legislature or the crown have the right to set up new counties on the frontier and to grant the inhabitants representation in the legislature? Did colony or crown pay the salaries of judges? Such questions caused friction even when British and American interests were not immediately involved.

The struggle between colonial legislatures and royal officials increased in bitterness during the decade preceding the Declaration of Independence. When the legislatures became a sounding board for colonial grievances, royal governors attempted to silence them. That failing, the legislatures were frequently dissolved and government came to a standstill.

Interference with Courts

8. He has obstructed the administration of justice, by refusing his assent to laws for establishing judiciary powers.

9. He has made judges dependent on his will alone for the tenure of their offices, and the amount and payment of their salaries.

Harassment by New Officials

10. He has erected a multitude of new offices, and sent hither swarms of officers to harass our people and eat out their substance.

Abuse of Military Power

11. He has kept among us in times of peace, standing armies, without the consent of our legislatures.

12. He has affected to render the military independent of, and superior to, the civil power.

There was a large measure of unfairness in these charges. George III was a stubborn, opinionated man, eager to increase royal power. He very much wanted to suppress the American Revolution. But he was no dictator, and did not begin the quarrel with the thirteen colonies. In fact, he detested George Grenville, the minister most responsible for the policy of stricter control of the colonies, and dismissed him from office. Not until 1774, as already indicated, did George III play any important role in shaping policy toward America. From then on he resisted all concessions, and so may justly be said to have helped bring on the Revolutionary War and the break with America. But total blame cannot truthfully be laid at his door.

Jefferson, however, was not writing a cool appraisal of the causes of the Revolution. He was appealing to world opinion in the heat of battle. Write about the unwarrantable actions of the majority in Parliament and you have to explain the British Constitution. How much easier to blame everything on George III and add this monarch to the long roll of tyrants who fill the pages of history—Xerxes, Herod, Nero, Caligula, King John, Genghis Khan. (Continued on p. 17)

Explanatory

Notes Grievance 10. This refers to the new customs offices and admiralty courts set up after 1764 to prevent smuggling.

Grievance 11. After the Seven Years' War ended and Pontiac's great Indian rebellion had been suppressed in 1763, the colonies saw no more use for British troops in America. The British government thought otherwise. It stationed redcoats in American cities and required the colonists to quarter them. Their presence caused a constant irritation that occasionally flared into violence such as the Boston Massacre. American leaders claimed, furthermore, that the British government had no right to send troops to America without colonial consent. According to the British Bill of Rights of 1689, "the raising or keeping of troops within this kingdom in time of peace unless it be with the consent of parliament is against law."

But according to Jefferson, Franklin, and others, each colonial legislature from the beginning had enjoyed the same status as Parliament; therefore it must decide if troops are to be stationed within its domain.

Grievance 12. This applies to the appointment of General Gage, commander-in-chief of British forces in America, as Governor of Massachusetts in 1774 as part of the general effort to force that colony into submission.

Unconstitutional and Oppressive Actions by Parliament

13. He has combined with others to subject us to a jurisdiction foreign to our constitutions, and unacknowledged by our laws; giving his assent to their acts of pretended legislation:

14. For quartering large bodies of armed troops among us;

15. For protecting them, by a mock trial, from punishment for any murders which they should commit on the inhabitants of these States;

16. For cutting off our trade with all parts of the world;

17. For imposing taxes on us without our consent;

18. For depriving us, in many cases, of the benefits of trial by jury;

19. For transporting us beyond seas, to be tried for pretended offences;

20. For abolishing the free system of English laws in a neighboring province, establishing therein an arbitrary government, and enlarging its boundaries, so as to render it at once an example and fit instrument for introducing the same absolute rule into these colonies;

21. For taking away our charters, abolishing our most valuable laws, and altering, fundamentally, the forms of our governments;

22. For suspending our own legislatures, and declaring themselves invested with power to legislate for us in all cases whatsoever.

Barbarous Warfare against the Colonies

23. He has abdicated government here, by declaring us out of his protection, and waging war against us.

24. He has plundered our seas, ravaged our coasts, burned our towns, and destroyed the lives of our people.

25. He is at this time transporting large armies of foreign mercenaries to complete the works of death, desolation and tyranny, already begun with circumstances of cruelty and perfidy scarcely paralleled in the most barbarous ages, and totally unworthy the head of a civilized nation.

26. He has constrained our fellow-citizens, taken captive on the high seas, to bear arms against their country, to become the executioners of their friends and brethren, or to fall themselves by their hands.

There was also a theoretical reason for pinning everything on the king. Jefferson was one of those who argued that the thirteen colonies had never been legally subordinate to Parliament. His idea of the constitutional position of the colonies was something very like dominion status in the British Commonwealth of Nations today. In a pamphlet entitled *A Summary View of the Rights of British America*, published in 1774, Jefferson wrote that when the original settlers came to this continent, they had established "new societies" with their own laws, tied to Britain only by submission "to the same common Sovereign, who was thereby made the central link connecting the several parts of the Empire. . . ." Now if the colonies had never been legally subject to Parliament, but only to the crown, it logically follows that every invasion of colonial rights was the fault of the king. Parliament, to be sure, had subverted American rights, but only because the king allowed it to do so.

Jefferson's catalogue of grievances is remarkably full, covering almost every phase of the dispute with England. For many years it served to keep hatred of Britain alive, and Fourth of July orators continued to denounce the tyranny of George III and the atrocities committed by British redcoats long after all who had participated in the Revolution were in their graves. This passage has also served through the years as a model for the makers of political platforms when they denounce and deplore the actions of their opponents. Thus the Democratic platform of 1932 echoed the Declaration in blaming the Republicans for the Great Depression:
(Continued on p. 19)

Explanatory

Notes Grievance 13. ". . . a jurisdiction foreign to our constitutions, and unacknowledged by our laws; . . ." This refers to Parliament. The king was conveniently blamed for every parliamentary invasion of American rights because parliamentary bills did not become law until he signed them. Actually, however, the royal right to refrain from signing bills, the veto power, had not been exercised since 1707.

Grievances 14–22. Anyone familiar with the background of the Revolution can spot "the acts of pretended legislation" here mentioned.

Grievance 20. "For abolishing the free system of English laws. . . ." This refers to the Quebec Act of 1774, which provided for the legal system, the government, and the boundaries of the Province of Quebec acquired from France in 1763. This law was not an instrument of oppression, but on the whole an act of statesmanship. It granted the people of Canada, who had no desire for "the free system of English laws," the right to use their own system of law, to speak their own language, and to practice their religion. The Act also extended the boundary of Quebec to the Ohio River. This was designed to protect the Indians and with them the fur trade; it was bitterly resented by those colonies, like Virginia, with western land claims.

17

27. He has excited domestic insurrection among us, and has endeavored to bring on the inhabitants of our frontiers the merciless Indian savages, whose known rule of warfare is an undistinguished destruction of all ages, sexes, and conditions.

ATTEMPTS AT RECONCILIATION REBUFFED

In every stage of these oppressions we have petitioned for redress in the most humble terms; our repeated petitions have been answered only by repeated injury. A prince whose character is thus marked by every act which may define a tyrant, is unfit to be the ruler of a free people.

Nor have we been wanting in our attentions to our British brethren. We have warned them, from time to time, of attempts by their legislature to extend an unwarrantable jurisdiction over us. We have reminded them of the circumstances of our emigration and settlement here. We have appealed to their native justice and magnanimity; and we have conjured them, by the ties of our common kindred, to disavow these usurpations, which would inevitably interrupt our connections and correspondence. They, too, have been deaf to the voice of justice and consanguinity. We must, therefore, acquiesce in the necessity which denounces our separation, and hold them, as we hold the rest of mankind, enemies in war, in peace friends.

They have ruined our foreign trade; destroyed the values of our commodities and products, crippled our banking system, robbed millions of our people of their life savings, and thrown millions more out of work, produced widespread poverty and brought the government to a state of financial distress unprecedented in time of peace.

Four years later the Republican platform used the same familiar cadences when denouncing the New Deal:

It has insisted on the passage of laws contrary to the Constitution.
It has intimidated witnesses and interfered with the right of petition.
It has dishonored our country by repudiating its most sacred obligations.
It has been guilty of frightful waste and extravagance, using public funds for partisan political purposes. . . .
It has created a vast multitude of new offices, filled them with its favorites, set up a centralized bureaucracy, and sent out swarms of inspectors to harass our people.

Explanatory

Notes ". . . we have petitioned for redress in the most humble terms; . . ." A petition to George III for redress of grievances was adopted by the First Continental Congress on October 26, 1774, and one by the Second Continental Congress on July 8, 1775. Neither one was answered; the second the king refused even to receive. The so-called "Olive Branch Petition" of 1775 began, "Most Gracious Sovereign: We, your Majesty's faithful subjects in the Colonies of . . . (names of the thirteen colonies). Attached to your Majesty's person, family, and government, with all the devotion that principle and affection can inspire. . . ."

"Nor have we been wanting in our attentions to our British brethren. . . . They, too, have been deaf to the voice of justice and consanguinity." Here Jefferson indicts the British people as well as their monarch. Along with the petitions to the king mentioned above, Congress had sent two solemn addresses to the people of England.

THEREFORE . . . .

We, therefore, the Representatives of the United States of America, in General Congress assembled, appealing to the Supreme Judge of the world for the rectitude of our intentions, do, in the name and by the authority of the good people of these colonies, solemnly publish and declare, That these united Colonies are, and of right ought to be, free and independent states; that they are absolved from all allegiance to the British crown, and that all political connection between them and the state of Great Britain is, and ought to be, totally dissolved; and that, as free and independent states, they have full power to levy war, conclude peace, contract alliances, establish commerce, and do all other acts and things which independent states may of right do. And, for the support of this declaration, with a firm reliance on the protection of Divine Providence, we mutually pledge to each other our lives, our fortunes, and our sacred honor.

Therefore . . . .

Having established the right, indeed the duty, of an oppressed people to revolt, and having described "a long train of abuses and usurpations," there was now no other possible conclusion but separation from England. The essential clause here ("That these united Colonies . . . totally dissolved; . . .") is taken directly from Richard Henry Lee's motion presented to the Congress on June 7, and approved on July 2. This may underline the fact that the Declaration of Independence simply explained a decision already made.

After asserting independence, the Declaration goes on to explain the powers of "free and independent states"—"to levy war, conclude peace," etc. Taken together these powers are known as "sovereignty," a term defined by political theorists of the seventeenth and eighteenth centuries as "supreme power." But while everyone agreed that there was no higher earthly power than that of the sovereign state, they disagreed as to whether sovereignty could be divided. Could it be shared between different branches of government, such as king and parliament? Could it be shared between a central government and subordinate agencies such as provincial or colonial assemblies?

This problem of division of sovereignty is suggested in the Declaration. Jefferson begins by referring to the Americans with a singular noun—"one people"—but a plural pronoun—"they." And in this final statement the different colonies are described as becoming "free and independent states," each with sovereign power, and yet they are somehow "united." Are the Americans forming a nation or a temporary military alliance? Does power lie with the states or is it shared with the Congress? A great deal of the later political history of the United States consisted in hammering out answers to these difficult questions.

Explanatory Notes

". . . we mutually pledge to each other our lives, our fortunes, and our sacred honor." In his war message to Congress on April 2, 1917, calling for a crusade on behalf of democracy against German militarism, Woodrow Wilson concluded by echoing the Declaration of Independence:

> To such a task we can dedicate our lives and our fortunes, everything that we are and everything that we have, with the pride of those who know that the day has come when America is privileged to spend her blood and her might for the principles that gave her birth and happiness and the peace which she has treasured. God helping her, she can do no other.

THE SIGNERS

The foregoing Declaration was, by order of Congress, engrossed, and signed by the following members:

JOHN HANCOCK

New Hampshire
JOSIAH BARTLETT
WILLIAM WHIPPLE
MATTHEW THORNTON

Massachusetts Bay
SAMUEL ADAMS
JOHN ADAMS
ROBERT TREAT PAINE
ELBRIDGE GERRY

Rhode Island
STEPHEN HOPKINS
WILLIAM ELLERY

Connecticut
ROGER SHERMAN
SAMUEL HUNTINGTON
WILLIAM WILLIAMS
OLIVER WOLCOTT

New York
WILLIAM FLOYD
PHILIP LIVINGSTON
FRANCIS LEWIS
LEWIS MORRIS

New Jersey
RICHARD STOCKTON
JOHN WITHERSPOON
FRANCIS HOPKINSON
JOHN HART
ABRAHAM CLARK

Pennsylvania
ROBERT MORRIS
BENJAMIN RUSH
BENJAMIN FRANKLIN
JOHN MORTON
GEORGE CLYMER
JAMES SMITH
GEORGE TAYLOR
JAMES WILSON
GEORGE ROSS

Delaware
CÆSAR RODNEY
GEORGE READ
THOMAS M'KEAN

Maryland
SAMUEL CHASE
WILLIAM PACA
THOMAS STONE

CHARLES CARROLL, of
 Carrollton

Virginia
GEORGE WYTHE
RICHARD HENRY LEE
THOMAS JEFFERSON
BENJAMIN HARRISON
THOMAS NELSON, JR.
FRANCIS LIGHTFOOT LEE
CARTER BRAXTON

North Carolina
WILLIAM HOOPER
JOSEPH HEWES
JOHN PENN

South Carolina
EDWARD RUTLEDGE
THOMAS HEYWARD, JR.
THOMAS LYNCH, JR.
ARTHUR MIDDLETON

Georgia
BUTTON GWINNETT
LYMAN HALL
GEORGE WALTON

The Signers

Most of those who signed the Declaration of Independence did so on August 2, 1776, Congress meanwhile having authorized for the purpose a fair copy engrossed on vellum. Some members who were not present signed later, as did one man not elected to the Congress until September.

The familiar pictures of the signing of the Declaration that show an array of grave gentlemen in knee breeches—men who might otherwise be attending a church service or a trustees' meeting—obscure the fact that this was a desperate step. These men were not acting casually. Each of them was now a traitor in the eyes of the British government, and treason was regarded as so horrid a crime that it was punished by a barbarous form of execution, confiscation of the criminal's property, and disgrace for his family. Should the Americans lose the Revolutionary War, the signers of the Declaration could expect indeed to lose their lives, their fortunes, and their sacred honor.

These "reluctant rebels," as they have been called, were not the kind one might expect to find leading a revolution. They were people of prominence in their communities, and for the most part well off. Most of them brought along private servants to Philadelphia. They were at least as well educated as the members of the British Parliament. Their devotion to public service and their unwillingness to use official position to fill their pockets were an astonishment to Europe.

It must still amaze us that a country of perhaps three million people, strung along the Atlantic coast on farms, in villages, and in small towns, should produce such a galaxy of able and disinterested politicians. How

(Continued on p. 25)

Explanatory

Notes State delegations. Each of the thirteen states decided upon what men should represent it in Congress, how large the delegation should be, and what he should be paid. Each state, as later in the Confederation Congress and in the Senate today, had equal voting rights.

DISTRIBUTION

Resolved, That copies of the Declaration be sent to the several assemblies, conventions, and committees, or councils of safety, and to the several commanding officers of the continental troops; that it be proclaimed in each of the United States, at the head of the army.

did it happen? There is no certain answer to this question, but it may perhaps be found in the fact that during the colonial period the Americans had developed one of the freest societies in the world. To be sure, it was neither a free nor an egalitarian society in modern terms. Negro slavery, although concentrated in the South because of economic circumstances, existed and was protected by law in all the thirteen colonies. Indentured servitude and apprenticeship often came close to temporary slavery for many whites as well. It was noted on tombstones whether a dead man was a "gentleman," a "yeoman" (small landholder), or "goodman" (laborer). The class lists at Harvard were arranged not alphabetically but by social rank. The higher positions in government almost invariably were occupied by the upper class. Yet compared to Europe this was a society where men could get ahead on their merits, as did Franklin. It was the policy of the British government—quite different from that of the Spanish or French—to allow the Americans to run their own affairs through county governments, town meetings, and colonial legislatures. Colonial leaders had therefore a practical training in politics that stood them well when they attempted to set up a new nation. Partly this freedom was the result of distance and indifference on the part of Britain (later called "salutary neglect"). Partly, too, it stemmed from the fact that the English colonists had inherited from the mother country very useful political institutions and a tradition of individual rights. So it may be regarded as a left-handed tribute to the mother country that the thirteen colonies should be the first in the modern world to revolt against their imperial masters.

Explanatory

Notes Distribution. As has already been explained, the Declaration was distributed as soon as it was voted on, although the formal signing did not take place until nearly a month later.

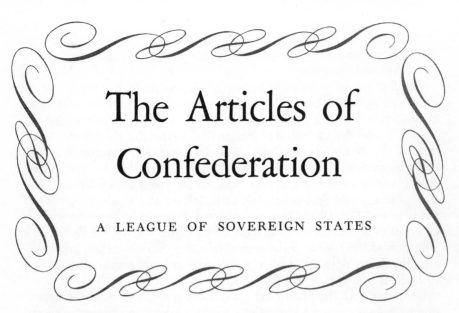

The Articles of
Confederation

A LEAGUE OF SOVEREIGN STATES

T HE ORIGINS of American independence can be traced back to the very beginning of the English settlement. All the thirteen colonies were founded through private initiative, and often by people who wanted to evade the control of Great Britain. Separated from Europe by three thousand miles of ocean, and by uncomfortable sea voyages lasting from one to three months, from the very first the colonies enjoyed local self-government. Even in their external affairs Parliament generally pursued a policy of "salutary neglect" and did not enforce laws that might have restricted the colonial economy, such as the Laws of Trade and Navigation. By the time of the Revolution the Americans had acquired a habit of pretty much running their own affairs and the Declaration of Independence may therefore be regarded as the natural climax of a long development.

There was little tradition of union, however, among the English colonies. There had been two short-lived New England Confederacies in the seventeenth century, and whenever war threatened there was talk of some kind of league of defense. For the most part, however, the different colonies had little to do with each other—just enough to develop rather strong suspicions and dislikes toward the people of other regions. New Englanders regarded other Americans as less thrifty, less cultured, and less moral than they. In return, other colonists regarded New Englanders as sanctimonious, sly, and sharp in business dealing. Gouverneur Morris' father even stipulated in his will that on no account were any of his children to be educated among the coarse and dishonest people of Connecticut. The Quakers of Pennsylvania deplored the gambling and horse-racing that went on below their southern boundary. Southern planters in turn were not sure that any "gentlemen" dwelt north of the Mason-Dixon line.

The first serious attempt at lasting union was made in 1754 when, on the eve of the Seven Years' War, delegates from seven northern states met at Albany to work out plans for cooperation with the Iroquois against the French. Under the leadership of Benjamin Franklin this conference recommended the Albany Plan of Union. Franklin urged the formation of a "general government," with a President-General appointed by the British crown, and a general legislature, selected by colonial legislatures. This government would deal principally with defense and would be given the power to tax. The Albany Plan was rejected, however, by the Americans as an invasion of the rights of the individual colonies and by the British as a reduction of the powers of the crown. Effective common action arose only after the Seven Years' War when the thirteen colonies organized resistance to English invasions of their rights.

Beginning with the Stamp Act Congress in 1765, leaders of the opposition to Britain created a revolutionary network, working through colonial legislatures and New England town meetings, through newspapers, the Sons of Liberty, and the Committees of Correspondence. The effectiveness of the radical organization was revealed when the First Continental Congress formed "the Association" in October, 1774. The Association was designed to force Parliament to repeal the Intolerable Acts by cutting off trade with Britain. Embargoes on British goods had been used effectively before to force the repeal of the Stamp Act and partial repeal of the Townshend Acts. What was extraordinary about the Association was the way it attempted to regulate details of life. Americans were told they should not drink East India tea or Madeira wine, that they should not import slaves, that they should give up "every species of extravagance and dissipation," including horse-racing, cock-fighting, plays, and elaborate funerals. Merchants were ordered not to use the scarcity of goods as an excuse to raise prices. To enforce these prohibitions committees were to be set up in every "county, city, and town attentively to observe the conduct of all persons touching this association." When they found violators, the committees were to publish their names in the newspapers as "enemies of American liberty" and see that they were shunned by their neighbors. With the power to compel obedience by the use of economic and social boycotting, the Association was a species of government.

Once hostilities had broken out in 1775, the Second Continental Congress raised troops, appointed George Washington commander-in-chief, sent two expeditions against Canada, issued currency, and carried on secret negotiations to get arms from France. In other words Congress became what is known as a *de facto* government (a government in fact). But it was not yet a *de jure* government (one based on right and law). Once independence was seriously considered, it became more than ever necessary to establish a formal central government, which, in the American colonial tradition, meant also drawing up a written frame of government. When Richard Henry Lee proposed that the colonies declare themselves "free and independent states," he also made a resolution "that a plan of confederation be prepared and transmitted to the respective Colonies for their consideration and approbation." A committee, therefore, prepared a draft of "Articles of Confederation and Perpetual Union" for the United States, and presented it to Congress on July 12, 1776. This first plan of union was largely the work of John Dickinson. Dickinson in turn was influenced by a plan that Benjamin Franklin had submitted to the Continental Congress in 1775 without gaining much support.

It was not until November, 1777, that Congress finally submitted a revised version of the Articles to the states, and not until March, 1781, nearly five years after Lee's first proposal, were they finally ratified. There were several reasons for the extraordinary delay in what would seem to be a pressing matter. One was that Congress had other things on its mind. As John Adams wrote his wife:

> When fifty or sixty men have a constitution to form for a great empire, at the same time they have a country fifteen hundred miles in extent to fortify, millions to arm and train, a naval power to begin, an extensive commerce to regulate, numerous tribes of Indians to negotiate with, a standing army of tweny-seven thousand men to raise, pay, victual, and officer, I really shall pity these fifty or sixty men.

Whenever Congress did get around to discussing the Articles of Confederation, various difficulties and disagreements were revealed. The greatest single obstacle to an effective union was the fact that each of the thirteen states was a law unto itself. That is, each regarded itself as free and sovereign. Having gained independence from England, they were inclined to remain independent of each other. The first loyalty of the members of the Continental Congress was to the states they represented, and when discussing the Articles of Confederation they insisted that each state retain its full sovereignty. They resisted any suggestion that a central government might have the power to coerce a state. The actual debates in Congress were concerned less with general distrust of strong central government, however, and more with the practical ways in which a new government might tend to coerce the states. Three problems particularly stood out: representation in Congress, the basis of assessments for financial contributions, and the disposition of western lands.

The large states wanted representation on the basis of population; the small ones insisted on an equal voice for all. The large states eventually gave in and agreed that each one should have a single vote in the Confederation Congress. They insisted, though, that in certain important matters nine votes should be required for final action, so that the small states would not be able to outvote the larger.

An obvious way to find a formula for financial contributions to the Confederation treasury was to take a census and base state quotas on relative population. But how to count slaves? Southern delegates proposed that quotas be based on the number of white inhabitants, excluding Negroes on the ground that they were property like sheep and cattle. Northerners argued that slaves were people, and produced wealth, so quotas should be based on the total number of inhabitants. The Congress finally dodged this dispute by proposing that contributions be based on land values.

The most difficult practical problem that Congress had to face, and the one that longest delayed ratification of the Articles, was that of the trans-Appalachian West. Seven states had claims in this region, six of them going back to colonial charters in which they were granted lands extending from the Atlantic to the Pacific. Virginia's claim was far the largest, including nearly all of the modern states of Kentucky, Ohio, Indiana, Illinois, Michigan, and Wisconsin. Virginia, furthermore, could argue that the Ohio Valley was hers by right of conquest, since she had armed and equipped George Rogers Clark's successful expedition against British posts in the West.

Although there were as yet only a few widely scattered settlements in the western lands, it was already known that the area was potentially valuable, with great forests, rich soil, and navigable rivers. If only those states with land claims expanded westward, the others would be hopelessly surpassed, and the Confederation would be an alliance of pygmies and giants. Led by Maryland, the landless states, therefore, insisted that the West should be turned over to the Confederation Congress as the common property of all.

In July 1778 ten states ratified the Articles of Confederation and within a year two more came into the fold. But Maryland held out, insisting that the price of her ratification was the abandonment of the western claims. Finally New York gave up her claims, followed by Connecticut. It was now up to Virginia, but that state refused to give up her immense holdings. The dispute was complicated further by speculators from Virginia and the middle colonies who had formed rival stock companies to buy land in the Ohio Valley.

The Articles might never have been ratified if the year 1780 had not been in some ways the blackest of the Revolution. It was a year that saw British armies take Savannah and Charleston and wander seemingly at will through the southernmost states. In the North it was the year when Benedict Arnold committed treason and some of the best troops in the Continental Army turned mutinous. Finally, there was great discontent among civilians because of runaway inflation and skyrocketing prices, with beef selling at $8 and tea at $90 a pound.

With disaster imminent, it was more vital than ever that the United States finally unite. Virginia, therefore, generously gave up her claims north of the Ohio River, although with certain conditions, whereupon Maryland ratified the Articles at a ceremony held in Philadelphia on March 1, 1781. Thomas Rodney, a member of Congress, recorded the occasion in his diary:

> By a Signal given at the State House the Completion of this grand Union and Confederation was announced by Firing thirteen cannon on the Hill and the same number on board Captn. Paul Jones Frigate in the Harbour. At Two O'Clock the members of Congress and a great number of Gentlemen waited on the President of Congress to Congratulate him on this occasion. . . . In the evening there was a grand exhibition of fireworks at the State House, and also on board Paul Jones Frigate . . . and all the vessels in the Harbour were Decorated and illuminated and great joy appeared in every Countenance but those of the Disaffected.

These celebrations turned out to be premature because the Articles of Confederation was not an effective bond of union.

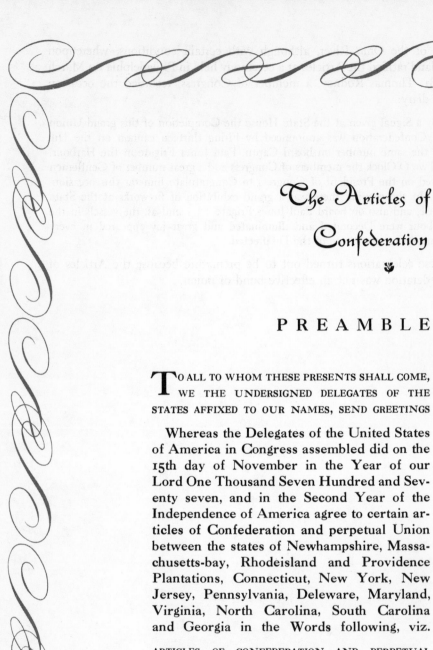

The Articles of Confederation

PREAMBLE

TO ALL TO WHOM THESE PRESENTS SHALL COME, WE THE UNDERSIGNED DELEGATES OF THE STATES AFFIXED TO OUR NAMES, SEND GREETINGS

Whereas the Delegates of the United States of America in Congress assembled did on the 15th day of November in the Year of our Lord One Thousand Seven Hundred and Seventy seven, and in the Second Year of the Independence of America agree to certain articles of Confederation and perpetual Union between the states of Newhampshire, Massachusetts-bay, Rhodeisland and Providence Plantations, Connecticut, New York, New Jersey, Pennsylvania, Deleware, Maryland, Virginia, North Carolina, South Carolina and Georgia in the Words following, viz.

ARTICLES OF CONFEDERATION AND PERPETUAL UNION BETWEEN THE STATES OF NEWHAMPSHIRE, MASSACHUSETTS-BAY, RHODEISLAND AND PROVIDENCE PLANTATIONS, CONNECTICUT, NEW YORK, NEW JERSEY, PENNSYLVANIA, DELAWARE, MARYLAND, VIRGINIA, NORTH CAROLINA, SOUTH CAROLINA AND GEORGIA

Preamble

The date of this agreement of November 15, 1777, means that on that day the Continental Congress finally voted to submit the Articles to the states for ratification. The Articles went into effect only after every one of the thirteen states ratified them. Ratification demanded a formal vote of a state legislature empowering its delegates to the Continental Congress to sign the document.

Note the deliberate mention of each one of the states, especially as compared to the famous phrase "We the People of the United States, . . ." that begins the preamble to our present Constitution. This enumeration suggests that each state was acting in its sovereign and independent capacity.

A LEAGUE OF SOVEREIGN STATES

Article I

Name. The Stile of this confederacy shall be "The United States of America."

Article II

States Retain Sovereignty. Each State retains its Sovereignty, freedom and independence, and every Power, Jurisdiction and right, which is not by this confederation expressly delegated to the United States in Congress assembled.

Article III

Mutual Assistance. The said states hereby severally enter into a firm league of friendship with each other, for their common defence, the security of their Liberties, and their mutual and general welfare, binding themselves to assist each other, against all force offered to, or attacks made upon them, or any of them, on account of religion, sovereignty, trade, or any other pretence whatever.

A League of Sovereign States

No member of the Continental Congress had broader views or more desire to see Americans unite than John Adams. Yet when Adams wrote about "our country," he meant Massachusetts; when he referred to the Massachusetts delegates in Congress, he called them "our embassy." This underlines the fact that at the time of the Revolution a man's first loyalty was to his state. By the Declaration of Independence the thirteen colonies became thirteen nations, each as independent of each other as they all were of Great Britain. The second and third of the Articles of Confederation make this clear. The key words here are "Sovereignty" in Article II and "league" in Article III.

The clause in the original draft of the Articles corresponding to Article II presented to Congress in July, 1776, read:

> Each Colony shall retain and enjoy as much of its present Laws, Rights, and Customs, as it may think fit, and reserves to itself the sole and exclusive Regulation and Government of its internal police, in all matters that shall not interfere with the Articles of this Confederation.

This statement implied that the entire control of external affairs was in the hands of the Confederation, and that even in matters of "internal police," state power was limited. The clause was therefore rewritten to make clear where ultimate power lay. Look again at Article II and note how the word "Sovereignty" comes first, reenforced by "freedom and independence." To be sure, state sovereignty is reduced by certain powers, jurisdictions, and rights granted to the Confederation, but the word "expressly" puts narrow limits on this subtraction. The final say remains with the states.

In Article III the phrase "league of friendship" reveals that the Confederation is not a national government, but a pact of mutual assistance. The Confederation has no legal power to coerce the states; such powers as it does exercise come from their good will and willingness to place "their mutual and general welfare" above their selfish interests.

Explanatory

Notes Article 1. ". . . Stile. . . ." (which today would be spelled "style") here means "title" or "name." Note that sometimes the United States is capitalized in this document and sometimes not. Rules of spelling and punctuation were less rigid in the eighteenth century than today. The words "confederacy" and "confederation" come from the Latin words *con*, meaning "with," and *foedare*, "to form a league."

MUTUAL DUTIES AND PRIVILEGES

Article IV

Exchange of Privileges; Freedom of Movement; No Taxation of Government Agencies. The better to secure and perpetuate mutual friendship and intercourse among the people of the different states in this union, the free inhabitants of each of these states, paupers, vagabonds and fugitives from Justice excepted, shall be entitled to all privileges and immunities of free citizens in the several states, and the people of each state shall have free ingress and regress to and from any other state, and shall enjoy therein all the privileges of trade and commerce, subject to the same duties, impositions and restrictions as the inhabitants thereof respectively, provided that such restrictions shall not extend so far as to prevent the removal of property imported into any state, to any other state of which the Owner is an inhabitant, provided also that no imposition, duties or restriction shall be laid by any state, on the property of the united states, or either of them.

Extradition. If any Person guilty of, or charged with treason, felony or other high misdemeanor in any state, shall flee from Justice, and be found in any of the united states, he shall upon demand of the Governor or executive power of the state from which he fled, be delivered up and removed to the state having jurisdiction of his offence.

Reciprocal Recognition. Full faith and credit shall be given in each of these states to the records, acts and judicial proceedings of the courts and magistrates of every other state.

Mutual Duties and Privileges

Up to July 2, 1776, all the free inhabitants of the thirteen colonies were subjects of one sovereign, the king of England, and as such they all enjoyed the privileges of British citizenship. This meant that they could move freely throughout the British Empire, that everywhere within the Empire they had the protection of the authorities, and that they nominally had equal rights in all courts of law.

Once the colonies declared their independence, the Americans were all of a sudden living under thirteen sovereignties, and they were citizens not of the United States, but of Virginia, Massachusetts, Pennsylvania, and so forth. One of the problems, therefore, of the Continental Congress in drawing up the Articles was how to preserve the advantages of the former common citizenship now that there was no longer a common sovereignty.

Article IV attempts to guarantee Americans the same advantages of free movement and the same protection by law that they had enjoyed earlier. This was a genuinely enlightened policy. It meant that there was free travel (except for "paupers, vagabonds and fugitives from Justice. . . ."). There were no passports or visas necessary for moving from state to state. It meant that the property of a citizen of New York, say, was safe in Connecticut (unless he had been a Loyalist!) and *vice versa*.

The essential provisions of Article IV were later incorporated in the Constitution and are in force in the United States today.

Explanatory Notes

". . . paupers, vagabonds, and fugitives from Justice. . . ." Pauperism and vagrancy were not as serious problems in eighteenth century America as they were in Europe because there was an abundance of work and land was cheap. In *Letters from an American Farmer*, the French nobleman Michel Guillaume Jean Crèvecoeur reported that even the American who lived in a log cabin had "a dry and comfortable habitation" compared to the clay-built huts of European serfs "where cattle and men keep each other warm." Other foreigners coming to these shores generally agreed with Crèvecoeur that there was little poverty in the thirteen colonies.

Where poverty did exist in America, it was generally dealt with according to the principles of the English Poor Law of 1601 that made each parish responsible for the relief of its own paupers, through local taxation if necessary. Other communities naturally wanted none of them. The Articles make clear that each state must take care of its own problem.

The phrase "fugitives from Justice" had a wider meaning in the eighteenth century than now since it included not only criminals, but runaway apprentices, indentured servants, and slaves.

CONGRESS

Article V

Chosen by States. For the more convenient management of the general interest of the united states, delegates shall be annually appointed in such manner as the legislature of each state shall direct, to meet in Congress on the first Monday in November, in every year, with a power reserved to each state, to recall its delegates, or any of them, at any time within the year, and to send others in their stead, for the remainder of the Year.

Number of Members; Restrictions on Membership. No state shall be represented in Congress by less than two, nor by more than seven Members; and no person shall be capable of being a delegate for more than three years in any term of six years; nor shall any person, being a delegate, be capable of holding any office under the united states, for which he, or another for his benefit receives any salary, fees or emolument of any kind.

Paid by States. Each state shall maintain its own delegates in a meeting of the states, and while they act as members of the committee of the states.

One State, One Vote. In determining questions in the united states, in Congress assembled, each state shall have one vote.

Privileges of Members. Freedom of speech and debate in Congress shall not be impeached or questioned in any Court, or place out of Congress, and the members of congress shall be protected in their persons from arrests and imprisonments, during the time of their going to and from, and attendance on congress, except for treason, felony, or breach of the peace.

Congress

Asked to define the word "congress," most Americans in the twentieth century would probably say, "legislature," but in the eighteenth century, and throughout Europe in the nineteenth, the word was more likely to mean "a meeting of diplomats," such as the Congress of Vienna, 1815, or the Congress of Berlin, 1878. The Confederation Congress was betwixt and between. It was granted severely limited powers of legislation, which made it to some degree resemble the United States Congress today. On the other hand, its members were delegates of sovereign states. They were supported by their states and might be recalled at any time. Thus they resembled ambassadors.

The sovereign equality of each of the thirteen states was shown by the fact that whether a state had a population of under 60,000 people, like Delaware, or over 600,000, like Virginia, it had just one vote in Congress. These arrangements were designed to reenforce the supremacy of the states over the Confederation.

The authors of the Articles not only feared centralized government, but political power in general. They shared the widely-held view expressed by Tom Paine in *Common Sense*: ". . . government, even in its best state, is but a necessary evil." Part of this evil comes from the fact that men like the authority, the prestige, and sometimes the graft that comes from office-holding. Furthermore, the desire for power is never sated; on the contrary, as a member of the Continental Congress wrote, "It gives the Passion of ambition a Velocity which Increases in its progress, and this is a passion which grows in proportion as it is gratified."

To prevent the members of the Confederation Congress from becoming entrenched in power the Articles provides for what is known as "rotation in office": no man might sit in Congress for more than three years in any six. The difficulties with this arrangement are obvious. It means that no sooner did a member of Congress learn his complex job, than he had to step down and let another, presumably less experienced, take his place. It also means that there would inevitably be less chance for continuity and consistency in policy.

Explanatory Notes

"Each state shall maintain its own delegates. . . ." This did not generally mean that the members of the Confederation Congress were paid salaries, but simply that their states paid the rather heavy expenses of attending sessions and journeying to and from them.

"Freedom of speech and debate. . . ." This and the other protections for members of Congress described in this paragraph are derived from those enjoyed by members of the British Parliament.

LIMITATIONS ON STATE ACTION

Article VI

Restrictions on Diplomacy; No Titles of Nobility. No state without the Consent of the united states in congress assembled, shall send any embassy to, or receive any embassy from, or enter into any conference, agreement, alliance or treaty with any King, prince or state; nor shall any person holding any office of profit or trust under the united states, or any of them, accept of any present, emolument, office or title of any kind whatever from any king, prince or foreign state; nor shall the united states in congress assembled, or any of them, grant any title of nobility.

Restrictions on Interstate Treaties. No two or more states shall enter into any treaty, confederation or alliance whatever between them, without the consent of the united states in congress assembled, specifying accurately the purposes for which the same is to be entered into, and how long it shall continue.

No Interference with French and Spanish Treaties. No state shall lay any imposts or duties, which may interfere with any stipulations in treaties, entered into by the united states in congress assembled with any king, prince or state, in pursuance of any treaties already proposed by congress to the courts of France and Spain.

Limitation of State Armaments. No vessels of war shall be kept up in time of peace by any state, except such number only, as shall be deemed necessary by the united states in congress assembled, for the defence of such state, or its trade; nor shall any body of forces be kept up by any state, in time of peace, except such number only, as in the judgment of the united states, in congress assembled, shall be deemed requisite to garrison the forts necessary for the defence of such state; but every state shall always keep up a well regulated and disciplined militia, sufficiently armed and accoutred, and shall provide and constantly have ready for use, in public stores, a due number of field-pieces and tents, and a proper quantity of arms, ammunition and camp equipage.

Limitations on State Action

Article VI details ways in which the Articles of Confederation restrict state sovereignty. This section is designed to provide a clear field for federal action within its own sphere. It is thus the counterpart to Article IX that details the powers of the Confederation.

These prohibitions on state action are in the field most clearly reserved to the Confederation Congress—foreign affairs and war. They make it explicitly clear that the diplomatic relations of the United States with the rest of the world are to be carried on through Congress. Nor has a state an independent right to wage war, except in the case of an invasion of its territory.

These restrictions were insufficient for their purpose. The most obvious example of this is the clause forbidding the states to lay duties or imposts conflicting with treaties with France and Spain. Why only France and Spain? Were the United States never to trade with any other countries? Yet trade with other countries demanded that Congress write trade treaties, and this in turn demanded that foreign ships and products get the same treatment in all ports of the United States. When John Adams, our first minister to Great Britain, approached the Foreign Office about a trade treaty, he is said to have received the reply, "Do you want thirteen treaties or one?" The only way to make effective commercial agreements was to ensure that foreign traders did not run into thirteen different sets of tariff duties. *(Continued on p. 43)*

Explanatory Notes

Restrictions on Interstate Treaties. There was a fear that a group of states, such as the middle colonies or New England, might form their own confederation and secede. This fear was expressed, for instance, when in both 1779 and 1780 the New England states and New York sent delegates to a conference at Hartford, Connecticut, to devise means of controlling prices and to prosecute the Revolutionary War more efficiently.

"... a well regulated and disciplined militia, ..." Because of the cost of maintaining them and because they might be used to repress liberties, Americans disliked standing armies. The success of the minutemen at Concord and at Bunker Hill encouraged the belief that a militia could take the place of a standing army. The history of the Revolutionary War and later of the War of 1812 revealed that this was a delusion, for the militia were very seldom well enough regulated or disciplined to be trusted in combat.

Restrictions on State War-making Powers. No state shall engage in any war without the consent of the united states in congress assembled, unless such state be actually invaded by enemies, or shall have received certain advice of a resolution being formed by some nation of Indians to invade such state, and the danger is so imminent as not to admit of a delay, till the united states in congress assembled can be consulted: nor shall any state grant commissions to any ships or vessels of war, nor letters of marque or reprisal, except it be after a declaration of war by the united states in Congress assembled, and then only against the kingdom or state and the subjects thereof, against which war has been so declared, and under such regulations as shall be established by the united states in congress assembled, unless such state be infested by pirates, in which case vessels of war may be fitted out for that occasion, and kept so long as the danger shall continue, or until the united states in congress assembled shall determine otherwise.

Article VII

Appointment of Officers. When land-forces are raised by any state for the common defence, all officers of or under the rank of colonel, shall be appointed by the legislature of each state respectively by whom such forces shall be raised, or in such manner as such state shall direct, and all vacancies shall be filled up by the state which first made the appointment.

There was never a real test of the prohibition on state war-making, but probably it was not effective. To prevent a state from making war the Confederation government would have needed overwhelming military force, a force superior to any state militia. But the only force under the direct control of Congress, the Continental Army, was rapidly being disbanded even before the Treaty of Paris was ratified. In June, 1784, Congress passed a resolution "that the commanding officer be, and is hereby directed to discharge the troops now in the service of the United States, except 25 privates, to guard the stores at Fort Pitt, and 55 to guard the stores of West Point and other magazines, with a proportionate number of officers; no officer to remain in service above the rank of captain. . . ." With a total force of 80 men, plus half a dozen officers, the Confederation was surely not going to overawe a state that decided to ignore its duties under the Articles.

Except for the restriction on interstate treaties and war in Article VI and the mutual guarantees of individual rights in Article IV, there was no restriction on how states could treat each other during the Confederation period. They were free to levy heavy tariff duties on each other's products, to favor their own ships in their ports, and to refuse to accept each other's currency. Some states deliberately carried on economic warfare with their neighbors, and there was nothing in the Articles to prevent them.

Explanatory Notes

". . . letters of marque or reprisal, . . ." These are licenses issued by a government in wartime authorizing individuals to arm privateers to prey on the commerce and shipping of the enemy. The owners of privateers were empowered to sell captured ships and cargoes for their own profit. This was a cheap way for a poor maritime nation to create a navy in a hurry. During the Revolution the states and Congress commissioned more than five hundred privateers, and the number of men in their crews at times exceeded those fighting on land. They were so effective that insurance rates on British trade to the West Indies rose to 28 percent. Robert Morris, the leading financier of the Revolutionary period, made a fortune of three or four hundred thousand pounds by privateering.

The line between privateering and piracy was a narrow one, as the career of the famous Captain Kidd reveals. When peace came, privateers were apt to go on doing business—which was now piracy—pretending, in an age before the radio and trans-oceanic cable, that they did not know the war was over. Most of the nations of Europe agreed to abolish privateering at an international peace congress in Paris in 1856, at the end of the Crimean War. Since then it has been used in warfare only once—by the Confederacy in the American War Between the States.

RAISING MONEY

Article VIII

Liability for Expenses of the CONFEDERATION. All charges of war, and all other expences that shall be incurred for the common defence or general welfare, and allowed by the united states in congress assembled, shall be defrayed out of a common treasury, which shall be supplied by the several states, in proportion to the value of all land within each state, granted to or surveyed for any Person, as such land and the buildings and improvements thereon shall be estimated according to such mode as the united states in congress assembled, shall from time to time direct and appoint.

State Taxation for Confederate Treasury. The taxes for paying that proportion shall be laid and levied by the authority and direction of the legislatures of the several states within the time agreed upon by the united states in congress assembled.

Inadequate Revenue

The most obvious single weakness of the Articles of Confederation was that they failed to grant Congress the power to tax. The Confederation was supposed to be supported by state contributions levied in proportion to land values. Congress could not, however, force the states to obey its requests. The states were heavily burdened with war debts of their own, and when Congress asked for money, they paid only a small share of the requisitions. For instance, on January 30, 1781, Congress requested $8,000,000. By January 1, 1784, the states had paid less than $1,500,000. The Confederation was unable to meet the interest on the war debts incurred by the Continental Congress, and the market value of United States bonds fell as low as fifteen cents on the dollar. Only timely new loans from Dutch bankers averted absolute bankruptcy.

Congress had two independent sources of revenue under the Confederation—income from the post office and money from the sale of the trans-Allegheny lands ceded to the Confederation at Maryland's insistence. Postal revenues were no more than enough to pay for the cost of the postal service. Land sales did not bring in much money because the Confederation lacked troops to defend the frontier from Indians, and this discouraged settlement, especially in the area north of the Ohio where the Congress had the clearest title.

Twice the states were asked to approve an amendment to the Articles granting Congress the right to levy moderate import duties. On both occasions the vote of a single state—Rhode Island in 1781, and New York in 1786—defeated the proposal. Had this amendment been ratified, the Confederation might have survived, at least for far longer than it did. With an independent source of revenue it could have met the charges on its debts, and might have pushed several of the other problems it faced toward solution. Once able to pay troops, for example, it could have raised an army to defend the frontier from Indians, thus ensuring the loyalty of western settlers and making it possible to sell more western lands.

Explanatory Notes

"The taxes for paying that proportion. . . ." This underlines the fact that the states were to raise the money to pay the requisitions of Congress in any way they pleased. One reason why there was unrest during the Confederation period, culminating in Shays's Rebellion in 1786, was that the burden of taxes fell most heavily on the poorer people. Thus Virginia taxed land at a shilling per hundred acres, whether the acres were in the rich tidewater region or in the back country where farms "lay edgeways." Massachusetts relied heavily on poll taxes that called on every man to pay the same amount.

POWERS OF CONGRESS

Article IX

Foreign Affairs: Conduct of War; Piracy. The united states in congress assembled, shall have the sole and exclusive right and power of determining on peace and war, except in the cases mentioned in the sixth article—of sending and receiving embassadors —entering into treaties and alliances, provided that no treaty of commerce shall be made whereby the legislative power of the respective states shall be restrained from imposing such imposts and duties on foreigners, as their own people are subjected to, or from prohibiting the exportation or importation of any species of goods or commodities whatsoever—of establishing rules for deciding in all cases, what captures on land or water shall be legal, and in what manner prizes taken by land or naval forces in the service of the united states shall be divided or appropriated —of granting letters of marque and reprisal in times of peace— appointing courts for the trial of piracies and felonies committed on the high seas and establishing courts for receiving and determining finally appeals in all cases of captures, provided that no member of congress shall be appointed a judge of any of the said courts.

Powers Without Power

It is instructive to compare this Ninth and longest of the Articles of Confederation with the corresponding section of the Constitution, Article I, Section 8 (pp. 110–112). Many of the same powers appear in both documents. Both grant the central government authority to borrow money, to deal with Indians, to regulate currency and coin money, to establish post offices, to punish piracy, to declare war, to grant letters of marque and reprisal, to raise armies, to maintain a navy, to regulate the armed forces, and to call out the militia. Why then have the Articles been accounted a failure and the Constitution a success? The answer is that the Confederation was granted *powers without power*. As we have seen, it needed the right to tax. With that alone it might well have survived. It also needed authority to regulate interstate and foreign commerce. So long as the states were permitted to regulate commerce, the Confederation government could neither write commercial treaties with other countries, nor prevent interstate tariff wars.

In one case an important power clearly granted by the Articles to Congress proved ineffective because the states were not specifically forbidden to act. The Ninth Article states that "The united states in congress assembled shall also have the sole and exclusive right and power of regulating the alloy and value of coin struck by their own authority, or by that of the respective states. . . ." This looks as though Congress regulated all currency, and during the Confederation period it did vote to establish the decimal system of coinage that we enjoy today. It was quite unable, however, to control state currency. Each state issued money as it pleased, usually paper money not backed by silver or gold, so that the value was constantly fluctuating, and money good in one state was not accepted in another.

The inability of Congress to control state currency is just one of many things that reveal the great underlying weakness of the Confederation— *the lack of power to coerce*. It could force neither individuals nor the states to do its bidding. This is another way of saying that it lacked sovereignty.

Explanatory

Notes ". . . appointing courts for the trial of piracies . . . on the high seas . . . and determining finally appeals in all cases of captures, . . ." These are the only courts provided for in the Confederation. Members of Congress were not allowed to sit on them, presumably because it would be a violation of the principle of "separation of powers" (see pp. 105–107) for a member of a legislature to hold a judicial position.

Arbitration of Interstate Disputes. The united states in congress assembled shall also be the last resort on appeal in all disputes and differences now subsisting or that hereafter may arise between two or more states concerning boundary, jurisdiction or any other cause whatever, which authority shall always be exercised in the manner following. Whenever the legislative or executive authority or lawful agent of any state in controversy with another shall present a petition to congress stating the matter in question and praying for a hearing, notice thereof shall be given by order of congress to the legislative or executive authority of the other state in controversy, and a day assigned for the appearance of the parties by their lawful agents, who shall then be directed to appoint by joint consent, commissioners or judges to constitute a court for hearing and determining the matter in question: but if they cannot agree, congress shall name three persons out of each of the united states, and from the list of such persons each party shall alternately strike out one, the petitioners beginning, until the number shall be reduced to thirteen; and from that number not less than seven, nor more than nine names as congress shall direct, shall in the presence of congress be drawn out by lot, and the persons whose names shall be so drawn or any five of them, shall be commissioners or judges, to hear and finally determine the controversy, so always as a major part of the judges who shall hear the cause shall agree in the determination: and if either party shall neglect to attend at the day appointed, without showing reasons, which congress shall judge sufficient, or being present shall refuse to strike, the congress shall proceed to nominate three persons out of each State, and the secretary of congress shall strike in behalf of such party absent or refusing; and the judgment and sentence of the court to be appointed, in the manner before prescribed, shall be final and conclusive; and if any of the parties shall refuse to submit to the authority of such court, or to appear or defend their claim or cause, the court shall nevertheless proceed to pronounce sentence, or judgment, which shall in like manner be final and decisive, the judgment or sentence and other proceedings being in either case transmitted to congress and lodged among the acts of congress for the security of the parties concerned: provided that every commissioner, before he sits in judgment, shall take an oath to be administered by one of the judges of the supreme or superior court of the state, where the cause shall be tried, "well

Arbitration of Interstate Disputes

It was one of the purposes of the Articles of Confederation to prevent civil war. At the time of the Declaration of Independence there were three interstate disputes that threatened to erupt into violence. Virginia had forcibly ejected Pennsylvania surveyors from lands both states claimed along the headwaters of the Ohio. Connecticut people had settled in the Wyoming Valley in northwestern Pennsylvania, and when the Pennsylvania legislature threatened to drive them off, Connecticut sent 800 soldiers to protect them. In the area now the state of Vermont, land claims of New York were resisted by the inhabitants. The Green Mountain Boys were quite as willing to fight the New York militia as Burgoyne's Hessians. All of these disputes continued into the Confederation period, and others were added.

The longest paragraph in the Articles is devoted to the settlement of quarrels between states. In the event of a controversy, no matter what its nature, each state has a right to ask Congress for a hearing and an eventual judgment. Congress in turn has the power to set up a court of arbitration, every effort being made to see that it should render an impartial judgment. By the fact of ratifying the Articles each state agreed to accept the decision of such a court.

This elaborate machinery of compulsory arbitration was never put into action, but the very fact that it was written into the Articles shows that the authors of the document were ahead of their age. The first use of courts of arbitration in an international dispute was in drawing up the Jay Treaty between the United States and Great Britain in 1795. John Jay had been a member of the Confederation Congress, and was of course familiar with the Articles. Not until the Hague Conference of 1899 was there any attempt to set up a general system of arbitration; never have the nations of the world declared their willingness to submit all disputes to peaceful judgment.

and truly to hear and determine the matter in question, according to the best of his judgment without favour, affection or hope of reward": provided also that no state shall be deprived of territory for the benefit of the united states.

Disputes over Private Land Claims. All controversies concerning the private right of soil claimed under different grants of two or more states, whose jurisdiction as they may respect such lands, and the states which passed such grants are adjusted, the said grants or either of them being at the same time claimed to have originated antecedent to such settlement of jurisdiction, shall on the petition of either party to the congress of the united states, be finally determined as near as may be in the same manner as is before prescribed for deciding disputes.

Coinage; Weights and Measures; Indians; Postal Service; Regulation of Armed Services. The united states in congress assembled shall also have the sole and exclusive right and power of regulating the alloy and value of coin struck by their own authority, or by that of the respective states—fixing the standard of weights and measures throughout the united states—regulating the trade and managing all affairs with the Indians, not members of any of the states, provided that the legislative right of any state within its own limits be not infringed or violated—establishing and regulating post-offices from one state to another, throughout all the united states, and exacting such postage on the papers passing thro' the same as may be requisite to defray the expences of the said office—appointing all officers of the land forces, in the service of the united states, excepting regimental officers—appointing all the officers of the naval forces, and commissioning all officers whatever in the service of the united states—making rules for the government and regulations of the said land and naval forces, and directing their operations.

Notes ". . . provided also that no state shall be deprived of territory for the benefit of the united states." Congress had no right to force states to cede land to the United States, but Maryland's refusal to ratify the Articles until the western land claims were given up accomplished the same object.

"All controversies concerning the private right of soil claimed under different grants of two or more states, . . ." Most of the interstate disputes were of this nature. Rival speculators, with grants from different states to the same area, would clash when they attempted to survey or settle the same or overlapping areas.

Coinage. Note that Congress did not have power to control all currency, but only to determine the proportions of gold, silver, and base metals in coins. Even this control proved to be a dead letter because the states issued paper money instead of minted coins. But the Confederation Congress made an important contribution to the country when it adopted Thomas Jefferson's proposal that the United States should adopt as its basic coin the Spanish dollar, but should divide it in tenths and hundredths instead of in eighths, as had been the previous practice. This scheme for a decimal coinage was adopted by the United States when Washington became President in 1789. It was a great improvement on the cumbersome British system of twelve pence to the shilling, and twenty shillings to the pound.

Postal Service. The postal system established by the Confederation Congress was quite efficient and more than paid its own way.

Executive Committee; Troop Levies on States. The united states in congress assembled shall have authority to appoint a committee, to sit in the recess of congress, to be denominated "A Committee of the States," and to consist of one delegate from each state; and to appoint such other committees and civil officers as may be necessary for managing the general affairs of the united states under their direction—to appoint one of their number to preside, provided that no person be allowed to serve in the office of president more than one year in any term of three years; to ascertain the necessary sums of Money to be raised for the service of the united states, and to appropriate and apply the same for defraying the public expences—to borrow money, or emit bills on the credit of the united states, transmitting every half year to the respective states an account of the sums of money so borrowed or emitted,—to build and equip a navy—to agree upon the number of land forces, and to make requisitions from each state for its quota, in proportion to the number of white inhabitants in such state; which requisitions shall be binding, and thereupon the legislature of each state shall appoint the regimental officers, raise the men and cloath, arm and equip them in a soldier like manner, at the expence of the united states; and the officers and men so cloathed, armed and equipped shall march to the place appointed, and within the time agreed on by the united states in congress assembled: But if the united states in congress assembled shall, on consideration of circumstances judge proper that any state should not raise men, or should raise a smaller number than its quota, and that any other state should raise a greater number of men than the quota thereof, such extra number of men shall be raised, officered, cloathed, armed and equipped in the same manner as the quota of such state, unless the legislature of such state shall judge that such extra number cannot be safely spared out of the same, in which case they shall raise, officer, cloath, arm and equip as many of such extra number as they judge can be safely spared. And the officers and men so cloathed, armed and equipped, shall march to the place appointed, and within the time agreed on by the united states in congress assembled.

Executive Power in the Confederation

One way in which the leaders of the American Revolution showed their distrust of concentrated political power was their fear of a strong executive. This fear was reenforced by their long, bitter experience with the British crown and with royal governors. The prevailing American attitude toward executive power was revealed in the state governments set up during the Revolution. In ten states the governor was elected for only a year at a time; in eleven, he had no power of veto.

The first draft of the Articles contained a provision for a separate executive, called a "Council of State," with one member from each state and with specified powers. The members of the Continental Congress refused to accept this. Instead, the only executive office they provided in the Articles was a "Committee of the States" to take care of routine business when Congress was not in session.

Even though the Articles provided for no permanent executive, Congress had executive duties that had to be undertaken. The day-to-day business of carrying on government must continue, and it cannot be done on the floor of a legislature. Some people must answer letters, send out instructions to diplomats, pay the troops, keep accounts, and so forth. The Confederation Congress therefore set up three executive departments—foreign affairs, war, and finance. Each department was under a single head, who in turn was answerable to Congress for his actions. It is possible that had the Confederation continued, the department heads might have formed an executive committee, holding office so long as they were supported by a majority in Congress; then the United States would have had something very like cabinet government in England.

Explanatory Notes

"The united states in congress assembled shall have authority . . . to appoint one of their number to preside, . . ." This "president" of the Confederation Congress was simply an arbiter of debate, like the Speaker in the English House of Commons or the Vice-President in the United States Senate today. The position carried with it no independent executive power like that of the President today.

". . . to agree upon the number of land forces, and to make requisitions from each state for its quota, in proportion to the number of white inhabitants in such state; which requisitions shall be binding, . . ." Observe that Congress was expected to raise troops in the same way it was supposed to raise money—by asking the states for them. The basis of the quota—the proportion of *white* inhabitants —was a victory for the southern delegates in Congress since their large Negro population was ignored.

Vote of Nine States Required for Important Matters. **The** united states in congress assembled shall never engage in a war, nor grant letters of marque and reprisal in time of peace, nor enter into any treaties or alliances, nor coin money, nor regulate the value thereof, nor ascertain the sums and expences necessary for the defence and welfare of the united states, or any of them, nor emit bills, nor borrow money on the credit of the united states, nor appropriate money, nor agree upon the number of vessels of war, to be built or purchased, or the number of land or sea forces to be raised, nor appoint a commander-in-chief of the army or navy, unless nine states assent to the same; nor shall a question on any other point, except for adjourning from day to day be determined, unless by the votes of a majority of the united states in congress assembled.

Explanatory

Notes **Vote of Nine States Required for Important Matters.** In every matter of any importance concerning either peace or war, the support of nine states was necessary to take action. This provision was inserted at the insistence of the large states who feared that if only a simple majority were required, they might be outvoted. Since it was seldom that all thirteen states were represented in Congress, or even as many as ten or eleven, this rule meant that in practice something close to unanimity was necessary to get action.

Note that nine of thirteen states meant in effect two-thirds. The device of requiring a two-thirds vote of Congress on certain important matters was carried over into the Constitution, most notably in relation to the power of Congress to override a presidential veto and the senatorial power to ratify treaties. (See the Explanatory Notes on Article I, Section 3, clause 6, p. 103.)

The last phrase here is ambiguous. Did it mean the majority of all the thirteen states, or merely a majority of the states whose representatives happened to be in Congress at a given session? The Congress, in the interest of getting as much business done as possible, decided on the second interpretation.

Congressional Procedures. The Congress of the united states shall have power to adjourn to any time within the year, and to any place within the united states, so that no period of adjournment be for a longer duration than the space of six Months, and shall publish the Journal of their proceedings monthly, except such parts thereof relating to treaties, alliances or military operations as in their judgment require secrecy; and the yeas and nays of the delegates of each state on any question shall be entered on the Journal, when it is desired by any delegate, and the delegates of a state, or any of them, at his or their request shall be furnished with a transcript of the said Journal, except such parts as are above excepted, to lay before the legislatures of the several states.

Article X

Recess Powers of Executive Committee. The committee of the states, or any nine of them, shall be authorized to execute, in the recess of congress such of the powers of congress as the united states in congress assembled, by the consent of nine states, shall from time to time think expedient to vest them with; provided that no power be delegated to the said committee, for the exercise of which, by the articles of confederation, the voice of nine states in the congress of the united states assembled is requisite.

The Wanderings of Congress

The Confederation Congress operated under immense handicaps. It lacked power, public support, and faith in the instrument of government it was called upon to administer. More often than not it lacked the quorum necessary to carry on business. For a time it resembled a traveling theatrical troupe, moving from town to town in search of a haven. The wonder is that it continued to exist.

A first great blow to congressional prestige occurred in June, 1783, when the Congress was in Philadelphia, engaged in the difficult business of disbanding the Continental Army. Eighty mutinous soldiers under the command of a sergeant marched into the city, roused some four or five hundred other troops stationed there, surrounded the State House where Congress was in session, and demanded pay. Using "offensive words," the soldiers emphasized their demands by pointing their muskets into the hall. With some courage Congress adjourned, and walked out through the picket line of jeering, half-drunken troops. It then moved to Princeton, New Jersey. Later, in 1783, it proved difficult to get representatives from nine states together in order to ratify the Treaty of Paris ending the Revolutionary War. Only by persuading a New Jersey member to leave a sick bed was ratification finally achieved in January, 1784.

Congress moved on to Annapolis, Maryland, early in 1784. There, complained a New England delegate, members amused themselves with "plays, Balls, Concerts, routs, hops, Fandangoes, and fox-hunting." Well might they enjoy themselves since they could seldom get a quorum. In November, 1784, they rode to Trenton, New Jersey, where they remained for two months, and then went on to New York City. There they remained until the Confederation passed out of existence in 1789.

With all these difficulties it is remarkable how many able men were willing to serve in the Confederation Congress, often at serious cost to themselves. No less than twenty-four of the thirty-seven who signed the Constitution in 1787 had been members. The Congress was a school of politics, giving its members a grasp of practical affairs that proved invaluable when the new Constitution was written and later put into effect.

The Confederation Congress produced three pieces of legislation of permanent value: the law establishing the decimal system of coinage that we use today; the Land Ordinance of 1785, providing for systematic survey of western lands; and the Northwest Ordinance, to which the next chapter of this book is devoted.

The Confederation was a necessary first step to the Constitution. Without having experienced the defects of this earlier, loose, ineffective machinery, the Americans never would have approved of the much stronger frame of government established by the Constitution.

Article XI

Admission of New States. Canada acceding to this confederation, and joining in the measures of the united states, shall be admitted into, and entitled to all the advantages of this union: but no other colony shall be admitted into the same, unless such admission be agreed to by nine states.

Article XII

Liability for Debts of Continental Congress. All bills of credit emitted, monies borrowed and debts contracted by, or under the authority of congress, before the assembling of the united states, in pursuance of the present confederation, shall be deemed and considered as a charge against the united states, for payment and satisfaction whereof the said united states, and the public faith are hereby solemnly pledged.

Explanatory

Notes Article XI. Note the latch string out for Canada. When Benjamin Franklin drew up a plan of union for the colonies in 1775, he hoped that the thirteen colonies would be joined by other British possessions —Florida, the West Indies, Bermuda, Nova Scotia, Canada, even Ireland. These ambitious hopes were dimmed, but the desire to get Canada to join the United States persisted for nearly a century. Once deprived of Canada the British would be unable either to invade the United States from the North or to enlist the help of the Indians.

Article XII. The Confederation was unable to make good on this pledge. The paper money issued by the Continental Congress became so completely worthless that the phrase "not worth a Continental" has persisted almost to this day. The Confederation managed to borrow enough money from Dutch bankers to head off absolute bankruptcy, and so it never repudiated its debts even though it could not pay them off.

By the terms of Hamilton's financial program voted by Congress during Washington's first term in office (1789–1793), the debts of the United States were ultimately paid at par. The Continental Currency was, however, never redeemed.

59

Article XIII

Obedience; Perpetual Union; Amendment. Every state shall abide by the determinations of the united states in congress assembled, on all questions which by this confederation are submitted to them. And the Articles of this confederation shall be inviolably observed by every state, and the union shall be perpetual; nor shall any alteration at any time hereafter be made in any of them; unless such alteration be agreed to in a congress of the united states, and be afterwards confirmed by the legislatures of every state.

RATIFICATION

AND WHEREAS it has pleased the Great Governor of the World to incline the hearts of the legislatures we respectively represent in congress, to approve of, and to authorize us to ratify the said articles of confederation and perpetual union. KNOW YE that we the undersigned delegates, by virtue of the power and authority to us given for that purpose, do by these presents, in the name and in behalf of our respective constituents, fully and entirely ratify and confirm each and every of the said articles of confederation and perpetual union, and all and singular the matters and things therein contained: And we do further solemnly plight and engage the faith of our respective constituents, that they shall abide by the determinations of the united states in congress assembled, on all questions, which by the said confederation are submitted to them. And that the articles thereof shall be inviolably observed by the states we respectively represent, and that the union shall be perpetual.

The Clause That Doomed the Articles

When the Confederation Congress first met in 1781, there was debate over the meaning of Article XIII. Some members, anxious to strengthen the Confederation, argued that the pledge of the states to obey the Confederation implied that Congress had the right to force a disobedient state to do its bidding, even if this meant using troops. The majority of the delegates did not, however, believe that Article XIII granted any such power. If the Articles were to be strengthened, it had to be through amendment.

Amendments designed to increase the powers of the Confederation were suggested again and again, but none were ever adopted because of the requirement that every state must agree to them. As has already been suggested, the Confederation might have survived if given the power to tax, but on two occasions the negative vote of a single state prevented granting this power.

The extreme difficulty of amending the Articles contradicted the brave declaration ". . . the union shall be perpetual." Change and growth are necessary for survival in institutions as well as people. By making amendment to the Articles almost impossible, Article XIII doomed the Confederation.

IN WITNESS whereof we have hereunto set our hands in Congress. DONE at Philadelphia in the state of Pennsylvania the ninth Day of July in the Year of our Lord one Thousand seven Hundred and Seventy-eight, and in the third year of the independence of America.

On the part and behalf of the State of New Hampshire.
JOSIAH BARTLETT,   JOHN WENTWORTH, JUNR. August 8, 1778.

On the part and behalf of the State of Massachusetts Bay.
JOHN HANCOCK,   FRANCIS DANA,
SAMUEL ADAMS,   JAMES LOVELI,
ELBRIDGE GERRY,   SAMUEL HOLTEN.

On the part and in behalf of the State of Rhode Island and Providence Plantations.
WILLIAM ELLERY,   JOHN COLLINS.
HENRY MARCHANT,

On the part and behalf of the State of Connecticut.
ROGER SHERMAN,   TITUS HOSMER,
SAMUEL HUNTINGTON,   ANDREW ADAMS.
OLIVER WOLCOTT,

On the part and behalf of the State of New York.
JAS DUANE,   WILLIAM DUER,
FRAS LEWIS,   GOUVR MORRIS.

On the part and in behalf of the State of New Jersey.
JNO WITHERSPOON,   NATHL SCUDDER, Nov. 26, 1778.

On the part and behalf of the State of Pennsylvania.
ROBT. MORRIS,   WILLIAM CLINGAN,
DANIEL ROBERDEAU,   JOSEPH REED, July 22nd, 1778.
JONA BAYARD SMITH,

On the part and behalf of the State of Delaware.
JOHN DICKINSON, May 5, 1779,   THO. M'KEAN, Feb. 12, 1779.
NICHOLAS VAN DYKE,

On the part and behalf of the State of Maryland.
JOHN HANSON, March 1, 1781,
DANIEL CARROLL   Do

On the part and behalf of the State of Virginia.
RICHARD HENRY LEE,   JNO HARVIE,
JOHN BANISTER,   FRANCIS LIGHTFOOT LEE.
THOMAS ADAMS,

On the part and behalf of the State of North Carolina.
JOHN PENN, July 21, 1778,   JNO WILLIAMS.
CORNS. HARNETT,

On the part and behalf of the State of South Carolina.
HENRY LAURENS,   RICHARD HUTSON,
WILLIAM HENRY DRAYTON,   THOS. HEYWARD, JUNR.
JNO MATHEWS,

On the part and behalf of the State of Georgia.
JNO WALTON, 24th July, 1778,   EDWD. LANGWORTHY.
EDWD TELFAIR,

Explanatory Notes

"DONE at Philadelphia in the state of Pennsylvania the ninth Day of July in the Year of our Lord one Thousand seven Hundred and Seventy-eight, . . ." Here the promoters of the Confederation proved to be more hopeful than accurate. For the word "DONE" should be substituted "BEGUN." Only six states signed the Articles on July 9, 1778. Five others ratified later in that year, and another in 1779. Maryland, for reasons already explained, held out until 1781.

Only fourteen of the forty-eight members of the Continental Congress who signed the Articles of Confederation had been signers of the Declaration of Independence two years earlier. This reveals a rapid turnover in membership in the Congress, and this in turn made for inefficiency because of inexperience.

The phrase "the third year of the independence of America" suggests that the members of the Continental Congress were aware that the Declaration of Independence was a great event in the history of mankind.

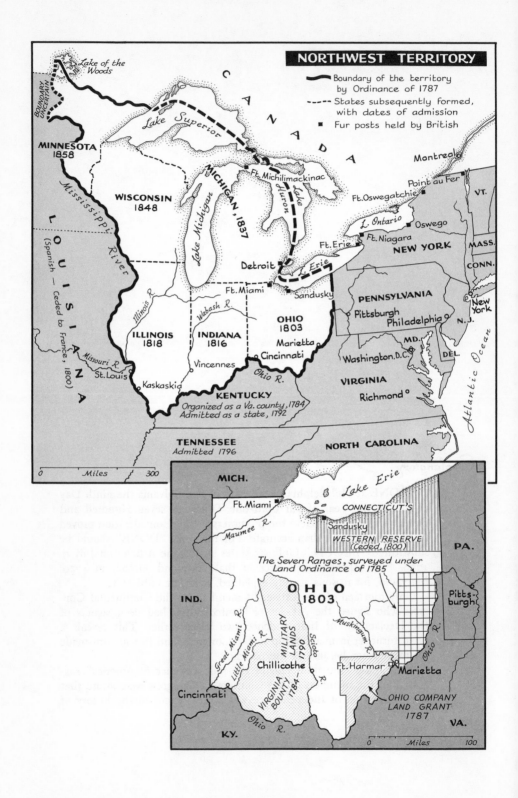

NORTHWEST TERRITORY

— Boundary of the territory
  by Ordinance of 1787
- - - States subsequently formed,
  with dates of admission
▪ Fur posts held by British

CANADA

Lake of the Woods

BOUNDARY UNCERTAIN

Lake Superior

MINNESOTA 1858

WISCONSIN 1848

MICHIGAN, 1837

Ft. Michilimackinac

Lake Huron

Montreal

Point au Fer

Ft.Oswegatchie

VT.

Lake Michigan

L. Ontario

Oswego

MASS.

Ft. Erie

Ft. Niagara

NEW YORK

CONN.

Detroit

L. Erie

Sandusky

Ft. Miami

PENNSYLVANIA

Pittsburgh

Philadelphia

New York

N.J.

Illinois R.

Wabash R.

OHIO 1803

MD.

DEL.

ILLINOIS 1818

INDIANA 1816

Marietta

Cincinnati

Washington, D.C.

Mississippi River

LOUISIANA (Spanish — Ceded to France, 1800)

Vincennes

Ohio R.

VIRGINIA

Richmond

Missouri R.

St.Louis

Kaskaskia

KENTUCKY
Organized as a Va. county, 1784
Admitted as a state, 1792

Atlantic Ocean

TENNESSEE
Admitted 1796

NORTH CAROLINA

0   Miles   300

MICH.

Ft.Miami

Lake Erie

CONNECTICUT'S

Maumee R.

Sandusky

WESTERN RESERVE
(Ceded, 1800)

PA.

The Seven Ranges, surveyed under
Land Ordinance of 1785

IND.

OHIO
1803

Pittsburgh

Great Miami R.

Little Miami R.

VIRGINIA
MILITARY
LANDS
1790

Chillicothe

Scioto R.

Muskingum R.

Ohio R.

Cincinnati

VIRGINIA
BOUNTY
1784-

Ft.Harmar

Marietta

OHIO COMPANY
LAND GRANT
1787

Ohio R.

KY.

VA.

0   Miles   100

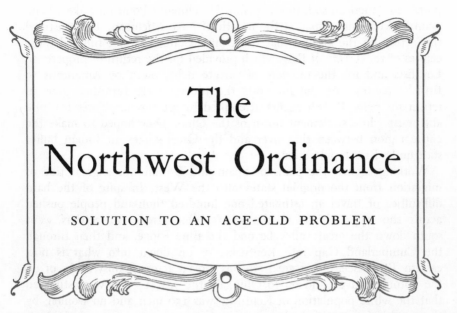

The
Northwest Ordinance

SOLUTION TO AN AGE-OLD PROBLEM

AT THE CLOSE of the Revolutionary War some knowledgeable people expected Washington to follow in the path of other military heroes, like Caesar and Cromwell, and make himself a dictator. Instead, he returned to his beloved Mount Vernon, hoping to spend the rest of his days as a farmer. He found it impossible, however, to withdraw from public affairs. From all over the United States men wrote, sending information and asking advice. Washington himself was especially interested in the West, where he had large land holdings, and he came to fear that the region would not remain part of the American Union. In 1786 he wrote a friend, "The West hangs by a hair."

Washington's fears were justified. Although the Treaty of Paris granted the United States the immense area between the Appalachians and the Mississippi, neither Spain nor Great Britain accepted this award as final. The Spanish hoped to restrict the southwestern boundary of the United States to the Tennessee River. They made allies of the Creek, Choctaw, and Chickasaw Indians who lived south of the Tennessee, and furnished them with guns so that they could defend their lands from white settlers. Spain's greatest weapon was her possession of New Orleans, the only port through which Westerners could send their lumber, hides, and grain to the rest of the world. By controlling the mouth of the Mississippi, the Spanish were in a position either to strangle western trade or to dictate the terms on which such trade could be carried on.

Meanwhile, the British refused to be dislodged from the Northwest. In defiance of the Treaty of Paris they held a string of "fur posts" on American soil, running from Dutchman's Point on Lake Champlain to Michilimackinac at the mouth of Lake Michigan. They justified this action on the ground that the United States had not fulfilled those clauses of the Treaty of Paris which provided for the return of property to Loyalists and for the recovery of private debts owed by Americans to British creditors. At the fur posts the Indians were furnished guns in return for pelts. British agents attempted to get the aborigines to unite and resist white settlement north of the Ohio. They hoped to make the entire region between that river and the Great Lakes an Indian buffer state under British protection.

Working against the plans of Spain and Britain was a great tide of migration from the original states into the West. In spite of the hard difficulties of travel an estimated one hundred thousand people pushed across the Appalachians in the 1780's. One stream of settlers went south down the great valley beyond the Blue Ridge, and then through the Cumberland Gap into Kentucky, or on down into what is now eastern Tennessee. Other great streams moved across Pennsylvania, or up the Potomac River, and on to Ohio. By the year 1775 it was estimated that the white population of Kentucky was 150 men and no women; by the census of 1790 this had grown to 73,677 men, women, and children. Such rapid settlement made it ultimately certain that neither Spain nor Britain could hope to control the trans-Appalachian West or any considerable part of it.

It was by no means certain, however, that the region would remain part of the United States. Often Westerners had no love for the East—many of them had left their homes because of accumulated debts or heavy taxation, or because they did not get on with their neighbors. They would be loyal to the United States only if they got what they desperately needed: protection against the Indians, removal of the British from the fur posts, and the opening of the Mississippi.

The cession of state land claims put the West under control of the Confederation Congress. The handicaps imposed on Congress by the Articles of Confederation hampered it here as in other matters. Unable to raise a revenue, it could not enlist an army strong enough to protect the frontiers. Commanding no respect abroad, it could neither force Britain to abandon the fur posts nor Spain to open the mouth of the Mississippi. Furthermore, in arranging a treaty with Spain, John Jay, foreign secretary of the Confederation, threatened to sacrifice western interests to eastern. By the terms of the Jay-Gardoqui Treaty, negotiated in 1785, Spain would open her Caribbean ports to United States shipping, but in return the United States agreed to give up any claim to free navigation of the Mississippi for twenty-five years. Only seven states voted to ratify this treaty, and so it did not go through, but the news of it infuriated the Westerners. Why be loyal to a helpless government that proposed to throttle western trade for the sake of eastern shippers and merchants? Committees of correspondence were formed in the West, and there was talk of setting up an independent republic.

Although unable to provide for the immediate demands of the West, the Confederation Congress did concern itself with long-time policy. In 1784 Thomas Jefferson introduced a plan for organizing a government in the area. The most striking feature of Jefferson's plan was that it provided for the ultimate creation of ten new states named Assenisippia, Cherronesus, Illinoia, Metropotamia, Michigania, Pelisipia, Polypotamia, Sarotaga, Sylvania, and Washington. When any state reached a population of 20,000, it was to have the right to local self-government. When it should have as many inhabitants as the least populous of the original thirteen states, it was to be admitted to the Union on terms of equality with the older states. Congress voted to embody most of Jefferson's plan in a measure known as the Land Ordinance of 1784. This never went into effect, but it was the basis for the later Northwest Ordinance.

Congress next debated the matter of the survey and sale of a strip of land just west of Pennsylvania. Should settlers have the right to claim land that suited their needs, with surveys to follow after their choice? Or should surveys follow natural boundaries such as rivers and ridges? Or should there be a uniform system according to a geometrical formula? Should the public lands be regarded principally as a source of quick revenue, in which case they should be divided into large areas and sold to speculators, or should they be divided into smaller plots and reserved for actual settlers? In the Land Ordinance of 1785 Congress decided on the geometrical system of survey. The land was divided into townships six miles square, with 36 "sections" each a mile square. The Ordinance became a precedent followed later and accounts for the rectangular landscape that is so striking a feature of the Middle West as seen today from the air. As regards sale the Ordinance offered land in no smaller piece than a section, at one dollar an acre; thus it was designed to raise revenue by quick sales to speculators, who later would retail the land to settlers.

In 1786 a group of New Englanders organized the Ohio Company and dispatched a lobbyist to Congress, Rev. Manasseh Cutler, with an offer to buy over a million acres of land bordering the Ohio River. Congress accepted this offer, and then Cutler further insisted that a regular system of government in the area must be set up. Congress again obliged, and after only three days of debate produced the famous Northwest Ordinance.

Together with the Declaration of Independence and the Constitution, this is one of the great documents of American political history. The reasons why it is a landmark in the history of this country, and of the world, will appear in the following page-by-page study of the document.

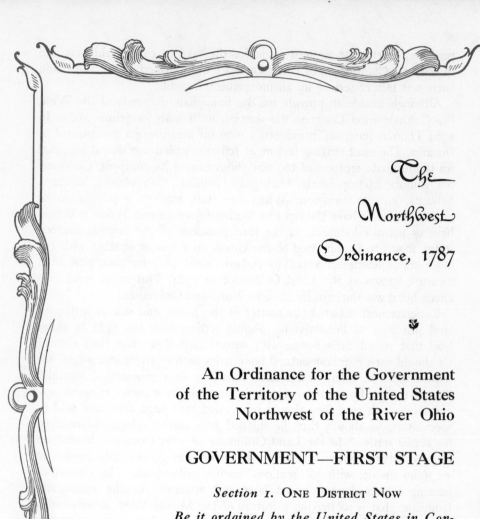

The
Northwest
Ordinance, 1787

An Ordinance for the Government of the Territory of the United States Northwest of the River Ohio

GOVERNMENT—FIRST STAGE

Section 1. ONE DISTRICT NOW

Be it ordained by the United States in Congress assembled, That the said Territory, for the purpose of temporary government, be one district, subject, however, to be divided into two districts, as future circumstances may, in the opinion of Congress, make it expedient.

Section 2. INHERITANCE AND WILLS

Be it ordained by the authority aforesaid, That the estates both of resident and non-resident proprietors in the said territory, dying intestate, shall descend to, and be distributed among their children and the descendants of a deceased child in equal parts . . . [since it is long and of slight importance, the remainder of this section is omitted.]

Government—First Stage

The first stage of government provided for the Northwest Territory resembles that designed for civilians living in a military outpost, such as the Panama Canal Zone today. Political power is wholly concentrated in the hands of a governor, assisted by a secretary and three judges. The governor is sole executive and commander-in-chief; he and the three judges constitute the legislature. Their actions may be overruled only by the distant Congress that appointed them.

The authoritarian government here described accorded with the needs of those who started to settle the north bank of the Ohio in the late 1780's. These first white inhabitants of the region were in constant danger from Indian attack. Their most important town, Marietta, grew up under the guns of Fort Harmar, built to guard the junction of the Muskingum and Ohio Rivers. The first governor of the Northwest Territory was a military man, General Arthur St. Clair, whose headquarters was in Fort Harmar.

(Continued on p. 71)

Explanatory Notes ". . . the Territory of the United States Northwest of the River Ohio." Eventually all the western land claims of the original states were ceded to the United States, but in 1787 the only area where the cessions had been completed was bounded by the Great Lakes, the western boundary of Pennsylvania, the Ohio River, and the Mississippi River. This region was the so-called "Northwest Territory." Later, after the United States acquired the Oregon Territory, it was also called the "Old Northwest."

Section 2. One result of the American Revolution was greater equality in land-holding. In many cases large estates belonging to Loyalists were confiscated, broken up into smaller lots, and sold. The new states promoted subdivision of property by discouraging primogeniture, which provided that all property should descend to the eldest son, and by abolishing entail, whereby a family was prevented from selling or in any way subdividing its lands. Section 2 follows this trend by providing for equal inheritance of the property of those who die intestate (without making a will).

Part of Section 2, omitted here, guaranteed the French and Canadian inhabitants of the Illinois region the right to sell and bequeath property according to their own laws and customs.

Section 3. GOVERNOR

Be it ordained by the authority aforesaid, That there shall be appointed, from time to time, by Congress, a governor whose commission shall continue in force for the term of three years, unless sooner revoked by Congress; he shall reside in the district, and have a freehold estate therein, in one thousand acres of land, while in the exercise of his office.

Section 4. SECRETARY, JUDGES

There shall be appointed from time to time, by Congress, a secretary, whose commission shall continue in force for four years, unless sooner revoked; he shall reside in the district, and have a freehold estate therein, in five hundred acres of land, while in the exercise of his office. It shall be his duty to keep and preserve the acts and laws passed by the legislature, and the public records of the district, and the proceedings of the governor in his executive department, and transmit authentic copies of such acts and proceedings every six months to the Secretary of Congress. There shall also be appointed a court, to consist of three judges, any two of whom to form a court, who shall have a common-law jurisdiction, and reside in the district, and have each therein a freehold estate, in five hundred acres of land, while in the exercise of their offices; and their commissions shall continue in force during good behavior.

Section 5. LAWS OF ORIGINAL STATES MAY BE TEMPORARILY IN FORCE

The governor and judges, or a majority of them, shall adopt and publish in the district such laws of the original States, criminal and civil, as may be necessary, and best suited to the circmstances of the district, and report them to Congress from time to time, which laws shall be in force in the district until the organization of the general assembly therein, unless disapproved of by Congress; but afterwards the legislature shall have authority to alter them as they shall think fit.

So long as they had military protection, the Ohio pioneers did not immediately demand the right to govern themselves. In any case they were so busy carving farms out of the wilderness that it would have been difficult, if not impossible, for them to get together for public meetings or elections.

Observe that one way in which the first stage of government in the Northwest Territory differs from that in a modern military post is that the officials appointed by Congress must own land in the area. They thus have a stake in the success of the government they administer.

Also note that the government set up by Sections 3 through 8 of the Northwest Ordinance is to be temporary. Sections 5, 6, 7, and 8 state that the great powers enjoyed by the governor and the three judges shall last only until the time comes when the people shall elect a legislature, or "general assembly." *(Continued on p. 73)*

Explanatory

Notes "There shall also be appointed a court, to consist of three judges, any two of whom to form a court, who shall have a common-law jurisdiction, . . ." The United States inherited the English common law. This system of law was described by the eighteenth century English jurist Sir William Blackstone as *lex non scripta*—law not written down in any statute or ordinance, but depending on "immemorial usage" as defined from the thirteenth century on by English judges. This law depended on "precedents"; that is, it followed former court decisions, and has therefore been called "case law," or "judge-made law." The common law is still the basis of law and procedure in all of the states of the Union except Louisiana, where French law as defined in the Napoleonic code is the principal guide.

71

Section 6. GOVERNOR AS COMMANDER-IN-CHIEF

The governor, for the time being, shall be commander-in-chief of the militia, appoint and commission all officers in the same below the rank of general officers; all general officers shall be appointed, and commissioned by Congress.

Section 7. APPOINTMENTS

Previous to the organization of the general assembly the governor shall appoint such magistrates, and other civil officers, in each county or township, as he shall find necessary for the preservation of the peace and good order in the same. After the general assembly shall be organized the powers and duties of magistrates and other civil officers shall be regulated and defined by the said assembly; but all magistrates and other civil officers, not herein otherwise directed, shall, during the continuance of this temporary government, be appointed by the governor.

Section 8. LAW ENFORCEMENT

For the prevention of crimes and injuries, the laws to be adopted or made shall have force in all parts of the district, and for the execution of process, criminal and civil, the governor shall make proper divisions thereof, and he shall proceed, from time to time, as circumstances may require, to lay out the parts of the district in which the Indian titles shall have been extinguished, into counties and townships, subject, however, to such alterations as may thereafter be made by the legislature.

In the Ohio region this first stage of government lasted for eleven years. During that time the Indians had been defeated by General Anthony Wayne in the Battle of Fallen Timbers, 1794, and the next year they ceded about half of Ohio to the United States. In 1795 Great Britain signed the Jay Treaty and thereby agreed to abandon the fur posts. Now that the Indian menace was removed, settlers poured into Ohio. Soon they demanded of Governor St. Clair that he take a census, and he ordered one in 1798. Its result showed that the time had come to move on to the second stage of government.

73

GOVERNMENT—SECOND STAGE

Section 9. ELECTION OF LEGISLATURE; QUALIFICATIONS OF REPRESENTATIVES AND VOTERS

So soon as there shall be five thousand free male inhabitants, of full age, in the district, upon giving proof thereof to the governor, they shall receive authority, with time and place, to elect representatives from their counties or townships, to represent them in the general assembly: *Provided,* that for every five hundred free male inhabitants there shall be one representative, and so on, progressively, with the number of free male inhabitants, shall the right of representation increase, until the number of representatives shall amount to twenty-five; after which the number and proportion of representatives shall be regulated by the legislature: *Provided,* That no person be eligible or qualified to act as a representative, unless he shall have been a citizen of one of the United States three years, and be a resident in the district, or unless he shall have resided in the district three years, and, in either case, shall likewise hold in his own right, in fee-simple, two hundred acres of land within the same: *Provided also,* That a freehold in fifty acres of land in the district, having been a citizen of one of the States, and being resident in the district, or the like freehold and two years' residence in the district, shall be necessary to qualify a man as an elector of a representative.

Section 10. TERMS OF OFFICE

The representatives thus elected shall serve for the term of two years; and in case of the death of a representative, or removal from office, the governor shall issue a writ to the county or township, for which he was a member, to elect another in his stead, to serve for the residue of the term.

Section 11. COMPOSITION OF LEGISLATURE; POWERS OF GOVERNOR

The general assembly, or legislature, shall consist of the governor, legislative council, and a house of representatives. The legislative council shall consist of five members, to continue in office five years, unless sooner removed by Congress; any three of whom to be a quorum; and the members of the council shall be nominated and appointed in the following manner, to wit: As

Territorial Government

The importance of the census referred to on the last page of commentary is revealed in the first sentence of Section 9. As soon as there were five thousand free male inhabitants, the people of the territory had a right to elect representatives to the legislature. As Section 11 makes clear the "general assembly" consisted of three parts—a governor, a legislative council, and a house of representatives. Only the last was directly elected by the people.

This second stage of government was closely modeled after that of the English "royal" or "crown" colony. In both the crown colony and the territorial government the governor was appointed by the central government; in both, the upper house of the legislature was chosen by the central government and the lower house by the people. The non-voting representative to Congress described in Section 12 had a position rather like that of the colonial agents who were sent to London by the colonies to look after their interests. Benjamin Franklin was for many years a colonial agent. *(Continued on p. 77)*

Explanatory

Notes Section 9. ". . . Provided, That no person be eligible or qualified to act as a representative, unless he shall . . . hold in his own right, in fee-simple, two hundred acres of land. . . . Provided also, That a freehold . . . of land in the district, . . . shall be necessary to qualify a man as an elector of a representative." In the Northwest Territory, as in the older states, only property holders had full political rights. If one talked of "the people" of a territory as having the right to choose legislators, one really meant "free adult male citizens owning fifty or more acres of land." The requirement that one must own land to hold the franchise was based on the idea that men with a stake in society would vote more responsibly than men who had little or nothing to lose. The graduated qualifications for officials, rising from two hundred acres for a representative in the assembly to a thousand acres for the governor, express the same idea—the more a man had at stake the more he was likely to be interested in good government.

The terms "fee-simple" and "freehold" come from the English common law. Land held in fee-simple is in absolute possession of the owner and he may dispose of it in any way he pleases. A freehold may be either absolute ownership of a piece of land or possession for life. The two terms are often used interchangeably; both rule out day laborers, squatters, and tenants.

soon as representatives shall be elected the governor shall appoint a time and place for them to meet together, and, when met they shall nominate ten persons, resident in the district, and each possessed of a freehold in five hundred acres of land, and return their names to Congress, five of whom Congress shall appoint and commission to serve as aforesaid; and whenever a vacancy shall happen in the council, by death or removal from office, the house of representatives shall nominate two persons, qualified as aforesaid, for each vacancy, and return their names to Congress, one of whom Congress shall appoint and commission for the residue of the term; and every five years, four months at least before the expiration of the time of service of the members of the council, the said house shall nominate ten persons, qualified as aforesaid, and return their names to Congress, five of whom Congress shall appoint and commission to serve as members of the council five years, unless sooner removed. And the governor, legislative council, and house of representatives shall have authority to make laws in all cases for the good government of the district, not repugnant to the principles and articles in this ordinance established and declared. And all bills, having passed by a majority in the house, and by a majority in the council, shall be referred to the governor for his assent; but no bill or legislative act whatever, shall be of any force without his assent. The governor shall have power to convene, prorogue, and dissolve the general assembly, when, in his opinion, it shall be expedient.

Section 12. OATH OF OFFICE; NON-VOTING REPRESENTATIVES TO CONGRESS

The governor, judges, legislative council, secretary, and such other officers as Congress shall appoint in the district, shall take an oath or affirmation of fidelity, and of office; the governor before the President of Congress, and all other officers before the governor. As soon as a legislature shall be formed in the district, the council and house assembled, in one room, shall have authority, by joint ballot, to elect a delegate to Congress, who shall have a seat in Congress, with a right of debating, but not of voting, during this temporary government.

In the territorial government, as in the crown colony, the local legislature was not free to pass laws as it pleased. The governor had the power to call the legislature together and to dissolve it whenever he chose to do so; he had the right to veto ("refuse his assent to") all bills. In other words, during this second stage of government, a territory had the status of a colony. The ultimate sovereignty remained with the Congress of the United States, just as during the colonial period the British claimed that Parliament had the right to make laws binding on the colonies "in all cases whatsoever."

The great difference between the colonial status of the thirteen colonies and that of the territorial governments carved out of the Northwest Territory is found in the last phrase of Section 12—"this temporary government." While the British had intended to keep their colonies in a state of permanent subordination and dependence, the Americans intended territorial government only as a transitional phase.

While Sections 9 through 12 applied strictly only to the Northwest Territory, they originated a method for the government of other areas that was in continuous operation until the last territory, Hawaii, was granted statehood in 1959. Only six states outside the original thirteen were admitted to the Union without having undergone a period of territorial status—Vermont, Kentucky, Maine, Texas, California, and West Virginia.

A GUARANTEE OF BASIC RIGHTS

Section 13. PURPOSE

And for extending the fundamental principles of civil and religious liberty, which form the basis whereon these republics,
their laws and constitutions, are erected; to fix and establish those
principles as the basis of all laws, constitutions, and governments,
which forever hereafter shall be formed in the said territory;
to provide, also, for the establishment of States, and permanent
government therein, and for their admission to a share in the
Federal councils on an equal footing with the original States, at
as early periods as may be consistent with the general interest:

Section 14. A SOLEMN CONTRACT

It is hereby ordained and declared, by the authority aforesaid,
That the following articles shall be considered as articles of
compact, between the original States and the people and States
in the said territory, and forever remain unalterable, unless by
common consent, to wit:

Article I. Religious Freedom. No person, demeaning himself
in a peaceable and orderly manner, shall ever be molested on
account of his mode of worship, or religious sentiments, in the
said territories.

Article II. Political Rights; Protection of Property. The inhabitants of the said territory shall always be entitled to the benefits of the writs of *habeas corpus,* and of the trial by jury; of a
proportionate representation of the people in the legislature, and
of judicial proceedings according to the course of the common
law. All persons shall be bailable, unless for capital offences,
where the proof shall be evident, or the presumption great. All
fines shall be moderate; and no cruel or unusual punishment
shall be inflicted. No man shall be deprived of his liberty or property, but by the judgment of his peers, or the law of the land,
and should the public exigencies make it necessary, for the common preservation, to take any person's property, or to demand
his particular services, full compensation shall be made for the
same. And, in the just preservation of rights and property, it is
understood and declared, that no law ought ever to be made or
have force in the said territory, that shall, in any manner whatever, interfere with or affect private contracts, or engagements,
bona fide, and without fraud previously formed.

A Solemn Contract and a Blueprint for the Future

Sections 13 and 14 give the Northwest Ordinance its enduring importance. Here is set down the principle stated by John Locke, that the rightful basis of government is a solemn contract (here called "compact") between the people and their rulers, its purpose being to guarantee the people their inalienable rights. Here the "glittering generalities" of the Declaration of Independence are translated into concrete terms; the broad phrases, "life, liberty, and the pursuit of happiness" and "consent of the governed" are spelled out. "Liberty" is defined as freedom to worship as conscience dictates; protection from arbitrary arrest, imprisonment, or punishment; and—see Article VI—the abolition of slavery. The "pursuit of happiness" here consists both of protection of private property and encouragement of education.

Explanatory

Notes Article I. This grant of complete religious toleration, subject only to good order, went farther than most of the thirteen states in 1787. Although the Revolution resulted in general progress toward greater freedom of worship, restrictions were retained in most of the states. In New England (except for Rhode Island) the Congregational Church was still supported by taxation and only Protestants could hold office. Pennsylvania demanded of officials that they recognize the divine inspiration of the Bible. South Carolina tolerated only those who believed in one God and in rewards and punishments in a future life.

Article II. Most of the protections of the individual in this section are derived from the traditional "rights of Englishmen." The writ of *habeas corpus* is a court order to prevent a person from being imprisoned without hearing the charge against him and guarantees his receiving a prompt trial. "Judicial proceedings according to the course of the common law" protect the rights of those accused of crimes or misdemeanors—many of these protections are detailed in the Bill of Rights of the Constitution (see Amendments IV–VIII, pp. 138–142). "Bailable" means an accused person may put up a sum of money as security that he will return to court for trial. The phrase "no cruel or unusual punishment" comes from the English Bill of Rights, 1689, and "the judgment of his peers or the law of the land" from Magna Carta, 1215.

Article III. Encouragement of Education; Fair Treatment of Indians. Religion, morality, and knowledge being necessary to good government, and the happiness of mankind, schools and the means of education shall forever be encouraged. The utmost good faith shall always be observed towards the Indians; their lands and property shall never be taken from them without their consent; and in their property, rights, and liberty they never shall be invaded or disturbed, unless in just and lawful wars authorized by Congress; but laws founded in justice and humanity shall, from time to time, be made, for preventing wrongs being done to them, and for preserving peace and friendship with them.

Article IV. Duties and Prohibitions. The said territory, and the States which may be formed therein, shall forever remain a part of this confederacy of the United States of America, subject to the Articles of Confederation, and to such alterations therein as shall be constitutionally made; and to all the acts and ordinances of the United States in Congress assembled, conformable thereto. The inhabitants and settlers in the said territory shall be subject to pay a part of the Federal debts, contracted, or to be contracted, and a proportional part of the expenses of government to be apportioned on them by Congress, according to the same common rule and measure by which apportionments thereof shall be made on the other States; and the taxes for paying their proportion shall be laid and levied by the authority and direction of the legislatures of the district, or districts, or new States, as in the original States, within the time agreed upon by the United States in Congress assembled. The legislatures of those districts, or new States, shall never interfere with the primary disposal of the soil by the United States in Congress assembled, nor with any regulations Congress may find necessary for securing the title in such soil to the *bona-fide* purchasers. No tax shall be imposed on lands the property of the United States; and in no case shall non-resident proprietors be taxed higher than residents. The navigable waters leading into the Mississippi and Saint Lawrence, and the carrying places between the same, shall be common highways, and forever free, as well to the inhabitants of the said territory as to the citizens of the United States, and those of any other States that may be admitted into the confederacy, without any tax, impost, or duty therefor.

Explanatory

Notes Article III. ". . . schools and the means of education shall forever be encouraged." The Confederation Congress had already put this principle into practice. The Land Ordinance of 1785, following a New England precedent, stipulated that one section in each of the six-mile-square townships should be reserved "for the maintenance of public schools." This was the first federal support of education in the United States.

"**The utmost good faith shall always be observed towards the Indians; . . .**" This admonition was not followed. The treatment of the natives of the Northwest Territory was like that followed everywhere on the frontier until the last Indians were cooped up in reservations about 1890. Over and over again Indian chiefs were forced or cajoled into giving up their hunting lands to the whites, and then were guaranteed what was left in treaties that were to last "as long as the sun shall climb the heavens or the waters shall run in the streams." But frontiersmen refused to be bound by such agreements and hunted, trapped, or settled in Indian lands until Indians were provoked into taking the warpath. Invariably they were sooner or later defeated by the whites. After each defeat they would cede more land and be guaranteed the rest "as long as the sun shall climb the heavens, etc."

Article IV. "**The legislatures . . . shall never interfere with the primary disposal of the soil by the United States in Congress assembled, . . .**" Although the inhabitants of the Northwest Territory were guaranteed the right to govern themselves, all land not yet sold to private purchasers or assigned to some public purpose, such as a fort or a school, remained under the control of the United States. In 1787 this land was expected to be one of the major sources of income for the Confederation.

"**. . . in no case shall non-resident proprietors be taxed higher than residents.**" Some members of Congress were land speculators and had holdings in the West. This may explain the prohibition on taxing non-resident property higher than that of residents. However, the Fourth Article of Confederation guarantees that free men shall enjoy within every state ". . . all the privileges of trade and commerce, subject to the same duties, impositions and restrictions as the inhabitants thereof. . . ." (see p 36).

81

GOVERNMENT—THIRD STAGE

Article V. New States. There shall be formed in the said territory not less than three nor more than five States; and the boundaries of the States, as soon as Virginia shall alter her act of cession and consent to the same, shall become fixed and established as follows, to wit: The western State, in the said territory, shall be bounded by the Mississippi, the Ohio, and the Wabash Rivers; a direct line drawn from the Wabash and Post Vincents, due north, to the territorial line between the United States and Canada; and by the said territorial line to the Lake of the Woods and Mississippi. The middle State shall be bounded by the said direct line, the Wabash from Post Vincents to the Ohio, by the Ohio, by a direct line drawn due north from the mouth of the Great Miami to the said territorial line, and by the said territorial line. The eastern State shall be bounded by the last-mentioned direct line, the Ohio, Pennsylvania, and the said territorial line: *Provided, however,* And it is further understood and declared, that the boundaries of these three States shall be subject so far to be altered that, if Congress shall hereafter find it expedient, they shall have authority to form one or two States in that part of the said territory which lies north of an east and west line drawn through the southerly bend or extreme of Lake Michigan. And whenever any of the said States shall have sixty thousand free inhabitants therein, such State shall be admitted, by its delegates, into the Congress of the United States, on an equal footing with the original States, in all respects whatever; and shall be at liberty to form a permanent constitution and State

New States

Important above all is the way the fifth of these "articles of compact" defines "consent of the governed" as the eventual right of the people of the Northwest Territory to set up new states ". . . on an equal footing with the original States, in all respects whatever; . . ." Here the Confederation Congress showed its devotion to the principles of the American Revolution. It also found a solution to an age-old problem of politics. Athens in the fifth century B.C. was a self-governing republic, proud of its liberties; but Athens fell because it failed to grant its subject cities equal rights, and the cities revolted. The ancient Roman Republic was wiser. It not only guaranteed Roman citizens their rights in perpetuity whenever and wherever they founded colonies, but it also granted citizenship to conquered peoples as a reward for loyalty. Thus St. Paul, a Jew, could demand his rights as a Roman citizen to be tried in Rome itself. The Romans, however, failed to find a method of combining rule over a large area with effective self-government. It was partly because of this failure that the Roman Republic was eventually replaced by a dictatorship under Caesar Augustus who made himself the first Roman emperor. It was generally believed in the eighteenth century that only government ruled by an absolute king or emperor could long govern an extended territory.

The Northwest Ordinance set forth a means whereby a nation governed colonies as long as they could not fend for themselves, keeping their loyalty meanwhile by a guarantee of eventual equality and self-government. It

(Continued on p. 85)

Explanatory

Notes Article V. The most important section of this article, the promise that new states were to be formed and admitted into the Union on terms of full equality, has been dealt with on pages 78–79.

"There shall be formed in the said territory not less than three nor more than five States; and the boundaries of the States, . . . shall become fixed and established as follows, . . ." The number and size of the new states to be created in the West was a matter of dispute in the Congress. The delegates representing the agrarian South favored creating numerous states and admitting them to the Confederation on easy terms. The commercial interests of the North foresaw that the principal occupation of the western people would be agriculture. They feared a future political alliance of southern and western farmers and therefore advocated fewer western states and more difficult admission. The arrangement in the Northwest Ordinance is a compromise, but one more favorable to the North than those of the Land Ordinance of 1784 (see p. 67).

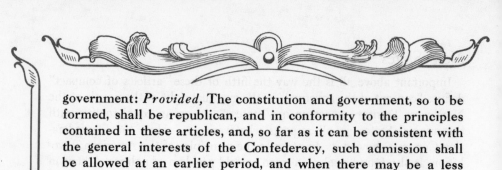

government: *Provided,* The constitution and government, so to be formed, shall be republican, and in conformity to the principles contained in these articles, and, so far as it can be consistent with the general interests of the Confederacy, such admission shall be allowed at an earlier period, and when there may be a less number of free inhabitants in the State than sixty thousand.

declared that a perpetual Union could be maintained not through force, but through ties of mutual respect and mutual devotion to the principle that government exists to protect human rights.

Although the promise of eventual statehood in Article V applied only to the Northwest Territory, it supplied a precedent for other areas. When North Carolina ceded her western land claims in 1790, a territorial government was immediately established in Tennessee and full statehood was granted in 1796. So it happened again and again as the people of the United States moved into the vast area stretching across the Great Plains and the Rocky Mountains to the Pacific Ocean. Once pioneers had settled a region and established orderly government, they could look forward with certainty to forming new states and entering the Union on terms of absolute equality.

The principle that colonial status is but a way station to full equality has proven significant outside the United States. The British learned from the American Revolution that the attempt to rule peoples against their will could lead to disaster. In the twentieth century Great Britain has allowed one colony after another to assume the status of a "dominion" or "commonwealth" on terms of full equality with the mother country, bound to her by mutual ties of good will and self-interest.

Explanatory Notes

"Provided, The constitution and government, so to be formed, shall be republican, . . ." This insistence on a "republican" form of government appears again in Article IV, Section 4, of the Constitution, drawn up in the same year as this Ordinance. It is obvious that the authors of the two documents believed republican government to be vital for the success of the American experiment; but what did they mean by the term? This is not an easy question because they themselves did not agree, nor do modern historians. This much can be said: A republican government was one that rested on popular consent, one in which the officials were elected, and one in which the people participated either directly or through their representatives. Such a state existed to protect and preserve the natural rights of man. While active citizenship (the right to vote and hold office) might be limited to property holders, property should be widely distributed. Privileges carried on from generation to generation, such as hereditary monarchy and a nobility, were banned.

According to both ancient Greek and Roman authors and the political thinkers of the eighteenth century, republican government was difficult to maintain because it depended on the "virtue" of its citizens—their loyalty to principles rather than to a monarch, their devotion to public service, and their self-restraint.

Article VI. No Slavery. There shall be neither slavery nor involuntary servitude in the said territory, otherwise than in the punishment of crimes, whereof the party shall have been duly convicted: *Provided always,* That any person escaping into the same, from whom labor or service is lawfully claimed in any one of the original States, such fugitive may be lawfully reclaimed, and conveyed to the person claiming his or her labor service as aforesaid.

ORDINANCE OF 1784 REPEALED

Be it ordained by the authority aforesaid, That the resolutions of the 23d of April, 1784, relative to the subject of this ordinance, be, and the same are hereby, repealed, and declared null and void.

Done by the United States, in Congress assembled, the 13th day of July, in the year of our Lord 1787, and of their sovereignty and independence the 12th.

CHARLES THOMSON,
Sec'y.

No Slavery

The Fathers of the American Revolution were perfectly aware of the glaring contradiction between the principles of the Declaration of Independence and slavery. None of them was more sensitive upon this point than a man who owned as many as 210 slaves and who sold as many as 55 at one time—Thomas Jefferson. In his *Notes on Virginia*, published in Paris in 1785, Jefferson wrote: "The whole commerce between master and slave is a perpetual exercise of the most boisterous passions, the most unremitting despotism on the one part, and degrading submissions on the other. . . . can the liberties of a nation be thought secure when we have removed their only firm basis, a conviction in the minds of the people that these liberties are the gift of God? That they are not to be violated but with His wrath? Indeed I tremble for my country when I reflect that God is just. . . ."

Before, during, and after the Revolution, Jefferson attempted to persuade the Virginia House of Burgesses to pass an emancipation act, but without success. Although in the eighteenth century the Virginia planters generally deplored slavery, they saw overwhelming practical difficulties in the way of its abolition.

Jefferson's one chance to strike a blow at slavery came when he was appointed head of a committee of Congress to draw up regulations for the West in 1784. Jefferson's first draft for the Land Ordinance of that year prohibited slavery in the West, but this was voted down by a narrow vote in Congress. The provision was revived in 1787 and written into the Northwest Ordinance.

This Article VI vitally affected the future of the United States by making the Ohio River a boundary line between slavery and freedom. It also provided a precedent for the prohibition of slavery in the Louisiana Purchase above the 36°30' line by the Missouri Compromise of 1820.

Explanatory Notes **Ordinance of 1784 Repealed.** This repeal of the Ordinance of 1784 was necessary because it was to have gone into effect when the states completed their western land cessions.

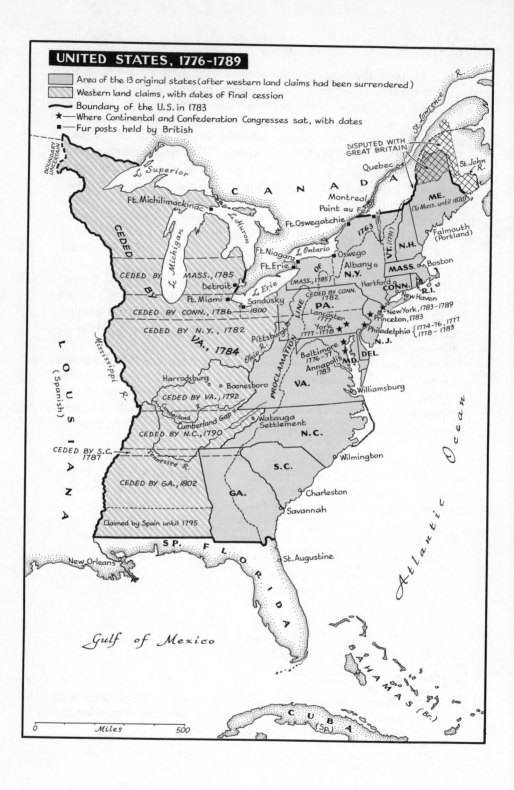

UNITED STATES, 1776-1789

Area of the 13 original states (after western land claims had been surrendered)

Western land claims, with dates of final cession

Boundary of the U.S. in 1783

★ Where Continental and Confederation Congresses sat, with dates

■ Fur posts held by British

BOUNDARY UNCERTAIN

CANADA

DISPUTED WITH GREAT BRITAIN

St. Lawrence R.

Quebec

St. John R.

Montreal

Point au Fer

Ft. Oswegatchie

L. Superior

Ft. Michilimackinac

L. Huron

L. Michigan

Ft. Niagara

L. Ontario

Oswego

1763

ME. (To Mass. until 1820)

Falmouth (Portland)

N.H.

VT. (1791)

CEDED BY

Ft. Erie

Albany

MASS.

Boston

CEDED BY MASS., 1785

Detroit

L. Erie

Sandusky

(MASS., 1785)

N.Y.

Hartford

CONN.

R.I.

New Haven

CEDED BY CONN., 1786

Ft. Miami

1800

PA.

CEDED BY CONN. 1782

New York, 1783-1789

Princeton, 1783

CEDED BY N.Y., 1782

Pittsburgh

Ohio R.

Lancaster 1777

York 1777-1778

Philadelphia {1774-76, 1777
                1778 - 1783}

VA., 1784

PROCLAMATION

LINE

OF

Baltimore 1776-77

MD.

Annapolis 1783

N.J.

DEL.

Mississippi R.

LOUISIANA (Spanish)

Harrodsburg

Boonesboro

CEDED BY VA., 1792

VA.

Williamsburg

Cumberland R.

Cumberland Gap

CEDED BY N.C., 1790

Watauga Settlement

N.C.

CEDED BY S.C., 1787

Tennessee R.

Wilmington

CEDED BY GA., 1802

GA.

S.C.

Charleston

Claimed by Spain until 1795

Savannah

SP. FLORIDA

New Orleans

St. Augustine

Gulf of Mexico

Atlantic Ocean

BAHAMAS (Br.)

CUBA (SP.)

0 — Miles — 500

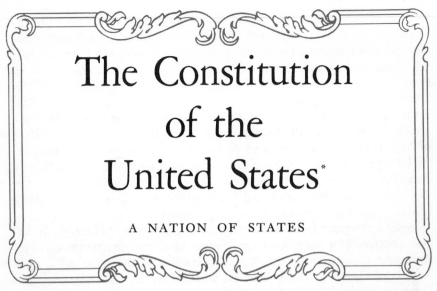

The Constitution
of the
United States*

A NATION OF STATES

T HE YEARS during which the Articles of Confederation were in
operation used to be called the "critical period" of the history
of the United States. Carrying out this notion, textbooks have
usually portrayed this period in somber tones. The Americans
were said to be in a state of acute economic distress because of
the loss of foreign markets, currency inflation, and interstate
tariff wars. Shays's Rebellion was evidence that civil war was
imminent. It was said to be touch and go whether the Union of
American states would survive. The country was saved from
anarchy and financial chaos only by the formation and ratification
of the Constitution.

Recent scholarship has challenged this long-held interpretation.
It is historically inaccurate to talk of any era as being *the* critical
period. There have been plenty of critical periods in our history—
the decade before the War Between the States, for instance; or
the Great Depression; or the present era, when mankind faces
the horrible prospect of atomic annihilation. Nor were the 1780's
as black as they have been painted. Of course there were commercial dislocations and difficulties, as after every major war, but
taken as a whole the postwar years saw the United States making
remarkable economic progress. In almost every city there was
a building boom. New foreign markets opened up to take the
place of those lost, and the exports of agricultural products rose

* Much of this introduction to the Constitution and nearly all of the page-
by-page explanation of the document is taken from *History of a Free People*,
Bragdon and McCutchen. Copyright © 1954, 1956, 1958, 1960, 1961 by
The Macmillan Company.

to twice what they had been before the Revolution. The picture of financial chaos has been exaggerated. Only in Rhode Island and North Carolina was there anything approaching runaway inflation. Most states established effective systems of taxation and stabilized their currency; most of them even assumed payment of a share of the war debts owed by the Confederation Congress. As it was pointed out in a previous chapter, if the Articles of Confederation had been amended so as to give the Congress the power to tax, the Confederation might have survived. The failure of New York to agree to such an amendment in 1786 was one of the precipitating causes of the movement to create a stronger government. Shays's Rebellion in Massachusetts that same year was influential in the same direction, because it revealed that the Confederation Congress was totally unable to assist the states in suppressing insurrection.

In 1786 delegates from five states met at Annapolis, Maryland, to discuss stronger and more uniform control of interstate commerce. The Annapolis Convention asked the Confederation Congress to call a convention of all the states for the next year. Acting on this suggestion, the Congress urged the thirteen states to send representatives to a meeting in Philadelphia "for the sole and express purpose of revising the Articles of Confederation."

Twelve states answered the call of Congress and sent delegates to a convention that convened in Philadelphia in May, 1787, and sat continuously for over four months. Only 55 of the 73 men chosen as delegates bothered to go, and the average attendance was around 30. But although small, the membership was able and experienced. Many of the delegates had read widely in political theory, and nearly all had practical experience in government.

The convention probably owed most to two members from Virginia, George Washington and James Madison. Washington was so universally trusted that his presence alone helped to make the work of the convention acceptable to the country. Chosen to preside, he kept the debates orderly and in good temper through his dignity and fairness.

Madison, only thirty-six years old, came to Philadelphia better prepared than any other delegate. He had studied confederations and leagues, ancient and modern, and he brought with him a scheme for a new government of the United States. This so-called "Virginia Plan" was presented to the convention by Edmund Randolph. The Virginia Plan became the basis for discussion and provided the main ideas for the government as finally set up.

Benjamin Franklin represented Pennsylvania. Over eighty years old, and so weak that he had to be carried to the meetings in a sedan chair, Franklin took little part in the debates. His tact and cheerfulness, however, helped to keep the convention from breaking up when disputes developed and tempers rose. Furthermore, he was so popular that, like Washington, he helped to make the convention a success by his mere presence.

From New York came Alexander Hamilton, one of the youngest men in the convention and perhaps the most brilliant. He was not influential, however, because his views were too extreme. He proposed a government that would reduce the states to mere provinces under governors appointed by the President of the United States. And the President, once elected, was to hold office for life. Hamilton's attitude may have been useful, since it made other plans to strengthen the central government seem comparatively mild.

Most of the delegates to the Philadelphia Convention were more or less wealthy. They tended to be lawyers, merchants, and plantation owners. Many held western land claims, government bonds, and private mortgages. Such people would benefit from a stronger government. Landowners wanted better prices for their produce, and these would come with the commercial treaties a strong government could arrange. Merchants wanted better protection for American shipping and a national currency. Owners of western lands wanted protection from Indians. Creditors hoped for more severe bankruptcy laws, an end to state paper money, and a government that could pay its debts.

Because the propertied classes wanted a stronger Union and would benefit by it, the creation of the Constitution is sometimes portrayed as a sort of plot whereby the wealthy created a government for their own selfish purposes. This theory overlooks several facts. As the prompt ratification of the Constitution soon showed, small property holders as well as large wanted more stable finances along with a government that could control interstate and foreign commerce. The Constitution at the time it was created and ever since has benefited the poor as well as the rich. A new government in any case could be formed *only* by the well-to-do, since at the time the Constitution was created, they alone had the necessary education, political experience, and ability to see the needs of the whole country.

Human motives are always mixed. The men who worked during all of a long, hot summer at Philadelphia were certainly aware that a stronger central government might eventually benefit most of them personally. They were also performing, at some cost to themselves, what they believed to be their public duty. The more one studies their work, the more one is likely to agree with James Madison, who later wrote:

> . . . there never was an assembly of men, charged with a great and obvious trust, who were more pure in their motives, or more exclusively and anxiously devoted to the object committed to them than were the members of the Federal Convention of 1787.

A principal reason why it took all summer to hammer out the Constitution was the reappearance of some of the same disputes that had plagued Congress when trying to write the Articles of Confederation (see p. 29).

The same dispute between the large and small states over representation in Congress almost broke up the convention. The large states, led by Virginia, demanded representation according to population; the small states insisted on retaining the sovereign equality they enjoyed in the Confederation Congress.

Over this conflict the Philadelphia Convention came to "a full stop," as one delegate described it. For a week, during a spell of especially hot weather, there was bitter debate, while flies buzzed over the delegates' heads and settled on legs exposed by knee breeches. There seemed no middle ground between the demands of the large and small states. Franklin proposed that each session be opened with prayer.

The log jam was broken when the delegates took a day off to celebrate the Fourth of July. During the recess a committee worked out what has since been called the Great Compromise. According to this arrangement one branch of Congress, the House of Representatives, would be chosen on the basis of population, while in the other house, the Senate, each state would have an equal vote. This was accepted by a vote of six states to five, one state not voting. And so it is that while Nevada sends but one representative to Congress and the adjoining state of California sends 38, each state is represented by two Senators.

Once the dispute between small and big states was settled, the other dangerous conflict was between the commercial interests of the North and the plantation interests of the South. One point of dispute was how to count slaves for representation and taxation. This was settled by arbitrarily counting the slave population as three-fifths of its number for both purposes, that is, five slaves were equal to three free people. The delegates from Georgia and South Carolina, the only states where slavery was profitable in the 1780's, feared the immediate abolition of the slave trade. At their insistence it was arranged that for twenty years the federal government might not interfere with the importation of slaves.

The other point of dispute between North and South concerned commerce. Southerners feared taxes on exports (which would fall heavily on their staples such as tobacco and naval stores) and navigation laws which would favor northern shipping at the cost of higher carrying charges for southern exports. As a compromise it was arranged that Congress be forbidden to levy duties on exports, but that navigation laws could be passed by a simple majority.

The disputes at the Philadelphia Convention tend to obscure the fact that on most important matters the Founding Fathers were agreed.

1. They believed that the Articles of Confederation were so inadequate for the needs of the country that they decided to create an entirely new Constitution. In doing this they exceeded their instructions which said they were merely to propose amendments to the Articles. They agreed with Washington who said that the members of the convention must create a frame of government that they believed would work.

2. They wanted to protect property rights from assaults such as Shays's Rebellion in Massachusetts and the Rhode Island laws requiring creditors to accept depreciated paper money in payment of debts.

3. While they feared that too much democracy made governments "turbulent and changeable," they never considered setting up a monarchy or an oligarchy (government of the few). Instead, they sought to set up a republic in which, while the ultimate power rested with the majority of the people, minority rights were protected.

4. The convention members knew that they could not go too far in the direction of strong government or abolition of state sovereignty or their new Constitution would never be ratified by the states.

5. In devising a workable government the Founding Fathers were guided by their experience with British and colonial government, as well as by certain political theorists, especially John Locke, and Montesquieu, a Frenchman who had written an analysis of the British constitution.

The new Constitution clearly granted to the federal government the powers it had most needed under the Articles. It could now levy and collect taxes, with certain minor restrictions; thus it could pay its way. It could regulate commerce with foreign nations and between the states; thus it could write and enforce commercial treaties. It had the sole right to coin money and regulate its value, establishing one national standard of money instead of state currencies with different values.

Many of the powers granted the federal government were simply carried over from the Confederation. For instance, under the Articles Congress had power to borrow money, as well as to raise an army and navy. But because the Confederation Congress could not tax, such powers existed only on paper. Now the federal government could carry out all the powers granted to it. This was especially true because *it could exert its powers directly upon individuals and compel them to obey.*

In certain matters the states were put under federal control. No longer might state legislatures relieve debtors by scaling down debts or issuing paper money. No state might levy tariffs on goods from another state. All state officials had to swear to support the Constitution of the United States; this made all of them, from governors to constables, agents of the federal government as well as of their own states. The state militia was put under the control of Congress.

The new Constitution provided a well worked out system of government, based on British experience. There was a separate executive department, centering on the President, to carry out the laws of the United States and conduct foreign relations. The Congress, divided into two houses, was carefully defined as to membership and powers. A federal judiciary was to deal with offenses against federal laws and with interstate disputes.

On September 17, 1787, the Founding Fathers held their last meeting and signed the document they had written. In the evening they held a farewell dinner. But their work was by no means over. It remained to be seen whether the country would accept the new Constitution. It was provided that the Constitution would go into effect after it had been ratified by nine states. It was impossible to propose unanimous acceptance, as provided in the Articles of Confederation, because Rhode Island was certain not to ratify and other states were doubtful. Ratification was to be carried out by state conventions called for the purpose, a democratic process following out the idea of the Declaration of Independence that governments "derive their just powers from the consent of the governed."

To get nine states to ratify the Constitution was no small task. There was suspicion of any sort of strong central government. Why revolt from Great Britain, it was asked, simply to transfer power to an even more powerful central government? There was fear that the President would make himself a kind of king. "This Constitution," said Patrick Henry, "squints toward monarchy; and does not this raise indignation in the breast of every true American?"

Henry was only one of several popular leaders, including Governor George Clinton of New York, Samuel Adams and John Hancock of Massachusetts, and Richard Henry Lee of Virginia, who maintained that a federal government as powerful as that provided in the Constitution would eventually suppress the liberties of the people.

Those who supported the new Constitution made a shrewd move when they called themselves "Federalists," even though they could perhaps have been more accurately described as "Nationalists." This foisted on the opposition the meaningless name of "Anti-Federalists." The Federalists had other advantages. They were united and the Constitution they supported was a definite program to meet the difficulties of the country. The Anti-Federalists were disunited, and they had nothing better to offer than to continue with the discredited Confederation or to call a second constitutional convention. The Federalists included men who commanded great popularity and respect, such as Franklin and Washington. They had the support of most of the clergymen, and many ministers used their pulpits to persuade their congregations to support the proposed frame of government. The Federalists also had the better of the debate in newspapers, pamphlets, and debates in state ratifying conventions. The electioneering over ratification produced, in fact, one of the finest pieces of political writing of all time. This is a collection of eighty-five articles called *The Federalist*, written by Hamilton, Madison, and John Jay to explain how the Constitution would work and how it would benefit the country. Even though written for the needs of the moment and originally published serially in a New York newspaper, *The Federalist* papers reveal so much of the intentions of the framers of the Constitution and contain so much political wisdom that they have become a classic.

In general, the Federalists represented the wealthier classes, the coastal districts, and professional men such as lawyers, ministers, and doctors. The Anti-Federalists tended to find support among the poorer people, especially among debt-burdened small farmers. But there were many exceptions to this division. For instance, in New York the great patroons, who owned land along the Hudson River, tended to oppose the Constitution. They feared heavier state taxes on their land if the federal government took over the taxes on which the government of New York State had previously depended for its support. The artisans of New York City and the small farmers up the Mohawk Valley supported it because they hoped a more stable government would bring a revival of trade and better wages. The smaller states tended to favor the Constitution because they had more need of union, while the big states were inclined to hold off. But even here it is dangerous to generalize, because one finds that Pennsylvania was among the first to ratify and that Rhode Island, the smallest state of all, did not ratify until the new government had been in operation for over a year.

In several important states the votes in the conventions were uncomfortably close; thus in Virginia it was 88 to 78 in favor, in Massachusetts 187 to 168, in New York 30 to 27. By mid-summer 1788, however, eleven states had ratified, and preparations were begun to set up the new government in 1789.

When the news of ratification came in, great celebrations were held in several cities. That on July 4, 1788, in Philadelphia included about five thousand participants and had eighty-eight separate displays. The framing and adoption of the Constitution were indeed events worthy of celebration. The Constitution is a unique document whose influence on the course of world history cannot even now be estimated. It created a new kind of government, the so-called *federal* type, which combines a powerful national government with vigorous localism. It has provided a pattern for uniting large areas, such as Canada, India, Australia, and South Africa. People who believe the free nations of the world should unite have also recommended it as a model. And this new, strong government was not formed by military leaders bent on conquest, nor by a seizure of government by a strong man or a clique, but by a group of citizens acting for what they considered to be the good of the country and submitting their work to their fellow countrymen for approval.

To the Reader

In studying the following pages the reader should note that:

1. Portions of the Constitution which are no longer in operation are printed in light-face type.

2. The descriptive headings at the beginning of Articles, Sections, and clauses of the Constitution are not part of the document itself, but have been added for the convenience of the reader.

The Constitution

of the

United States of America

PREAMBLE

WE THE PEOPLE of the United States, in Order to form a more perfect Union, establish Justice, insure domestic Tranquility, provide for the common defence, promote the general Welfare, and secure the Blessings of Liberty to ourselves and our Posterity, do ordain and establish this Constitution for the United States of America.

The Preamble

"The preamble is not, strictly speaking, a part of the Constitution, but 'walks before it.'" It explains the *source* of the Constitution and its *purposes*. When the preamble states, "We the People of the United States . . . do ordain and establish this Constitution. . . ." it follows the principle expressed in the Declaration of Independence: that governments derive "their just powers from the consent of the governed." The Constitution was drawn up by representatives of the people and ratified in conventions elected by them.

In 1789, however, "We the People" did not mean *all* the people, but only the minority possessing political rights. The right to vote was limited to white adult males with a certain amount of property. The proportion of voters varied from state to state, but everywhere a greater or lesser amount of property was required for the privilege of voting, and no Negroes or women could vote. In the many years since the Constitution went into effect, however, the advance of democracy has broadened the meaning of "We the People" so much that today it means "nearly all adults."

For many years there was dispute as to whether "We the People of the United States" meant "We the people of the different states" or "We the people of an American nation." In 1789 the former meaning was probably more accurate, since the delegates to the Philadelphia Convention were chosen by states, the Constitution was ratified state by state, and a man's first loyalty was to his state. As time went on, however, the loyalty of the American people to the nation became stronger than that to the states.

Each purpose of the Constitution described in the preamble had a special meaning in 1789. The authors of the Constitution were trying to create "a more perfect Union" than the Articles of Confederation. They sought to "establish Justice" for creditors, to "insure domestic Tranquility" by suppressing disorders such as Shays's Rebellion, and to "provide for the common defence" against Indians and Barbary pirates. They hoped the new government would "promote the general Welfare" by increasing interstate and foreign commerce. Finally, the purpose of the Constitution was to "secure the Blessings of Liberty" by creating a stronger government to protect people in their rights. This was different from the purpose of the Declaration of Independence which had been to obtain liberty by freeing the United States from the strong government of England.

Today, then, the preamble to the Constitution has a far broader meaning than in 1789. Then the few set up the federal government to provide for the simple needs of a small rural population living on the edge of an isolated continent. Now the federal government represents the great majority of the people, and the Constitution must provide for the complex needs of a great industrial nation in a world which has been made small by instantaneous communication and rapid transportation.

97

Article I. LEGISLATIVE DEPARTMENT

Section 1. CONGRESS

The Two Houses of Congress. All legislative Powers herein granted shall be vested in a Congress of the United States, which shall consist of a Senate and House of Representatives.

Section 2. HOUSE OF REPRESENTATIVES

1. *House Members Elected by the People.* The House of Representatives shall be composed of Members chosen every second Year by the People of the several States, and the Electors in each State shall have the Qualifications requisite for Electors of the most numerous Branch of the State Legislature.

2. *Qualifications of Representatives.* No Person shall be a Representative who shall not have attained to the Age of twenty five Years, and been seven Years a Citizen of the United States, and who shall not, when elected, be an Inhabitant of that State in which he shall be chosen.

3. *House Membership Based on State Populations.* Representatives and direct Taxes shall be apportioned among the several States which may be included within this Union, according to their respective Numbers, [which shall be determined by adding to the whole Number of free Persons, including those bound to Service for a Term of Years, and excluding Indians not taxed, three fifths of all other Persons.] The actual Enumeration shall be made within three Years after the first Meeting of the Congress of the United States, and within every subsequent Term of ten Years, in such Manner as they shall by Law direct. The Number of Representatives shall not exceed one for every thirty Thousand, but each State shall have at Least one Representative; [and until such enumeration shall be made, the State of New Hampshire shall be entitled to chuse three, Massachusetts eight, Rhode-Island and Providence Plantations one, Connecticut five, New-York six, New Jersey four, Pennsylvania eight, Delaware one, Maryland six, Virginia ten, North Carolina five, South Carolina five, and Georgia three.]

4. *Election for Vacancies in the House.* When vacancies happen in the Representation from any State, the Executive Authority thereof shall issue Writs of Election to fill such Vacancies.

5. *Election of Speaker of the House, Impeachment.* The House of Representatives shall chuse their Speaker and other Officers; and shall have the sole Power of Impeachment.

How Congress Is Organized and Does Business

The Congress of the United States under the Constitution differed from that under the Articles of Confederation in being "bicameral," that is, having two legislative chambers. This was a return to the English system whereby Parliament is divided into a House of Lords and a House of Commons. The Senate was originally designed to resemble the House of Lords in being somewhat removed from popular control, and the House of Representatives to resemble the Commons in being more democratic. In the American system, a further difference between the two branches of Congress resulted from the Great Compromise (see pp. 91–92). The House, chosen on a basis of population, represented the idea of a nation. The Senate, in which each state is equally represented, retained the idea of a league.

Usually in a bicameral legislature one house or the other becomes dominant, and it is usually the house more directly responsible to the people that gains the upper hand. The culmination of this process can be seen most clearly in Great Britain where nearly all legislative power is now lodged in the House of Commons, and the House of Lords has become little more than a ceremonial body. *(Continued on p. 101)*

Explanatory Notes

Article I, Section 2, clause 1. "Electors" here means simply "voters." Until the Fifteenth Amendment (1870) forbade states to deny the right to vote on grounds of race, the decision as to who might vote in federal elections was entirely a matter of state legislation.

Article I, Section 2, clause 3. "Those bound to Service for a Term of Years" means "indentured servants and apprentices." "Other Persons" means "slaves." Note that the latter were formerly counted for representation in the House at three-fifths of their number.

If there had continued to be one Representative for each thirty thousand people, the House would today contain over five thousand members. Its number is now fixed at 435.

Article I, Section 2, clause 5. The Speaker is chosen from the majority party in the House. This is in contrast to the British Parliament where the Speaker is an impartial umpire and is considered "above party." The powers of the Speaker of the House have varied. At one time his control over debate and over appointments to congressional committees was so great that he had more influence on legislation than the President.

As it is employed in this clause, "impeachment" means "indictment," "bringing charges against." Thus President Johnson was impeached by the House in 1868, but when the Senate failed to convict him, he remained in office.

99

Section 3. SENATE

1. *Number of Senators, Election, Term of Office.* **The Senate of the United States shall be composed of two Senators from each State,** [chosen by the Legislature thereof,] **for six Years; and each Senator shall have one Vote.**

2. *One-Third Senate Chosen Every Two Years.* **Immediately after they shall be assembled in Consequence of the first Election, they shall be divided as equally as may be into three Classes.** [The Seats of the Senators of the first Class shall be vacated at the Expiration of the second Year, of the second Class at the Expiration of the fourth Year, and of the third Class at the Expiration of the sixth Year,] **so that one third may be chosen every second Year;** [and if Vacancies happen by Resignation, or otherwise, during the Recess of the Legislature of any State, the Executive thereof may make temporary Appointments until the next Meeting of the Legislature, which shall then fill such Vacancies.]

3. *Qualifications of Senators.* **No Person shall be a Senator who shall not have attained to the Age of thirty Years, and been nine Years a Citizen of the United States, and who shall not, when elected, be an Inhabitant of that State for which he shall be chosen.**

4. *Vice-President Presides over Senate.* **The Vice President of the United States shall be President of the Senate, but shall have no Vote, unless they be equally divided.**

5. *Other Officers.* **The Senate shall chuse their other Officers, and also a President pro tempore, in the Absence of the Vice President, or when he shall exercise the Office of President of the United States.**

In the United States neither the House nor the Senate has gained any ascendancy over the other, although individual Senators generally enjoy more prestige than individual Congressmen, if only because the Senators are fewer in number and serve longer terms. But the two bodies retain practically equal powers of legislation. Since every law must be passed by both houses, each acts as a check on the other. Each house judges the qualifications of its own members, and enjoys the same privileges of free speech and freedom from arrest during sessions. On the other hand, each branch of Congress has special powers. The House has the right to impeach members of the executive and judicial departments for "high crimes and misdemeanors," and first proposes bills which involve raising money. The Senate acts as a court to try impeachments brought by the House, and has the right to accept or reject the President's appointments. The most famous special power of the Senate lies in the field of foreign affairs. The President must submit treaties to the Senate before they go into operation. It requires a vote of two-thirds of the Senators to ratify a treaty. This provision was inserted to make sure that no treaty would sacrifice the interests of one section to those of another, as the 1785 Jay-Gardoqui Treaty had sacrificed western interests to those of the Northeast. (Continued on p. 103)

Explanatory

Notes Article I, Section 3, clause 1. The Seventeenth Amendment provided that Senators should be chosen by direct popular vote, instead of by state legislatures.

Article I, Section 3, clause 4. One of the supposed weaknesses of the Constitution is that the Vice-President has so little to do. His only constitutional function is to preside over the Senate, his only constitutional power to cast a vote in those rare cases when there is a tie vote. Prominent men have not in the past sought an office regarded as "a political graveyard." Parties have usually chosen their vice-presidential candidates with a view to "balancing the ticket" by giving representation to a different section of the country or a different faction of the party from that of the presidential candidate. Under the Truman, Eisenhower, and Kennedy administrations, however, Vice-Presidents Alben Barkley, Richard Nixon, and Lyndon Johnson have been brought into the inner circle of presidential advisers and given important jobs involving both domestic and foreign policy.

6. *Senate a Court in Cases of Impeachment*. The Senate shall have the sole Power to try all Impeachments. When sitting for that Purpose, they shall be on Oath or Affirmation. When the President of the United States is tried the Chief Justice shall preside: And no Person shall be convicted without the Concurrence of two thirds of the Members present.

7. *Punishment for Officials Convicted in Cases of Impeachment*. Judgment in Cases of Impeachment shall not extend further than to removal from Office, and disqualification to hold and enjoy any Office of honor, Trust or Profit under the United States: but the Party convicted shall nevertheless be liable and subject to Indictment, Trial, Judgment and Punishment, according to Law.

Section 4. ELECTION AND MEETING OF CONGRESS

1. *Regulation of Elections*. The Times, Places and Manner of holding Elections for Senators and Representatives, shall be prescribed in each State by the Legislature thereof; but the Congress may at any time by Law make or alter such Regulations, except as to the Places of chusing Senators.

2. *Sessions of Congress*. [The Congress shall assemble at least once in every Year, and such Meeting shall be on the first Monday in December, unless they shall by Law appoint a different Day.]

In the course of time, the two branches of Congress have developed different ways of doing business. The House of Representatives became so unwieldy in size (435 members) that debate had to be severely restricted to get anything done at all. Nearly all the work of the House is done by committees dealing with particular problems, such as agriculture, government finances, foreign affairs, immigration, military affairs, commerce, education, and labor. The chairmen of these immensely powerful committees reach their position by seniority, and their average age is generally close to seventy years. Debate and the order of business in the House is strictly controlled by the Speaker and a nine-man Committee on Rules.

The Senate because of its smaller size (as of 1962 it contains 100 members) has been able to retain "freedom of debate," which means that any Senator may speak on any motion. This leads to the practice of "filibustering," whereby a few Senators, or even a single one, may block legislation they dislike by unlimited talk. A closure rule to prevent this practice has proved ineffective. Full-scale debate in the Senate, on the other hand, often educates the public on major issues. It can also insure thorough consideration of legislation which might otherwise be passed hurriedly. In general, however, the Senate like the House transacts most of its business in committee.

Explanatory Notes

Article I, Section 3, clause 6. When trying a case of impeachment brought by the House, the Senate becomes a court. The two-thirds vote necessary to convict an official under impeachment and remove him from office is one of several cases where the Constitution demands a two-thirds majority of either or both houses of Congress. Actions demanding a two-thirds vote involve matters of more than ordinary importance, or ones in which a simple majority vote might be unfair to individuals or minority groups. The complete list is as follows: (1) *trial of impeachments*—Article I, Section 3, clause 6 (two-thirds of the Senate); (2) *expulsion of members from either house of Congress*—Article I, Section 5, clause 2 (two-thirds of the house in which the member holds a seat); (3) *passing a bill over the President's veto*—Article I, Section 7, clause 2 (two-thirds of both houses); (4) *ratification of treaties*—Article II, Section 2, clause 2 (two-thirds of the Senate); (5) *proposing amendments to the Constitution* (two-thirds of both houses of Congress, or a constitutional convention proposed by two-thirds of the state legislatures).

Article I, Section 4, clause 2. The Twentieth Amendment, ratified in 1933, has changed the date of the opening of the regular session of Congress to January 3.

Section 5. Organization and Rules of Each House

1. *Power over Membership and Sittings.* Each House shall be the Judge of the Elections, Returns and Qualifications of its own Members, and a Majority of each shall constitute a Quorum to do Business; but a smaller Number may adjourn from day to day, and may be authorized to compel the Attendance of absent Members, in such Manner, and under such Penalties as each House may provide.

2. *Power over Rules and Behavior.* Each House may determine the Rules of its Proceedings, punish its Members for disorderly Behaviour, and, with the Concurrence of two thirds, expel a Member.

3. *Keeping a Record of Proceedings.* Each House shall keep a Journal of its Proceedings, and from time to time publish the same, excepting such Parts as may in their judgment require Secrecy; and the Yeas and Nays of the Members of either House on any question shall, at the Desire of one fifth of those Present, be entered on the Journal.

4. *Adjournment.* Neither House, during the Session of Congress, shall, without the Consent of the other, adjourn for more than three days, nor to any other Place than that in which the two Houses shall be sitting.

Separation of Powers

The authors of the Constitution had a great fear of unlimited political power, no matter who wielded it. Concentration of power in the hands of one man generally resulted, they knew, in oppression of the people as a whole. The members of the Philadelphia Convention also distrusted a government dominated by the unrestrained will of the people. They were convinced that such a complete democracy would be weak and changeable, and that it would enable the poor to rob the rich. Finally, there was always danger that men in office would try to seize more power than the people wanted to grant them.

In order to avert what they regarded as the triple dangers of tyranny, mob rule, and seizure of power, the Founding Fathers created a government based on the principle of "separation of powers." According to this principle—which stemmed both from American colonial experience and from the writings of Montesquieu, a well-known French political scientist —the major powers of government should be divided among different officials. So in the American Constitution the first three Articles are devoted to defining the powers of the legislative, executive, and judicial branches of the federal government, *each branch being administered by different people.* How careful the authors of the Constitution were to preserve separation of powers can be seen by Article I, Section 6, clause 2; this forbids any man to hold both an executive or judicial office and a seat in Congress at the same time. *(Continued on p. 107)*

Explanatory Notes

Article I, Section 5, clauses 1 and 2. The power enjoyed by each house of Congress to judge the qualifications of its members is absolute; there is no appeal from it to any court or other governmental agency. Very seldom, however, is a member of Congress excluded or expelled, for such action robs the people of his district or state of their right to be represented in the national legislature.

Immediately after the War Between the States the Radical Republican Congressmen, who opposed President Johnson's leniency toward the South, excluded Senators and Representatives from the former Confederate States. Among the reasons why individual members of the House or Senate have been excluded or expelled have been the following: practising polygamy, using corruption and fraud in elections, advocating a socialist revolution, and bribing fellow members of Congress to vote generous land grants to railroads.

Section 6. CONGRESSIONAL PRIVILEGES AND RESTRAINTS

1. *Payment and Privileges.* The Senators and Representatives shall receive a Compensation for their Services, to be ascertained by Law, and paid out of the Treasury of the United States. They shall in all Cases, except Treason, Felony and Breach of the Peace, be privileged from Arrest during their Attendance at the Session of their respective Houses, and in going to and returning from the same; and for any Speech or Debate in either House, they shall not be questioned in any other Place.

2. *Congressmen not to Hold Other Federal Offices.* No Senator or Representative shall, during the Time for which he was elected, be appointed to any civil Office under the Authority of the United States, which shall have been created, or the Emoluments whereof shall have been encreased during such time; and no Person holding any Office under the United States, shall be a Member of either House during his Continuance in Office.

This American system of separation of powers is in contrast to the British system of "parliamentary" or "cabinet" government. In Britain the real heads of the government, the prime minister and his cabinet, are chosen from the legislature itself. They represent the party which commands a majority in the lower house of Parliament, the House of Commons. Thus instead of being separated the British executive and legislative powers are merged.

Explanatory Notes Article I, Section 6, clause 1. Members of Congress now receive a salary of $22,500 plus a tax free expense account of $2,500 and staff assistance in proportion to the size of their constituency and load of committee work. Very few Congressmen can more than break even on their salary because their expenses are heavy. Considering the importance of the work, Congressmen are probably underpaid.

The privileges of Congressmen—freedom from arrest during session and freedom of speech within the halls of Congress—are taken from the practice of the British Parliament. These rights were won by the British House of Commons during a long struggle with the Stuart kings of England in the seventeenth century. Such privileges may be abused, as when Congressmen make unsupported accusations against defenseless individuals. Congressional immunity is necessary, however, if Congressmen are to act independently and speak freely on public questions.

Article I, Section 6, clause 2. The purpose of this clause is to prevent the corrupt use of patronage that was a feature of British parliamentary government in the eighteenth century, and also to prevent the President from influencing Congressmen by promising or giving them jobs. Without this provision the President might use his power of appointment to break down the intended separation between executive and legislative power.

Section 7. How Bills Become Laws

1. *Revenue Bills.* All Bills for raising Revenue shall originate in the House of Representatives; but the Senate may propose or concur with Amendments as on other Bills.

2. *President's Veto.* Every Bill which shall have passed the House of Representatives and the Senate, shall, before it becomes a Law, be presented to the President of the United States; If he approve he shall sign it, but if not he shall return it, with his Objections to that House in which it shall have originated, who shall enter the Objections at large on their Journal, and proceed to reconsider it. If after such Reconsideration two thirds of that House shall agree to pass the Bill, it shall be sent, together with the Objections, to the other House, by which it shall likewise be reconsidered, and if approved by two thirds of that House, it shall become a Law. But in all such Cases the Votes of both Houses shall be determined by yeas and Nays, and the Names of the Persons voting for and against the Bill shall be entered on the Journal of each House respectively. If any Bill shall not be returned by the President within ten Days (Sundays excepted) after it shall have been presented to him, the Same shall be a Law, in like Manner as if he had signed it, unless the Congress by their Adjournment prevent its Return, in which Case it shall not be a Law.

3. *Veto Power Extended to Resolutions.* Every Order, Resolution, or Vote to which the Concurrence of the Senate and House of Representatives may be necessary (except on a question of Adjournment) shall be presented to the President of the United States; and before the Same shall take Effect, shall be approved by him, or being disapproved by him, shall be repassed by two thirds of the Senate and House of Representatives, according to the Rules and Limitations prescribed in the Case of a Bill.

Checks and Balances

To prevent any branch of the federal government from overstepping its powers, the Constitution sets up an elaborate system of "checks and balances" whereby each branch of government is given some power to oversee or interfere in the work of the others. Thus the lawmaking power of Congress is checked by the President's veto, which is a negative power of legislation. While it is the President's job as chief executive to appoint civil servants and judges, the Senate shares in this executive power since it must ratify all major appointments. Although it is the function of the federal judiciary to try persons accused of crime, the President has the judicial power of granting pardons and reprieves.

Separation of powers plus checks and balances have sometimes received criticism. If any two branches of the federal government disagree, decisive action may be difficult, even impossible. Especially if the President and Congress are in opposition, the government tends to go into "dead center," with Congress unwilling to take action recommended by the President, and the President able to veto bills passed by Congress. In any case, checks and balances tend to slow up federal action to such a degree that one authority has written, "The time element in the American Constitution makes it a luxury the United States cannot afford in the modern world."

On the other hand, checks and balances and separation of powers are an insurance against the unlawful seizure of the federal government by one man or an organized group. They are also a protection against rash, ill-considered action. These advantages probably more than outweigh the apparent inefficiency of such a system.

Explanatory

Notes **Article I, Section 7, clause 2.** The President's veto is what is known as a "suspensive veto." That is, it suspends action until Congress has a chance to try to "override" the veto, which must be by a two-thirds vote. The President within less than ten days before the end of a congressional sitting may also use the "pocket veto." In such a case the President may simply ignore a bill ("put it in his pocket"), and it automatically fails to become a law.

Section 8. POWERS GRANTED CONGRESS

1. *Taxation.* The Congress shall have Power To lay and collect Taxes, Duties, Imposts and Excises, to pay the Debts and provide for the common Defence and general Welfare of the United States; but all Duties, Imposts and Excises shall be uniform throughout the United States;

2. *Borrowing.* To borrow Money on the credit of the United States;

3. *Regulation of Commerce.* To regulate Commerce with foreign Nations, and among the several States, and with the Indian Tribes;

4. *Naturalization and Bankruptcies.* To establish an uniform Rule of Naturalization, and uniform Laws on the subject of Bankruptcies throughout the United States;

5. *Coinage.* To coin Money, regulate the Value thereof, and of foreign Coin, and fix the Standard of Weights and Measures;

6. *Punishing Counterfeiters.* To provide for the Punishment of counterfeiting the Securities and current Coin of the United States;

7. *Postal Service.* To establish Post Offices and post Roads;

8. *Copyrights and Patents.* To promote the Progress of Science and useful Arts, by securing for limited Times to Authors and Inventors the exclusive Right to their respective Writings and Discoveries;

9. *Lower Courts.* To constitute Tribunals inferior to the supreme Court;

10. *Punishing Piracy.* To define and punish Piracies and Felonies committed on the high Seas, and Offences against the Law of Nations;

11. *Declaring War.* To declare War, grant Letters of Marque and Reprisal, and make Rules concerning Captures on Land and Water;

12. *Army.* To raise and support Armies, but no Appropriation of Money to that Use shall be for a longer Term than two Years;

13. *Navy.* To provide and maintain a Navy;

14. *Regulating the Armed Forces.* To make Rules for the Goverment and Regulation of the land and naval Forces;

15. *Calling Out Militia.* To provide for calling forth the Militia to execute the Laws of the Union, suppress Insurrections and repel Invasions;

The Federal System

Article I, Section 8, has been called "the heart of the Constitution." It grants the federal government the great powers needed to govern the United States effectively. In the many years since the Constitution went into effect, it has been found necessary to add very few new powers to the list in the original Constitution.

As compared with other national governments, however, a striking thing about the government of the United States is that *its powers are limited.* Other national governments hold "unlimited sovereignty"—that is, all the power of government centers in them. The United States, however, has a system of "divided sovereignty" whereby the Constitution grants the federal government charge of interstate and foreign relations while the states control local affairs. This arrangement was probably a result of the fact that during the colonial period Americans had become used to a similar

(Continued on p. 113)

Explanatory Notes

Article I, Section 8, clauses 1 and 3. These clauses contain the most important of the new powers granted the federal government by the Constitution: taxation and control over interstate and foreign commerce.

Both these powers have been greatly expanded since the Constitution first went into effect. The taxing power has been used for other purposes than raising money. Protective tariffs have always been levied in order to promote American industry. Heavy taxation has also been employed to prevent the use of certain products, such as sulphur matches, by raising their price so high that no one would buy them. Congress has attempted to discourage gambling by a special tax on the activities of professional gamblers.

The word "Commerce" in clause 3 has extremely varied meanings. Under its power to regulate interstate and foreign commerce, the federal government fixes railroad rates, prevents misleading advertising, establishes frequencies for radio stations, protects migratory birds, and makes kidnaping a federal offense.

Article I, Section 8, clause 5. Control over money is an exclusive federal power since the states are forbidden to issue currency (Article I, Section 10, clause 1). This arrangement was designed to end the confusion which resulted when each state had its own standard of currency.

Article I, Section 8, clause 12. The condition that money may be voted for the armed forces for only two years reveals fear of a standing army. Tyrants have often used their countries' armies to suppress the liberties of the people. The Constitution endeavors to see that the military force of the United States shall be servant of the people, not their master.

16. *Regulating Militia.* To provide for organizing, arming, and disciplining, the Militia, and for governing such Part of them as may be employed in the Service of the United States reserving to the States respectively, the Appointment of the Officers, and the Authority of training the Militia according to the discipline prescribed by Congress;

17. *Areas under Exclusive Control of Congress.* To exercise exclusive Legislation in all Cases whatsoever, over such District (not exceeding ten Miles square) as may, by Cession of particular States, and the Acceptance of Congress, become the Seat of the Government of the United States, and to exercise like Authority over all Places purchased by the Consent of the Legislature of the State in which the Same shall be, for the Erection of Forts, Magazines, Arsenals, dock-Yards, and other needful Buildings; —And

18. *The "Elastic Clause."* To make all Laws which shall be necessary and proper for carrying into Execution the foregoing Powers, and all other Powers vested by this Constitution in the Government of the United States, or in any Department or Officer thereof.

Section 9. POWERS DENIED THE UNITED STATES

1. *May Not Interfere with Slave Trade Before 1808.* [The Migration or Importation of such Persons as any of the States now existing shall think proper to admit, shall not be prohibited by the Congress prior to the Year one thousand eight hundred and eight, but a Tax or duty may be imposed on such Importation, not exceeding ten dollars for each Person.]

2. *May not Suspend* Habeas Corpus *Except in Crisis.* The Privilege of the Writ of Habeas Corpus shall not be suspended unless when in Cases of Rebellion or Invasion the public Safety may require it.

3. *May Not Pass Bills of Attainder or* Ex Post Facto *Laws.* No Bill of Attainder or ex post facto Law shall be passed.

4. *May Not Levy Taxes Except in Proportion to Population.* No Capitation, or other direct, Tax shall be laid, unless in Proportion to the Census or Enumeration herein before directed to be taken.

arrangement. To try to prevent such an increase in the powers of the central government as had caused the American Revolution, the Founding Fathers made the federal government one of "enumerated powers." This means that the actions of the government of the United States are restricted to the powers specifically granted in the Constitution. All other power remained in the hands of the states.

In the course of time, the powers of the federal government have been expanded in accordance with the needs of a growing country. This has been accomplished by interpretation of the so-called "elastic clause" (Article I, Section 8, clause 18). This states that Congress may make all laws "necessary and proper" for putting into effect its stated powers. Just what "necessary and proper" means has been a matter of bitter dispute. Those who wish to interpret the phrase strictly, and so to restrain the power of the federal government, emphasize the word "*necessary.*" They are known as "strict constructionists," because they wish to interpret the Constitution strictly and to limit the federal government to the powers *enumerated* or *specified* in the document itself. Those who wish to interpret the phrase loosely, and so to extend the power of the federal government, emphasize the word "*proper.*" They are known as "loose constructionists," because they wish to interpret the Constitution loosely and to allow the federal government to exercise powers *implied* in the document. Loose constructionists argue, for instance, that the enumerated power to control interstate commerce meant that the federal government had an implied power to build roads and canals.

No matter how much the "elastic clause" may be stretched, it is always understood that federal power is limited to the purposes stated in the Constitution. As the Tenth Amendment says:

The powers not delegated to the United States by the Constitution, nor prohibited by it to the States, are reserved to the States respectively, or to the people. (*Continued on p. 115*)

Explanatory

Notes Article I, Section 9, clause 2. The "writ of *habeas corpus*" is a legal document which forces a jailer to release a citizen held in prison unless he has been formally charged with crime or convicted in a law court. It protects citizens from arrests based on dislike or suspicion.

Article I, Section 9, clause 3. A "bill of attainder" was a means whereby the British Parliament formerly punished officials and private individuals without a trial. An "*ex post facto* law" is one passed after an act has been committed making that act a crime, and prescribing punishment for it.

5. *May Not Levy Export Taxes.* No Tax or Duty shall be laid on Articles exported from any State.

6. *May Not Favor One Port over Another.* No Preference shall be given by any Regulation of Commerce or Revenue to the Ports of one State over those of another: nor shall Vessels bound to, or from, one State, be obliged to enter, clear, or pay Duties in another.

7. *May Not Spend Money without Appropriations or Maintain Secrecy in Finances.* No Money shall be drawn from the Treasury, but in Consequence of Appropriations made by Law; and a regular Statement and Account of the Receipts and Expenditure of all public Money shall be published from time to time.

8. *May Not Grant Titles of Nobility.* No Title of Nobility shall be granted by the United States: And no Person holding any Office of Profit or Trust under them, shall, without the Consent of the Congress, accept of any present, Emolument, Office or Title, of any kind whatever, from any King, Prince, or foreign State.

Section 10. Powers Denied the States

1. *Various Actions Forbidden to the States.* No State shall enter into any Treaty, Alliance, or Confederation; grant Letters of Marque and Reprisal; coin Money; emit Bills of Credit; make any Thing but gold and silver Coin a Tender in Payment of Debts; pass any Bill of Attainder, ex post facto Law, or Law impairing the Obligations of Contracts, or grant any Title of Nobility.

2. *May Not Levy Import or Export Duties.* No State shall, without the Consent of the Congress, lay any Imposts or Duties on Imports or Exports, except what may be absolutely necessary for executing its inspection Laws: and the net Produce of all Duties and Imposts, laid by any State on Imports or Exports, shall be for the Use of the Treasury of the United States; and all such Laws shall be subject to the Revision and Controul of the Congress.

3. *May Not Wage War Unless Invaded.* No State shall, without the Consent of Congress, lay any Duty of Tonnage, keep Troops, or Ships of War in time of Peace, enter into any Agreement or Compact with another State, or with a foreign Power, or engage in War, unless actually invaded, or in such imminent Danger as will not admit of delay.

The division of sovereignty between the state and federal governments has had fortunate results. It has provided strong rule for the country as a whole, and yet has put local affairs into the hands of those who know them best. The federal government has not lacked the powers to meet every major test, whether of peace or war. Yet the state and municipal governments remain vigorous and useful. They still control the matters which concern the day-to-day life of Americans most closely—their health, their schooling, their police and fire protection, their water supply. This promotes democracy by encouraging people to take an active interest in local politics.

Local democracy also promotes the effectiveness of the federal government. It is a school of politics for many men who later hold federal office. Many Congressmen have served in state legislatures, and nearly half our Presidents served previously as state Governors. Furthermore, the states have served as "political laboratories" where new kinds of laws to meet the ever-changing problems of an industrial civilization can be tested.

Explanatory Notes Article I, Section 9, clauses 4, 5, 6, and 7. The taxing and spending powers of the federal government are limited in order to prevent taxation falling more heavily on one part of the country than on another and to discourage misuse of public funds. The Sixteenth Amendment was needed to legalize a federal income tax in 1913.

Article I, Section 10. Much of this section is designed to reenforce the powers granted to the federal government in Article I, Section 8. The states are prohibited from taking any part in control of foreign affairs, war, and control of interstate and foreign commerce.

Article I, Section 10, clause 1. Several phrases in this clause protect creditors from state laws designed to make it easier for debtors to repay what they have borrowed. The states are forbidden to "emit Bills of Credit"—that is, to print paper money which would reduce the value of the currency. The prohibitions on making "any Thing but gold and silver Coin a Tender in Payment of Debts" and on passing any "Law impairing the Obligations of Contracts" were both designed to prevent the states from scaling down debts.

Article II. EXECUTIVE DEPARTMENT

Section 1. PRESIDENT AND VICE-PRESIDENT

1. *Term of Office.* The executive Power shall be vested in a President of the United States of America. He shall hold his Office during the Term of four Years, and, together with the Vice President, chosen for the same Term, be elected, as follows:

2. *Number of Electors.* Each State shall appoint, in such Manner as the Legislature thereof may direct, a Number of Electors, equal to the whole Number of Senators and Representatives to which the State may be entitled in the Congress: but no Senator or Representative, or Person holding an Office of Trust or Profit under the United States, shall be appointed an Elector.

3. *Election of President and Vice-President.* [The Electors shall meet in their respective States, and vote by Ballot for two Persons, of whom one at least shall not be an Inhabitant of the same State with themselves. And they shall make a List of all the Persons voted for, and of the Number of Votes for each; which List they shall sign and certify, and transmit sealed to the Seat of the Government of the United States, directed to the President of the Senate. The President of the Senate shall, in the Presence of the Senate and House of Representatives, open all the Certificates, and the Votes shall then be counted. The Person having the greatest Number of Votes shall be the President, if such Number be a Majority of the whole Number of Electors appointed; and if there be more than one who have such Majority, and have an equal Number of Votes, then the House of Representatives shall immediately chuse by Ballot one of them for President; and if no Person have a Majority, then from the five highest on the List the said House shall in like Manner chuse the President. But in chusing the President, the Votes shall be taken by States, the Representation from each State having one Vote: A quorum for this Purpose shall consist of a Member or Members from two thirds of the States, and a Majority of all the States shall be necessary to a Choice. In every Case, after the Choice of the President, the Person having the greatest Number of Votes of the Electors shall be the Vice President. But if there should remain two or more who have equal Votes, the Senate shall chuse from them by Ballot the Vice President.]

4. *Time for Choosing Electors.* The Congress may determine the Time of chusing the Electors, and the Day on which they shall give their Votes; which Day shall be the same throughout the United States.

The Presidency

No branch of the federal government gave the authors of the Constitution so much difficulty as the executive department. The Founding Fathers knew that a strong President was needed, but they also had to reckon with a widespread fear of a strong executive. This fear was a carry-over from the struggles with royal governors in colonial times.

Under these circumstances it is surprising how much power the President was given. He has been called "an elective monarch," and historically this is an accurate description. The President's major powers are those formerly enjoyed by the king of England. These are, briefly, (1) conduct of foreign affairs, (2) supreme command of the army and navy, (3) appointment of executive and judicial officers, (4) the right to reprieve or pardon those accused of crime, and (5) a veto on legislation. In addition to these great powers, the President had a four-year term and was allowed to succeed himself in office. Contrast this to the position of many state Governors, who in the 1780's were allowed to hold office for only one year, had no veto power, and were not allowed to succeed themselves.

(Continued on p. 119)

Explanatory

Notes Article II, Section 1, clause 2. The Philadelphia Convention had trouble deciding how the President should be chosen. A proposal to have him selected directly by Congress was voted down because this would violate the principle of separation of powers. Direct election was hardly even considered because of the fear that a President with a great popular following might seize power. A choice by state legislatures, each state having one vote, was considered, but the large states were naturally opposed to this. The system finally agreed upon was indirect election by "electors" chosen for the purpose. The presidential electors are collectively called the "electoral college." During the early years of the republic, the presidential electors were, like the Senators, chosen by state legislatures rather than by vote of the people. For further discussion of the method of electing the President, see notes on the Twelfth Amendment.

Article II, Section 1, clause 3. This clause has been largely replaced by the Twelfth Amendment. Note that in the original Constitution each elector had two votes, and that the man with the highest number of votes became President and the next highest became Vice-President. If there was no majority, the election would be thrown into the House of Representatives. The House, voting by states with each state having one vote, would make a choice from the highest five candidates. It was expected that this would happen frequently, on the assumption that electors would vote for "favorite sons" from their own states or regions. Actually the House has elected the President only twice, in 1800 and 1824.

5. *Qualifications for President.* No Person except a natural born Citizen, [or a Citizen of the United States, at the time of the Adoption of this Constitution,] shall be eligible to the Office of President; neither shall any Person be eligible to that Office who shall not have attained to the Age of thirty five Years, and been fourteen Years a Resident within the United States.

6. *Presidential Succession in Case of Vacancy.* In case of the Removal of the President from Office, or of his Death, Resignation, or Inability to discharge the Powers and Duties of the said Office, the same shall devolve on the Vice President, and the Congress may by Law provide for the Case of Removal, Death, Resignation or Inability, both of the President and Vice President, declaring what Officer shall then act as President, and such Officer shall act accordingly, until the Disability be removed, or a President shall be elected.

7. *Presidential Salary.* The President shall, at stated Times, receive for his Services, a Compensation, which shall neither be encreased nor diminished during the Period for which he shall have been elected, and he shall not receive within that Period any other Emolument from the United States, or any of them.

8. *Presidential Oath.* Before he enter on the Execution of his Office, he shall take the following Oath or Affirmation:—"I do solemnly swear (or affirm) that I will faithfully execute the Office of President of the United States, and will to the best of my Ability, preserve, protect and defend the Constitution of the United States."

Section 2. POWERS OF THE PRESIDENT

1. *Military Power; Executive Departments; Reprieves and Pardons.* The President shall be Commander in Chief of the Army and Navy of the United States, and of the Militia of the several States, when called into the actual Service of the United States; he may require the Opinion, in writing, of the principal Officer in each of the executive Departments, upon any Subject relating to the Duties of their respective Offices, and he shall have Power to grant Reprieves and Pardons for Offences against the United States, except in Cases of Impeachment.

Nearly every one of the President's stated powers has been expanded since the Constitution first went into effect. At first, for instance, the veto power was used sparingly, but since Andrew Jackson's time Presidents have used the veto to hold up any legislation they disliked. Lincoln used his power as commander-in-chief as the basis for issuing the Emancipation Proclamation which declared slaves free in the South.

Much of the President's power comes from the fact that he is head of one or the other of the two great political parties. The members of his party in Congress are under pressure to support legislation which he recommends. The President has also gained strength because, as Grover Cleveland said, "The Presidency is the people's office." While members of Congress represent particular states, he represents the whole country. His every action attracts nation-wide attention. No one can rival him in his ability to appeal to public opinion—especially since the invention of radio broadcasting and television.

In time of crisis, as in wartime or a depression, when quick, decisive action is called for, Congress may turn over many of its powers to the President "for the duration." On such an occasion he may come close to being a temporary dictator.

The influence of the Presidency varies according to the personality and purposes of men who hold the office. Andrew Jackson and Theodore Roosevelt increased their power by sheer force of personality. A President

(Continued on p. 121)

Explanatory Notes

Article II, Section 1, clause 6. In the case of the death or removal of both the President and the Vice-President, the law now provides that the Speaker of the House of Representatives shall succeed to the presidency. A question which has never been answered is: Who decides that a President is unable to discharge the duties of his office? In 1919 and 1920 the country was almost leaderless when President Wilson fell seriously ill and yet failed to give others authority to act for him. The problem reappeared in less acute form when President Eisenhower fell ill in 1955 and again in 1956. Yet up to 1962 Congress has failed to pass legislation empowering some man or group of men to decide that the Vice-President should take the reins of government.

Article II, Section 2. An important presidential power, the veto, is described not in this section, but in Article I, Section 7, clauses 2 and 3.

Article II, Section 2, clause 1. Mention of "the principal Officer in each of the executive Departments" is one of two suggestions (see clause 2, this section) of the cabinet in the Constitution. Washington started the cabinet by asking the heads of government departments to meet with him for discussion of public questions. The cabinet is a purely advisory body, and its power depends on the President.

2. *Treaties and Appointments.* He shall have Power, by and with the Advice and Consent of the Senate, to make Treaties, provided two thirds of the Senators present concur; and he shall nominate, and by and with the Advice and Consent of the Senate, shall appoint Ambassadors, other public Ministers and Consuls, Judges of the supreme Court, and all other Officers of the United States, whose Appointments are not herein otherwise provided for, and which shall be established by Law: but the Congress may by Law vest the Appointment of such inferior Officers, as they think proper, in the President alone, in the Courts of Law, or in the Heads of Departments.

3. *Recess Appointments.* The President shall have Power to fill up all Vacancies that may happen during the Recess of the Senate, by granting Commissions which shall expire at the End of their next Session.

Section 3. PRESIDENTIAL DUTIES

Presidential Messages; Congressional Sessions; Executing Laws. He shall from time to time give to the Congress Information of the State of the Union, and recommend to their Consideration such Measures as he shall judge necessary and expedient; he may, on extraordinary Occasions, convene both Houses, or either of them, and in Case of Disagreement between them with Respect to the Time of Adjournment, he may adjourn them to such Time as he shall think proper; he shall receive Ambassadors and other public Ministers; he shall take Care that the Laws be faithfully executed, and shall Commission all the Officers of the United States.

Section 4. IMPEACHMENT

Removal of Executive Officers. The President, Vice President and all Civil Officers of the United States, shall be removed from Office on Impeachment for, and Conviction of, Treason, Bribery, or other high Crimes and Misdemeanors.

with a program of legislation he wants to put through Congress will generally exert more power than a "stand-patter" who wants to continue things as they are.

The President is now more than President of the United States. He is the leader of the free world alliance against international communism, and his decisions therefore must affect profoundly the lives of men in other countries.

Greatly as the power of the President has expanded, there has never been serious danger of dictatorship. Only in times of crisis will Congressmen consent to be "rubber stamps." The Supreme Court also stands ready to check undue use of power, as when in 1952 it forbade President Truman to settle a strike by seizing the steel industry (see pp. 266–273). Nor do America's allies accept the President's decisions without question; he must persuade them of the wisdom of any course of action.

Explanatory Notes

Article II, Section 2, clause 2. The requirement that treaties be ratified by two-thirds of Senators present has had important results. This provision, for instance, prevented the United States from joining the League of Nations after World War I.

Article II, Section 3. By delivering special messages urging particular laws or by calling "special sessions" for Congress to consider some particular problem, the President can focus public attention on legislation which he wants passed. When a crisis comes up while Congress is not in session, the President may attempt to keep matters in his own hands by failing to call Congress into session before its regular time of meeting.

The President's duty to receive foreign diplomats carries with it the power to ask a foreign country to withdraw its diplomatic officials from this country. This is called "breaking diplomatic relations," and often carries with it the threat of war. The President likewise has the power of deciding whether or not to "recognize" a new foreign government. Thus in 1913 President Wilson refused to recognize a Mexican government headed by Victoriano Huerta because Huerta had gained power by violence. Presidents Truman, Eisenhower, and Kennedy have all refused to recognize the Communist government of China.

The President's duty to faithfully execute the laws carries with it a power to interpret laws according to his judgment. A President must decide what to do when two laws contradict each other—as they sometimes do. Or Presidents may vary in the degree to which they carry out a law. Thus the Sherman Anti-Trust Act was almost a dead letter until Theodore Roosevelt chose to enforce it more vigorously than his three predecessors.

Article II, Section 4. Remember that "impeachment" means merely to "bring charges against," not "to remove from office." Removal takes place only *after* the accused officer has been convicted of the offense for which he was impeached.

Article III. JUDICIAL DEPARTMENT

Section 1. FEDERAL COURTS

Supreme and Lower Courts; Term and Salary of Judges. The judicial Power of the United States, shall be vested in one supreme Court, and in such inferior Courts as the Congress may from time to time ordain and establish. The Judges, both of the supreme and inferior Courts, shall hold their Offices during good Behaviour, and shall, at stated Times, receive for their Services, a Compensation, which shall not be diminished during their Continuance in Office.

Section 2. JURISDICTION OF FEDERAL COURTS

1. *Kinds of Cases Tried in Federal Courts.* The Judicial Power shall extend to all Cases, in Law and Equity, arising under this Constitution, the Laws of the United States, and Treaties made, or which shall be made, under their Authority;—to all Cases affecting Ambassadors, other public Ministers and Consuls;—to all Cases of admiralty and maritime Jurisdiction;—to Controversies to which the United States shall be a Party;—to Controversies between two or more States; [—between a State and Citizens of another State;]—between Citizens of different States;—between Citizens of the same State claiming Lands under Grants of different States, and between a State, or the Citizens thereof, and foreign States, Citizens or Subjects.

The Federal Judiciary

Of the three branches of government, the judicial department is the one most sketchily described in the Constitution. It was simply stated that there was to be a Supreme Court and inferior courts. Other details were left for later decision by Congress. Soon after the first Congress met, during the administration of George Washington, it passed the Judiciary Act of 1789 which set up the federal courts on a plan which has been followed ever since. The lowest courts were the "district courts," each presided over by a district judge. Most cases involving federal laws were, and are, tried in district courts. Above the district courts were established the "circuit courts." Their principal business is to hear cases which have been appealed from district courts.

The Constitution was more precise about the types of cases which should go to federal courts than about how the courts should be set up. The principal function of the federal judiciary under the Constitution is plain: to try offenses against federal laws and treaties. Thus the new federal government differed from that established by the Articles of Confederation because *it could compel individual citizens to obey it*.

One of the most vital powers of the federal judiciary is not stated in the Constitution. This is the practice known as "judicial review," whereby the courts decide whether state and federal laws accord with the Constitution. If the judiciary decides that a law is unconstitutional, it ceases to have effect. Thus the federal judiciary, and especially the Supreme Court, exerts a veto power. Furthermore, this veto extends beyond legislation to the actions of state and federal executives, and to the decisions of state courts (see p. 168). In no other country in the world does the judiciary exert so much power. It is not clear whether the authors of the Constitution meant to grant the courts such immense authority, but judicial review was an obvi-

(Continued on p. 125)

Explanatory

Notes Article III, Section 2, clause 1. The phrase "in Law and Equity" reflects the fact that American courts took over two kinds of traditional law from England. The basic law was the "common law" which was based on over five centuries of judicial decisions. "Equity" was a special branch of law developed for cases where common law did not apply, or to prevent injustice (also see p. 165). Federal courts deal mostly in "statute law"—actual legislation passed by Congress, treaties, or the Constitution itself. "Admiralty and maritime Jurisdiction" is a branch of law inherited from Great Britain. It covers all sorts of cases involving ships and shipping on the high seas and on navigable waters such as rivers, canals, and the Great Lakes.

The meaning of the phrase "between a State and Citizens of another State" has been altered by the Eleventh Amendment.

123

2. *Original and Appellate Jurisdiction of Supreme Court.* In all Cases affecting Ambassadors, other public Ministers and Consuls, and those in which a State shall be Party, the supreme Court shall have original Jurisdiction. In all the other Cases before mentioned, the supreme Court shall have appellate Jurisdiction, both as to Law and Fact, with such Exceptions, and under such Regulations as the Congress shall make.

3. *Jury Trial Guaranteed; Place of Trial.* The Trial of all Crimes, except in Cases of Impeachment, shall be by Jury; and such Trial shall be held in the State where the said Crimes shall have been committed; but when not committed within any State, the Trial shall be at such Place or Places as the Congress may by Law have directed.

Section 3. TREASON

1. *Definition of Treason.* Treason against the United States, shall consist only in levying War against them, or in adhering to their Enemies, giving them Aid and Comfort. No Person shall be convicted of Treason unless on the Testimony of two Witnesses to the same overt Act, or on Confession in open Court.

2. *Punishment for Treason; How Limited.* The Congress shall have Power to declare the Punishment of Treason, but no Attainder of Treason shall work Corruption of Blood, or Forfeiture except during the Life of the Person attainted.

ous interpretation of Article VI, clause 2, which states that the Constitution is the "supreme Law of the Land."

Today the main business of the Supreme Court is to judge constitutional questions in cases brought on appeal from lower federal courts. The only way to override a Supreme Court decision is by the difficult process of amending the Constitution. This was done, for instance, by Amendment XVI, which permitted Congress to levy an income tax after the Supreme Court had declared such a tax unconstitutional. The Supreme Court is also controlled, less obviously, by other factors. For one thing, the Court has developed a tradition of self-restraint, and is generally cautious in declaring state or federal actions unconstitutional. Nor does it pass on all laws, but only on those brought before it. And while the judges do not face the people at election time, and so feel free to oppose the popular will, actually the Court sooner or later usually "follows the election returns"— in other words, it goes along with public opinion as expressed through the actions of state governments, of Congress, and of the federal executive.

Federal judges hold office "during good Behavior," which means for life, or until they choose to resign. Combined with the provision that judges' salaries may not be reduced, this is designed to make the federal courts "independent." As long as they are not guilty of "high crimes or misdemeanors" (for which they may be impeached), federal judges are free of popular, presidential, or congressional control. The idea of an independent judiciary originated in England in the seventeenth century in order to prevent judges from being controlled by the king. The idea was carried over into the United States Constitution to prevent judges from being controlled by anybody.

While the wisdom of the federal judiciary has often been questioned, the Court has never been touched by corruption, and has always behaved with the dignity fitting its high position as guardian of the Constitution.

Explanatory Notes

Article III, Section 2, clause 2. When a court has "original Jurisdiction" over certain types of cases, it means that such cases are referred to it first. A court with "appellate Jurisdiction" tries cases which have been appealed from lower courts. Notice that the Supreme Court has original jurisdiction in cases involving foreign diplomats and those in which a state is a party. Others it hears on appeal.

Article III, Section 3, clause 1. The charge of treason had been used by tyrants as a means of getting rid of people who opposed them in any way. To prevent this abuse the authors of the Constitution defined it carefully and insisted that it be clearly proved.

Article III, Section 3, clause 2. Under British law a person found guilty of treason not only received barbarous punishment, but also his descendants lost their right to inherit his property. The Constitution here forbids extending punishment for treason to a person's heirs.

125

Article IV. INTERSTATE RELATIONS

Section 1. OFFICIAL ACTS

Reciprocal Recognition. Full Faith and Credit shall be given in each State to the Public Acts, Records, and judicial Proceedings of every other State. And the Congress may by general Laws prescribe the Manner in which such Acts, Records and Proceedings shall be proved, and the Effect thereof.

Section 2. MUTUAL DUTIES OF STATES

1. *Exchange of Privileges of Citizenship.* The Citizens of each State shall be entitled to all Privileges and Immunities of Citizens in the several States.

2. *Extradition.* A Person charged in any State with Treason, Felony, or other Crime, who shall flee from Justice, and be found in another State, shall on Demand of the executive Authority of the State from which he fled, be delivered up, to be removed to the State having Jurisdiction of the Crime.

3. *Fugitive Slaves, Apprentices, and Indentured Servants.* [No Person held to Service or Labour in one State, under the Laws thereof, escaping into another, shall, in Consequence of any Law or Regulation therein, be discharged from such Service or Labour, but shall be delivered up on Claim of the Party to whom such Service or Labour may be due.]

Interstate and Federal-State Cooperation

As was shown in discussing congressional powers, the Constitution grants certain powers to the federal government and reserves others to the individual states. It also provides for cooperation between the states and between the states and the federal government. Article IV declares that the states shall respect each other's laws and court actions, shall aid each other in bringing persons accused of crime to justice, and shall return runaway apprentices, indentured servants, and slaves to their masters. It also says that the federal government shall aid states in preserving rights of self-government, in repelling invasion, and in keeping order.

In the twentieth century the area of interstate cooperation has been widened. Since state lines often cut across natural geographical regions, a single state may be incompetent to deal with important problems. With the approval of Congress, states may make compacts to provide for co-operative action. New Jersey and New York, for instance, have jointly established the Port of New York Authority and have turned over to it such

(Continued on p. 129)

Explanatory Notes

Article IV, Section 1. The "Full Faith and Credit" clause was carried over from the Articles of Confederation. It means that court judgments and legal actions such as contracts, wills, marriages, partnerships, and corporation charters should be valid throughout the United States. "Full Faith and Credit" does not extend, however, to many matters which fall within what is called the "police power" of the states. It does not extend, for instance, to licenses to practice medicine, law, or engineering.

Article IV, Section 2, clause 1. The "Privileges and Immunities" guaranteed by each state to citizens of other states do not include privileges which demand residential qualifications, such as the right to vote, to run a restaurant, or to sell drugs. By the so-called "insular decisions" in the early twentieth century, the Supreme Court decided that this provision of the Constitution did not extend to inhabitants of the overseas colonies of the United States. Such people became citizens only when Congress granted them the privilege by legislation.

Article IV, Section 2, clause 3. During the early nineteenth century the fixed labor contracts of apprentices and indentured servants were abandoned. In 1865 slavery was abolished. This clause thus became a dead letter.

127

Section 3. NEW STATES AND TERRITORIES

1. *Admission of New States.* New States may be admitted by the Congress into this Union; but no new State shall be formed or erected within the Jurisdiction of any other State; nor any State be formed by the Junction of two or more States, or Parts of States, without the Consent of the Legislatures of the States concerned as well as of the Congress.

2. *Control over Territory and Property of the United States.* The Congress shall have Power to dispose of and make all needful Rules and Regulations respecting the Territory or other Property belonging to the United States; and nothing in this Constitution shall be so construed as to Prejudice any Claims of the United States, or of any particular State.

Section 4. FEDERAL PROTECTION FOR STATES

Guarantees Against Invasion, Despotism, and Domestic Violence. The United States shall guarantee to every State in this Union a Republican Form of Government, and shall protect each of them against Invasion; and on Application of the Legislature or of the Executive (when the Legislature cannot be convened) against domestic Violence.

powers as are necessary to control certain aspects of shipping and docking in the Hudson River. Before it was worth while to build the Hoover Dam on the Colorado River, seven states had to make an agreement about the control and use of its water for electric power, navigation, flood control, and irrigation. States cooperate in many other ways. Thus every year the Governors hold a conference to discuss common problems.

Cooperation between the federal and state governments also extends far beyond what is specified in the Constitution. In certain fields, such as conservation and control of aviation, federal and state governments have arranged similar laws and joint enforcement. It is a federal offense to carry across a state line game killed in violation of local law. The state governments require that airplane pilots have federal licenses. The federal government also provides financial aid for a great variety of state activities such as road building, public health, control of insect pests, and agricultural education.

Explanatory Notes

Article IV, Section 3. It is remarkable that neither in this section, where one might logically expect it, nor anywhere else in the Constitution is there any statement that the federal government may acquire new territory, whether by conquest or purchase. This omission greatly embarrassed Jefferson when he negotiated the Louisiana Purchase in 1803. The Louisiana Purchase was a magnificent bargain, but it hurt Jefferson's conscience that he could find warrant for it in the Constitution only by extreme application of the doctrine of "implied powers" (see p. 113).

Article IV, Section 4. The assurance of federal aid to help state authorities suppress domestic violence was made with Shays's Rebellion of 1786 in mind. Note that it is up to the state authorities to ask for help before the federal government sends it. But in the Pullman strike in and around Chicago in 1894, Grover Cleveland sent in federal troops over the protest of Governor Altgeld of Illinois on the grounds that it was the President's duty to protect the mails.

Article V. THE AMENDING PROCESS

How Amendments Are Proposed and Ratified. **The Congress, whenever two thirds of both Houses shall deem it necessary, shall propose Amendments to this Constitution, or, on the Application of the Legislatures of two thirds of the several States, shall call a Convention for proposing Amendments, which, in either Case, shall be valid to all Intents and Purposes, as Part of this Constitution, when ratified by the Legislatures of three fourths of the several States, or by Conventions in three fourths thereof, as the one or the other Mode of Ratification may be proposed by the Congress; Provided** [that no Amendment which may be made prior to the Year One thousand eight hundred and eight shall in any Manner affect the first and fourth Clauses in the Ninth Section of the first Article; and] **that no State, without its Consent, shall be deprived of its equal Suffrage in the Senate.**

The Amending Process

If amendments to the Articles of Confederation had not required unanimous consent of the states, the Articles might have lasted much longer than they did. Twice during the Confederation period a single state blocked a proposal to give Congress the power it most needed—the right to levy taxes. The authors of the Constitution made the amending process easier by arranging (1) that amendments be *proposed* either by a two-thirds vote of Congress or through a convention called by Congress on request of two-thirds of the state legislatures, (2) that amendments be *ratified* by three-quarters of the states. Ratification might be either by state legislatures or by state conventions called for the purpose. Although these provisions made altering the Constitution easier than changing the Articles, the process of amendment was still so difficult and slow that the original Constitution has undergone few alterations and only a few additions have been made.

How is it possible that a Constitution devised in the eighteenth century to meet the needs of a sparsely settled, isolated agricultural country is still used by a great industrial nation with world-wide interests? As has already been suggested, the Constitution has been greatly altered by *interpretation* and by *usage*. It has constantly changed its meaning from generation to generation. New demands on government have tended to widen its sphere and to alter its methods. The Supreme Court, by its power of judicial review, generally controls how far and how fast this change in meaning may go. Ultimately, though, the power of modifying the Constitution rests with the people and the officials whom they elect.

Explanatory

Notes Article V. One of the two methods described in the Constitution for proposing amendments—through a convention called on request of two-thirds of the states—has never been used. Only one amendment, the twenty-first, has been ratified by state conventions.

Article VI. FEDERAL CREDIT AND FEDERAL SUPREMACY

1. *Public Debt of the United States.* All Debts contracted and Engagements entered into, before the Adoption of this Constitution, shall be as valid against the United States under this Constitution, as under the Confederation.

2. *The Supreme Law of the Land.* This Constitution, and the Laws of the United States which shall be made in Pursuance thereof; and all Treaties made, or which shall be made, under the Authority of the United States, shall be the supreme Law of the Land; and the Judges in every State shall be bound thereby, any Thing in the Constitution or Laws of any State to the Contrary notwithstanding.

3. *Official Oath: No Religious Test.* The Senators and Representatives before mentioned, and the Members of the several State Legislatures, and all executive and judicial Officers, both of the United States and of the several States, shall be bound by Oath or Affirmation, to support this Constitution; but no religious Test shall ever be required as a Qualification to any Office or public Trust under the United States.

Explanatory Notes

Article VI, clause 1. It is an accepted principle of international law that a new government, even one established by revolution, shall be responsible for the debts of the one it replaces.

Article VI, clause 2. The "supremacy clause" is one of the most important in the entire Constitution. It was principally on the basis of this clause that Chief Justice John Marshall wrote his classic statement of loose construction in *Marbury v. Madison* (see pp. 176–183). In *McCulloch v. Maryland* (see pp. 184–191), Marshall also made clear that the Constitution itself is superior to "Laws of the United States which shall be made in Pursuance thereof." Or, to put it another way, a law passed by Congress that conflicts with the Constitution is obviously not "in Pursuance thereof," and may therefore be regarded as void.

The Judiciary Act of 1789 (see pp. 161–169) and the Fourteenth Amendment (see pp. 146–149 and 274–281) reenforced the supremacy of federal over state law.

Article VI, clause 3. Notice that state as well as federal officials must solemnly agree to support the Constitution. This makes local officers, from policemen to governors, federal officials as well. If the Constitution, treaties, and federal legislation are to be really the "supreme Law of the Land," state officials must help to enforce them. Also, the Constitution put many duties on the states, such as choosing Senators and presidential electors, fixing times of congressional elections, extradition, and recognizing the official acts of other states. In all these activities the states act more or less as agents of the federal government.

The fact that the Constitution forbids a religious test as a qualification for office reveals that its authors thought that church and state should not mix. How or whether a man worships God should be, they felt, a private affair. This principle of "separation of church and state" is also found in the First Amendment, which forbids Congress to set up a state church or to interfere with religious freedom.

133

Article VII. RATIFICATION OF THE CONSTITUTION

Nine States Necessary for Ratification. The Ratification of the Conventions of nine States, shall be sufficient for the Establishment of this Constitution between the States so ratifying the Same. Done in Convention by the Unanimous Consent of the States present the Seventeenth Day of September in the Year of our Lord one thousand seven hundred and Eighty seven and of the Independence of the United States of America the Twelfth.

Ratification of the Constitution

The authors of the Constitution arranged that it should go into effect when ratified by special conventions in nine states. This followed out the idea expressed in the Declaration of Independence that governments "derive their just powers from the consent of the governed." As has already been pointed out, *all* the people did not have an opportunity to say whether or not they would accept the Constitution because in the 1780's voting rights were limited to men of property. At the time it was ratified, however, the new federal Union came nearer to expressing the will of the people than did the government of any other country in the world. As Jefferson said at the time, the United States had given an example to the world in altering its government "by assembling the wise men of the state, instead of assembling armies."

The Articles of Confederation had insisted on the unanimous consent of the states for amendment. Opponents of the Constitution therefore claimed that the Founding Fathers had been guilty of exceeding their powers by providing for ratification by only nine out of thirteen states. In fact, however, the Constitution was not an amendment to the Articles of Confederation, but an entirely new frame of government.

For many years it was not clear whether once a state had joined the Union it had the right to withdraw. The Constitution itself is silent on the point. The question was put to the ultimate test when in 1861 eleven southern states attempted to form a separate union of their own, the Confederate States of America. Northern victory in the war that followed decided that problem: once having joined the Union a state may not leave it.

Explanatory

Notes Article VII. "The Unanimous Consent of the States present" does not mean "the unanimous consent of delegates from all the states," because Rhode Island was not represented. Nor does this mean that all the delegates sent to the Convention approved of the Constitution. A few men were so much opposed to what was going on in Philadelphia that they went home.

The Constitution actually went into effect with Washington's inauguration in April, 1789. At that time two states, Rhode Island and North Carolina, had not yet ratified the Constitution.

In witness whereof We have hereunto subscribed our Names,
G⁰ WASHINGTON—*Presid*ᵗ
and deputy from
Virginia

New Hampshire	{ JOHN LANGDON { NICHOLAS GILMAN		{ GEO: READ { GUNNING BEDFORD JUN
		Delaware	{ JOHN DICKINSON
Massachusetts	{ NATHANIEL GORHAM { RUFUS KING		{ RICHARD BASSETT { JACO: BROOM
Connecticut	{ Wᵐ SAMˡ JOHNSON { ROGER SHERMAN	*Maryland*	{ JAMES MᶜHENRY { DAN OF Sᵗ THOˢ JENIFER { DANˡ CARROLL
New York	ALEXANDER HAMILTON		
		Virginia	{ JOHN BLAIR— { JAMES MADISON JR.
New Jersey	{ WIL: LIVINGSTON { DAVID BREARLEY. { Wᵐ PATERSON. { JONA: DAYTON	*North Carolina*	{ Wᵐ BLOUNT { RICHᵈ DOBBS SPAIGHT. { HU WILLIAMSON
Pennsylvania	{ B FRANKLIN { THOMAS MIFFLIN { ROBᵗ MORRIS { GEO. CLYMER { THOˢ FITZSIMONS { JARED INGERSOLL { JAMES WILSON { GOUV MORRIS	*South Carolina*	{ J. RUTLEDGE { CHARLES COTESWORTH { PINCKNEY { CHARLES PINCKNEY { PIERCE BUTLER.
		Georgia	{ WILLIAM FEW { ABR BALDWIN

The Signers

The Philadelphia Convention sat for nearly four months, from May 25 to September 17, 1787. When on the last day the completed Constitution was presented for signature, there were forty-two delegates present out of the fifty-five who had attended the sessions at one time or another. Thirty-nine signed the document. Elbridge Gerry, George Mason, and Edmund Randolph refused to sign, chiefly because there was no provision for a bill of rights. Five delegates—Benjamin Franklin, Robert Morris, Roger Sherman, George Clymer, and James Wilson—signed both the Declaration of Independence and the Constitution. Historians who have studied the work of the Founding Fathers generally agree with the judgment of Charles and Mary Beard, who wrote, "Among the many historic assemblies which have wrought revolutions in the affairs of mankind, it seems safe to say that there never has been one that commanded more political talent, practical experience, and sound substance than the Philadelphia Convention of 1787."

Following the procedure already established in the Confederation, each state enjoyed a single vote in the Constitutional Convention, no matter what the differences in population, nor how many delegates attended.

AMENDMENTS

Amendment I. FREEDOM OF OPINION (1791)

Religion, Speech, Press, Assembly, Petition. Congress shall make no law respecting an establishment of religion, or prohibiting the free exercise thereof; or abridging the freedom of speech, or of the press; or the right of the people peaceably to assemble, and to petition the Government for a redress of grievances.

Amendment II. RIGHT TO BEAR ARMS (1791)

States Retain Militia. A well regulated Militia, being necessary to the security of a free State, the right of the people to keep and bear Arms, shall not be infringed.

Amendment III. QUARTERING TROOPS (1791)

No Soldiers in Private Homes in Peace Time. No Soldier shall, in time of peace be quartered in any house, without the consent of the Owner, nor in time of war, but in a manner to be prescribed by law.

Amendment IV. SEARCHES AND SEIZURES (1791)

No General Search Warrants. The right of the people to be secure in their persons, houses, papers, and effects, against unreasonable searches and seizures, shall not be violated, and no Warrants shall issue, but upon probable cause, supported by Oath or affirmation, and particularly describing the place to be searched, and the persons or things to be seized.

The Bill of Rights

One of the principal objections to the Constitution when it was presented for ratification in 1787 was that it contained no section spelling out the rights and liberties of American citizens. Several states were persuaded to ratify only on the assurance that such a statement would be added immediately. The first ten amendments, ratified in 1791, are known as the Bill of Rights. They were designed to make sure that the new federal government would not abuse its great powers by oppressing the people or the states. They underline the basic principle of the Declaration of Independence: that the purpose of government is to protect individual rights.

The rights of the individual stated here are not unlimited. In general, a citizen's rights end where his abuse of them hurts other individuals or threatens public safety. Freedom of speech does not include the right to utter slander (defaming a person by word of mouth) or to publish libel (defaming a person in writing). Freedom of assembly does not include the right to organize a lynching mob, nor does freedom of religion give the right to practices, such as polygamy, which offend the public sense of morality.

Most of the rights and privileges stated in the Bill of Rights are drawn from the "liberties of Englishmen" won in Great Britain during the long struggle between king and parliament which came to a head in the seventeenth century. It was to these rights Americans had first appealed in the struggle with the British Parliament which finally resulted in the Revolutionary War. (Continued on p. 141)

Explanatory

Notes Amendment II. "The right of the people to keep and bear Arms" means here only for purposes of protection. The conditions under which a person may possess, carry, and use weapons is almost entirely a matter for state legislation.

Amendments III and IV. These are based on an ancient principle of English law: "a man's house is his castle." They also reflect grievances against the British government before the Revolution. The British had quartered redcoats in private houses and had used "writs of assistance" (general search warrants) to seek out smuggled goods.

Amendments IV–VIII. These amendments carefully protect the rights of the person most at the mercy of society: the man accused of crime. They reflect two principles of Anglo-Saxon law: that a man is assumed to be innocent until proved guilty, and that it is better to let the guilty go free than to punish the innocent.

139

Amendment V. Rights of Accused Persons (1791)

Protection of Individual Rights in Criminal Prosecutions. No person shall be held to answer for a capital, or otherwise infamous crime, unless on a presentment or indictment of a Grand Jury, except in cases arising in the land or naval forces, or in the Militia, when in actual service in time of War or public danger; nor shall any person be subject for the same offence to be twice put in jeopardy of life or limb; nor shall be compelled in any criminal case to be a witness against himself, nor be deprived of life, liberty, or property, without due process of law; nor shall private property be taken for public use, without just compensation.

The exact meaning of the provisions of the Bill of Rights is partly determined by Congress. At various times Congress has, for instance, passed laws which define sedition (conspiring against the government). In general, however, the definition of the rights and liberties of citizens is the function of the federal judiciary.

Since during each passing year new conditions are constantly arising, the courts are constantly engaged in bringing the Bill of Rights up to date. Some of the questions which the courts have had to answer in applying ancient rights to modern situations are as follows: Have federal officials the right to tap telephone wires in gathering evidence against suspected

(Continued on p. 143)

Explanatory

Notes Amendment V. "A presentment or indictment" means to bring charges against a person. It is the function of a "Grand Jury" to see whether there appears to be enough evidence against a man to warrant his being brought to trial.

"The land or naval forces" and "Militia" are, while in actual service, subject to "military law," breaches of which may be tried in a "court martial." In times of emergency, such as invasion or natural disasters, civilians may temporarily be controlled by the armed forces under "martial law."

This significant phrase "nor shall be compelled in any criminal case to be a witness against himself" means that an accused person may refuse to answer questions on the ground that his answers might tend to incriminate him. This does not weaken his right to be assumed innocent until proved guilty.

There has been much debate as to whether a witness appearing before a Congressional investigating committee may refuse to testify on the ground that his testimony may incriminate him. Those who maintain that in this situation a witness may *not* "plead the Fifth Amendment" argue that a Congressional investigating committee is *not* a court of law trying a "criminal case." Instead, it is simply asking information which may be useful in making laws. Those who claim that the Fifth Amendment *does* apply here point out that testimony given before a Congressional committee may be used as evidence against a witness if he is later tried in court.

"Nor shall private property be taken for public use, without just compensation." This refers to the "right of eminent domain" which allows governments to take land or other property for public use if they pay a fair price. There are many cases where the "general welfare" outweighs an individual's right to possess property—as when a government needs to build a road, erect a fort, or lay out a park. Governments may employ the right of eminent domain to assist a private corporation in building a public utility such as a railroad or an electric power plant.

Amendment VI. Rights of Accused Persons (continued)
(1791)

Conduct of Trials. In all criminal prosecutions, the accused shall enjoy the right to a speedy and public trial, by an impartial jury of the State and district wherein the crime shall have been committed, which district shall have been previously ascertained by law, and to be informed of the nature and cause of the accusation; to be confronted with the witnesses against him; to have compulsory process for obtaining witnesses in his favor, and to have the Assistance of Counsel for his defence.

Amendment VII. Suits at Common Law (1791)

Right to Trial by Jury. In Suits at common law, where the value in controversy shall exceed twenty dollars, the right of trial by jury shall be preserved, and no fact tried by a jury, shall be otherwise reexamined in any Court of the United States, than according to the rules of the common law.

Amendment VIII. Bails, Punishments (1791)

Moderation in Bails, Fines, Punishments. Excessive bail shall not be required, nor excessive fines imposed, nor cruel and unusual punishments inflicted.

Amendment IX. Rights Not Enumerated (1791)

People Retain Rights Not Stated in Constitution. The enumeration in the Constitution, of certain rights, shall not be construed to deny or disparage others retained by the people.

Amendment X. Powers Not Delegated (1791)

Retention of Undelegated Powers by People and States. The powers not delegated to the United States by the Constitution, nor prohibited by it to the States, are reserved to the States respectively, or to the people.

Amendment XI. Suits Against States (1798)

No Right of Individual to Sue a State in Federal Courts. The Judicial power of the United States shall not be construed to extend to any suit in law or equity, commenced or prosecuted against one of the United States by Citizens of another State, or by Citizens or Subjects of any Foreign State.

criminals? Have the members of a religious sect the right to insist that their children not be required to salute the American flag in school? May a gangster refuse to give testimony to a committee of Congress on the ground that if he did so he would tend to incriminate himself?

In times of crisis, such as the War Between the States, the First and Second World War, and the "Cold War" against communism, there has been a natural tendency to reduce individual rights for the sake of the public safety. Such times produce an intense feeling of patriotism and along with it an intolerance for any who are even suspected of disloyalty. There is a temptation to deny to suspects the protection of the individual which is found in the Bill of Rights. Such periods of excitement reveal the advantage of putting judges beyond direct popular control by allowing them to hold office "during good Behaviour" (Article III, Section 1). Unswayed by the emotions of the moment, the federal judiciary preserves the liberties which the Constitution guarantees to the suspect and the fanatic as much as to the man whose loyalty is unquestioned and whose opinions are those of the majority.

Explanatory Notes

Amendment VI. "An impartial jury" here refers to a "petit" (pronounced "petty") or "trial" jury, which must reach unanimous agreement before a person charged with crime is held guilty.

Amendment IX. In other words, the people retain rights, even if these rights are not specifically described in the Constitution.

Amendment X. While most of the Bill of Rights deals with the rights of the individual, the Tenth Amendment is specifically directed toward protecting the states from over-extension of federal power. It limits the federal government to those powers which are clearly "delegated" (granted) in the Constitution.

Amendment XI. This amendment, like those preceding it, reflects distrust of federal power. No sooner had the Constitution gone into effect than private individuals began to sue state governments in federal courts. In the case of *Chisholm v. Georgia* in 1793, the Supreme Court upheld a decision in which the state of Georgia was ordered to pay damages to the heirs of a Britisher whose property had been confiscated during the Revolution. This decision caused such a howl of protest that Congress proposed and the states soon ratified this Eleventh Amendment which forbids individuals to sue states in the federal courts.

The Eleventh Amendment does not prevent a state from being sued before the Supreme Court by another state or by a foreign country. If State A, for instance, dumps garbage into a river running into State B, State B may bring charges before the Supreme Court to end the nuisance.

Amendment XII. PRESIDENTIAL ELECTION (1804)

Separate Ballot for President and Vice-President. The Electors shall meet in their respective states, and vote by ballot for President and Vice-President, one of whom, at least, shall not be an inhabitant of the same state with themselves; they shall name in their ballots the person voted for as President, and in distinct ballots the person voted for as Vice-President, and they shall make distinct lists of all persons voted for as President, and of all persons voted for as Vice-President, and of the number of votes for each, which lists they shall sign and certify, and transmit sealed to the seat of the government of the United States, directed to the President of the Senate;—The President of the Senate shall, in the presence of the Senate and House of Representatives, open all the certificates and the votes shall then be counted;—The person having the greatest number of votes for President, shall be the President, if such number be a majority of the whole number of Electors appointed; and if no person have such majority, then from the persons having the highest numbers not exceeding three on the list of those voted for as President, the House of Representatives shall choose immediately, by ballot, the President. But in choosing the President, the votes shall be taken by states, the representation from each state having one vote; a quorum for this purpose shall consist of a member or members from two-thirds of the states, and a majority of all the states shall be necessary to a choice. And if the House of Representatives shall not choose a President whenever the right of choice shall devolve upon them, [before the fourth day of March next following,] then the Vice-President shall act as President, as in the case of the death or other constitutional disability of the President.—The person having the greatest number of votes as Vice-President, shall be the Vice-President, if such number be a majority of the whole number of Electors appointed, and if no person have a majority, then from the two highest numbers on the list, the Senate shall choose the Vice-President; a quorum for the purpose shall consist of two-thirds of the whole number of Senators, and a majority of the whole number shall be necessary to a choice. But no person constitutionally ineligible to the office of President shall be eligible to that of Vice-President of the United States.

The Electoral College

According to the original Constitution, there was a single ballot in the electoral college for President and Vice-President. This caused serious difficulty in the election of 1800 when Jefferson and Burr, the candidates of the Republican party for President and Vice-President, each received 73 electoral votes. Although it was clear that the Republicans intended Jefferson to hold the higher position and Burr the lower, the Constitution provided that in case of a tie the election should be thrown into the House of Representatives. The House finally chose Jefferson, but only after several ballots. To prevent such confusion, the Twelfth Amendment states that there shall be separate ballots for President and Vice-President. In case of a tie or no majority in the vote for President, the House of Representatives, voting by states with each state having a single vote, chooses the President from the three men receiving the highest number of electoral votes.

The authors of the Constitution set up the electoral college to prevent direct popular choice of the President. It was their intention that the electors should make up their own minds as to who would be the best man for the office. Ever since the first party election in 1796, however, electors have been pledged to the support of party candidates. Thus they have become simply "rubber stamps" registering the popular will.

May a presidential elector still use his individual judgment or does a century and a half of custom outweigh the original purpose of the Founding Fathers? The evidence on this point is confused. In 1952 the Supreme Court ruled that a party might legally require a binding pledge that an elector should vote for the party nominee. Yet in 1956 an Alabama elector pledged to Adlai Stevenson voted for a local judge who had never been mentioned for the Presidency, and the action was accepted by Congress.

The Twelfth Amendment tries to insure that the President and Vice-President come from different states. In practice, they usually have come not only from different states but from different sections of the country. For many years, as an example, it was the practice of the Republicans to nominate their presidential candidates from the Middle West and to "balance the ticket" by nominating Easterners for the Vice-Presidency.

The electoral college system does not provide for an accurate determination of the popular will. The small states are over-represented to start with. When there are more than two candidates, it may be possible for a man to poll a minority of the popular vote and yet win a majority of the electoral college, as happened when Lincoln was elected in 1860 and Wilson was elected in 1912. In 1888, when there were only two major candidates, Harrison with a minority of the popular vote won over Cleveland, who had a larger proportion of the popular vote than in 1884 when he had been elected to the Presidency.

145

Amendment XIII. ABOLITION OF SLAVERY (1865)

1. *No Slavery in U. S.* Neither slavery nor involuntary servitude, except as a punishment for crime whereof the party shall have been duly convicted, shall exist within the United States, or any place subject to their jurisdiction.

2. *Power of Congress to Enforce.* Congress shall have power to enforce this article by appropriate legislation.

Amendment XIV. LIMITATIONS ON STATE ACTION (1868)

1. *Negroes Made Citizens; No State Discriminations.* All persons born or naturalized in the United States, and subject to the jurisdiction thereof, are citizens of the United States and of the State wherein they reside. No State shall make or enforce any law which shall abridge the privileges or immunities of citizens of the United States; nor shall any State deprive any person of life, liberty, or property, without due process of law, nor deny to any person within its jurisdiction the equal protection of the laws.

2. *Loss of Representation in Congress by States Denying Right to Vote.* Representatives shall be apportioned among the several States according to their respective numbers, counting the whole number of persons in each State, excluding Indians not taxed. But when the right to vote at any election for the choice of electors for President and Vice President of the United States, Representatives in Congress, the Executive and Judicial officers of a State or the members of the Legislature thereof, is denied to any of the male inhabitants of such State, being twenty-one years of age, and citizens of the United States, or in any way abridged, except for participation in rebellion, or other crime, the basis of representation therein shall be reduced in the proportion which the number of such male citizens shall bear to the whole number of male citizens twenty-one years of age in such State.

3. *Confederate Leaders Disqualified from Public Office.* No persons shall be a Senator or Representative in Congress, or elector of President and Vice President, or hold any office, civil or military, under the United States, or under any State, who, having previously taken an oath, as a member of Congress, or as an officer of the United States, or as a member of any State

The "National Supremacy Amendments"

During the reconstruction period which followed the War Between the States, three amendments were added to the Constitution. All of them attempted to define the position of the Negroes of the southern states. The Thirteenth Amendment declared all slaves free, the Fourteenth Amendment granted them citizenship, and the Fifteenth Amendment was intended to give them the vote.

The War Between the States resulted not only in the freeing of the slaves, but decided once and for all the supremacy of the nation over the states. Until the war, the supporters of "states' rights" had insisted that the federal government was simply an "agent" of the states, that states might "nullify" (ignore) federal laws they considered unconstitutional, and that states might secede from the Union. The northern victory over the South marked a final defeat for such ideas. It is therefore natural that the National Supremacy Amendments limited state action and deprived states of powers they formerly claimed. (Continued on p. 149)

Explanatory Notes

Amendment XIII. This was only the final act in freeing the slaves. Other slaves had been freed earlier by state legislation, and by Lincoln's Emancipation Proclamation of January 1, 1863.

In the First World War men wishing to avoid being drafted into the army claimed that conscription was a form of "involuntary servitude" and therefore a violation of the Thirteenth Amendment. The Supreme Court declared, however, that the federal government had the right to draft men into service through its power "to raise and support Armies" (Article I, Section 8, clause 12).

Amendment XIV, clauses 2, 3, and 4. The authors of this amendment were Radical Republicans who wanted to make sure that the South accepted defeat in the War Between the States. Clauses 2, 3, and 4 are designed to penalize southern states not granting Negroes the vote, to keep former Confederate leaders out of politics, to forbid payment of the Confederate debt, and to insure payment of the war debt of the Union. Southern states were obliged to ratify this amendment before their political powers, such as representation in Congress, were fully restored.

147

legislature, or as an executive or judicial officer of any State, to support the Constitution of the United States, shall have engaged in insurrection or rebellion against the same, or given aid or comfort to the enemies thereof. But Congress may by a vote of two-thirds of each House, remove such disability.

4. *Confederate Debt Declared Void.* The validity of the public debt of the United States, authorized by law, including debts incurred for payment of pensions and bounties for services in suppressing insurrection or rebellion, shall not be questioned. But neither the United States or any State shall assume or pay any debt or obligation incurred in aid of insurrection or rebellion against the United States, or any claim for the loss or emancipation of any slave; but all such debts, obligations and claims shall be held illegal and void.

5. *Enforcement.* The Congress shall have power to enforce, by appropriate legislation, the provisions of this article.

Amendment XV. NEGRO SUFFRAGE (1870)

Negroes Made Voters. The right of citizens of the United States to vote shall not be denied or abridged by the United States or by any State on account of race, color, or previous condition of servitude.

2. *Enforcement.* The Congress shall have power to enforce this article by appropriate legislation.

Of these amendments, the most important has been the Fourteenth. Through its first clause, which says that a state may not "deprive any person of life, liberty, or property without due process of law," the federal courts have gained the power to oversee state legislation. Thus a New York law which fixed a 10-hour day for employees of bakeries was declared unconstitutional; the Supreme Court said that it deprived workers of their "liberty" to make their own contracts with employers as to how long they worked (*Lochner v. New York*, 1905). A Minnesota law which set up a commission to fix railroad rates was declared unconstitutional on the ground that it deprived railroad corporations (which are "persons" under the law) of "property" by lowering rates. This first clause of the Fourteenth Amendment also protects individuals from unfair trial by state courts and from state violations of fundamental liberties such as freedom of speech and religion. In the case of *Brown v. Board of Education* in 1954 (see pp. 274–281), the Supreme Court declared that to segregate school children on account of race was a denial of "the equal protection of the laws."

Explanatory

Notes **Amendment XV.** Although this amendment limits the power of the states to define voting rights, as does the Nineteenth Amendment which established woman suffrage, the states still retain a large share of authority in this area. Nothing in the Constitution forbids the states to establish voting qualifications on the basis of age, literacy, length of residence, or payment of taxes. The states may also reduce the power of one set of voters and increase the power of another by "gerrymandering." This is the practice of so dividing electoral districts, whether for Congress or state legislatures, that one political group gets more than its share of seats.

Amendment XVI. INCOME TAX (1913)

Congress Given Power to Levy Income Taxes. The Congress shall have power to lay and collect taxes on incomes, from whatever source derived, without apportionment among the several States, and without regard to any census or enumeration.

Amendment XVII. DIRECT ELECTION OF SENATORS (1913)

1. *Qualifications of Voters in Senatorial Elections.* The Senate of the United States shall be composed of two Senators from each State, elected by the people thereof, for six years; and each Senator shall have one vote. The electors in each State shall have the qualifications requisite for electors of the most numerous branch of the State legislatures.

2. *Vacancies; Interim Appointments.* When vacancies happen in the representation of any State in the Senate, the executive authority of such State shall issue writs of election to fill such vacancies: *Provided,* That the legislature of any State, may empower the executive thereof to make temporary appointments until the people fill the vacancies by election as the legislature may direct.

3. *Not Applied to Senators Already in Office.* [This amendment shall not be so construed as to affect the election or term of any Senator chosen before it becomes valid as part of the Constitution.]

The "Progressive Amendments"

After passage of the three National Supremacy Amendments of 1865–1870, it was forty years before others were added to the Constitution. Then there occurred a period, 1913–1920, when four amendments were ratified within a space of seven years. These may be called the "Progressive Amendments" because they reflect the reforming spirit of the progressive movement of the early twentieth century.

The Sixteenth, Seventeenth, Eighteenth, and Nineteenth Amendments are characteristic of their period. It was a time when there was resentment against men of great wealth, and the Sixteenth (income tax) Amendment gave the federal government power to make them pay a larger share of taxes. It was a time when there was increasing belief that government

(Continued on p. 153)

Explanatory Notes

Amendment XVI. The demand for this amendment went back to 1895 when the Supreme Court declared that a federal income tax was unconstitutional. Such a tax, said a majority of the Court, violated Article I, Section 9, clause 4, which states that the federal government may levy no direct tax unless in proportion to population. The only lawful way to overrule a Supreme Court decision on the Constitution is to pass an amendment.

Amendment XVII. In clause 1 of this amendment, as in Article I, Section 2, clause 1, of the original Constitution, "electors" means simply "voters."

The Seventeenth Amendment had been urged for many years before it was finally passed. It was designed not only to make the choice of Senators more democratic, but also to reduce corruption and to improve state government. When choosing Senators, state legislatures had been too often influenced by bribery or by political bosses. The task of electing Senators was an extra burden on the states; the proper business of a legislature is to pass laws for the good of the state, not to choose federal officials.

Amendment XVIII. PROHIBITION (1919)

1. No Intoxicating Beverages in U. S. [After one year from the ratification of this article the manufacture, sale, or transportation of intoxicating liquors within, the importation thereof into, or the exportation thereof from the United States and all territory subject to the jurisdiction thereof for beverage purposes is hereby prohibited.]

2. Enforcement. [The Congress and the several States shall have concurrent power to enforce this article by appropriate legislation.]

3. Must Be Ratified in Seven Years. [This article shall be inoperative unless it shall have been ratified as an amendment to the Constitution by the legislatures of the several States, as provided in the Constitution, within seven years from the date of the submission hereof to the States by the Congress.]

Amendment XIX. WOMAN SUFFRAGE (1920)

1. Women Made Voters. The right of citizens of the United States to vote shall not be denied or abridged by the United States or by any State on account of sex.

2. Enforcement. Congress shall have power to enforce this article by appropriate legislation.

should actively intervene to make people's lives better. By the Eighteenth (prohibition) Amendment the federal government was given power to interfere with the personal habits of American citizens. It was a time when there was widespread belief that "the cure for the evils of democracy is more democracy." The Seventeenth Amendment made the federal government more democratic by declaring that Senators should be elected directly by the voters. The Nineteenth Amendment gave women the right to vote.

World War I helped to bring to a successful climax two reform movements that had been active since the Jacksonian period, the temperance crusade and the agitation for women's rights. The enactment of nationwide prohibition by the Eighteenth Amendment was aided by the fact that the American people were in a self-denying mood. "Meatless Mondays" and "Wheatless Wednesdays" made liquorless all the time seem more possible. Women's contributions to the war effort caused many who had opposed woman suffrage, including President Wilson, to change their minds, and hastened the passage of the Nineteenth Amendment.

Explanatory

Notes **Amendment XVIII.** This amendment was repealed by the passage of the Twenty-first Amendment in 1933.

In providing for the enforcement of this amendment, Congress in 1919 passed the Volstead Act which defined intoxicating beverages as those having an alcoholic content of more than one half of one per cent. One reason why this amendment was widely violated was that some states, especially those with a large urban population, made little effort to supplement the work of federal authorities to enforce prohibition.

Amendments XVIII and XIX. These amendments marked the triumph of reform movements which had been demanding prohibition and woman suffrage for many years. The temperance movement, which started in the 1820's and 1830's, had won its first great triumph in 1851 when Maine passed a state prohibition law. The women's rights movement, dating from the same time, first gained full voting rights for women in four western states before 1900.

Amendment XX. ABOLITION OF "LAME DUCK" SESSIONS (1933)

1. *Beginning of Terms of Federal Elective Officers.* The terms of the President and Vice President shall end at noon on the 20th day of January, and the terms of Senators and Representatives at noon on the 3rd day of January, of the years in which such terms would have ended if this article had not been ratified, and the terms of their successors shall then begin.

2. *Regular Congressional Sessions.* The Congress shall assemble at least once in every year, and such meeting shall begin at noon on the 3rd day of January, unless they shall by law appoint a different day.

3. *Election of President in Unusual Circumstances.* If, at the time fixed for the beginning of the term of the President, the President elect shall have died, the Vice President elect shall become President. If a President shall not have been chosen before the time fixed for the beginning of his term, or if the President elect shall have failed to qualify, then the Vice President elect shall act as President until a President shall have qualified; and the Congress may by law provide for the case wherein neither a President elect nor a Vice President elect shall have qualified, declaring who shall then act as President, or the manner in which one who is to act shall be selected, and such person shall act accordingly until a President or Vice President shall have qualified.

4. *Provision for Death of Minority Candidates for President and Vice-President.* The Congress may by law provide for the case of the death of any of the persons from whom the House of Representatives may choose a President whenever the right of choice shall have devolved upon them, and for the case of death of any of the persons from whom the Senate may choose a Vice President whenever the right of choice shall have devolved upon them.

5. *When Amendment Goes into Effect.* [Sections 1 and 2 shall take effect on the 15th day of October following the ratification of this article.]

6. *Must Be Ratified in Seven Years.* [This article shall be inoperative unless it shall have been ratified as an amendment to the Constitution by the legislatures of three-fourths of the several States within seven years from the date of its submission.]

Explanatory

Notes **Amendment XX.** This amendment had two major purposes: (1) to abolish the "lame duck" session of Congress, and (2) to shorten the time between a President's election and his inauguration.

The lame duck sessions were those which took place every other year in December after the congressional elections in November. The Congress which met in December of an election year was *not* the newly elected Congress but that which had been elected over two years before. It therefore contained many "lame ducks"—Congressmen who had failed to be reelected. In order to make Congress more responsive to the will of the people, the Twentieth Amendment abolishes the lame duck session and provides that Congress hold its first session soon after election.

When the Constitution first went into effect, means of transportation and communication were slow and uncertain. It was necessary to arrange for quite a long period, November to March, between the President's election and his inauguration. With the development of rapid travel and instant communication, however, such a prolonged gap between election and taking office was unnecessary. In a time of crisis it was also dangerous. Between Lincoln's election in November, 1860, and his inauguration in March, 1861, seven southern states left the Union and nothing was done to prevent it. Buchanan, the outgoing President, was unable to act because he had lost the confidence of the people. Lincoln, the President-elect, could take no action because he was not yet in office.

Clauses 3 and 4 of the Twentieth Amendment provide for various situations where choice of a President or of his successor might be difficult. Congress has also passed laws which make arrangements for the succession to the Presidency should both the President and Vice-President die. An Act of 1947 provides that in such a case the Presidency would pass first to the Speaker of the House of Representatives, and then to the President pro tempore of the Senate (the Senator who presides in the absence of the Vice-President). There is as yet no law which says what to do if the President becomes so incapacited that he is unable to perform his official duties.

Amendment XXI. REPEAL OF PROHIBITION (1933)

1. *Eighteenth Amendment Repealed.* The eighteenth article of amendment to the Constitution of the United States is hereby repealed.

2. *Federal Guarantee of Local "Dry" Laws.* The transportation or importation into any State, Territory, or possession of the United States for delivery or use therein of intoxicating liquors, in violation of the laws thereof, is hereby prohibited.

3. *Must Be Ratified in Seven Years by State Convention.* [This article shall be inoperative unless it shall have been ratified as an amendment to the Constitution by conventions in the several States, as provided in the Constitution, within seven years from the date of the submission hereof to the States by the Congress.]

The Unwritten Constitution

Containing only 7,500 words, the Constitution of the United States is remarkably brief. Most state Constitutions are much longer, that of Louisiana running to 200,000 words. By its very brevity the Constitution left a great deal to be filled in later, either by legislation or by custom. This legislation and custom may be called the "Unwritten Constitution." The Unwritten Constitution includes the power of the Supreme Court to decide on the constitutionality of state and federal laws, and the practice whereby the President calls the heads of executive departments together to form an advisory body known as the cabinet. It includes laws such as those which established the lower courts of the federal judiciary and those which provided for the succession if both President and Vice-President should die in office.

Institutions never dreamed of by the Founding Fathers have been added to the governmental system. Among these are the commissions which regulate much of the nation's economic life, such as the Interstate Commerce Commission and the National Labor Relations Board. Other later inventions include the two-party system and such institutions as primary elections and national conventions. (Continued on p. 159)

Explanatory

Notes Amendment XXI, clause 2. This clause was inserted to protect states which wanted to continue their own prohibition laws. It also helps to prevent people from avoiding state taxes by importing alcoholic beverages from states where taxes are lower. No liquor, for instance, may be sent by the United States mails. This is one way the federal government assists the states in enforcing their laws.

Amendment XXI, clause 3. The Twenty-first Amendment was the only one ever submitted to special ratifying conventions; all others have been ratified by state legislatures. The convention method is considered to be more democratic because the voters express their opinion of a proposed amendment in choosing the convention members.

Amendment XXII. LIMITATION OF PRESIDENTIAL TERMS (1951)

1. *Number of Terms.* No person shall be elected to the office of the President more than twice, and no Person who has held the office of President, or acted as President, for more than two years of a term to which some other person was elected President shall be elected to the office of the President more than once. But this Article shall not apply to any person holding the office of President when this Article was proposed by the Congress, and shall not prevent any person who may be holding the office of President, or acting as President, during the term within which this Article becomes operative from holding the office of President or acting as President during the remainder of such term.

2. *Must be Ratified in Seven Years.* [This article shall be inoperative unless it shall have been ratified as an amendment to the Constitution by the legislatures of three-fourths of the several States within seven years from the date of its submission to the States by the Congress.]

Amendment XXIII. VOTING RIGHTS FOR WASHINGTON, D. C. RESIDENTS (1961)

1. *Electors.* The District constituting the seat of Government of the United States shall appoint in such manner as the Congress may direct:

A number of electors of President and Vice President equal to the whole number of Senators and Representatives in Congress to which the District would be entitled if it were a State, but in no event more than the least populous State; they shall be in addition to those appointed by the States, but they shall be considered, for the purposes of the election of President and Vice President, to be electors appointed by a State; and they shall meet in the District and perform such duties as provided by the twelfth article of amendment.

2. *Power to Enforce.* The Congress shall have power to enforce this article by appropriate legislation.

The Twenty-second Amendment is a case where part of the Unwritten Constitution was transferred to the written Constitution itself. In the early days of the United States, Presidents Washington and Jefferson had limited themselves to two terms in office. The precedent they established was not broken until World War II. During the national crisis presented by this war, the American people elected Franklin Roosevelt to a third term in 1940 and a fourth term in 1944. After victory was won, however, the sentiment against this break in the two-term tradition became so strong that the Twenty-second Amendment was passed to prevent any President from serving more than twice.

The most important element in the Unwritten Constitution is the loyalty of Americans to the system established by the Founding Fathers. It is a system which for its successful operation demands self-discipline, patience, and generosity. In power, a majority must be willing to try to achieve its ends without violating the constitutional rights of the minority. Out of power, a minority must be willing to wait until it is able to gain control of the government by a peaceful victory at the polls. The basic principle of equal rights demands that people grant others the rights they claim for themselves.

Explanatory

Notes **Amendment XXII.** The two-term limitation did not apply to President Truman, who held office in 1951 when the Twenty-second Amendment was ratified, but early in 1952 he refused to run for another term.

Amendment XXIII. This grant of the franchise in presidential elections goes only part way to meet the charges that the inhabitants of the District of Columbia are second-class citizens. At one time the city of Washington had an elective mayor and the District of Columbia sent a non-voting representative to Congress. Since 1874, however, the District has been under the direct control of Congress and has had no say in the choice of its officials.

The Judiciary Act of 1789

FILLING OUT THE CONSTITUTION

A S HAS already been pointed out, the Constitution deals far more sketchily with the judiciary than with either the President or Congress. The only court mentioned is the Supreme Court. It is for Congress "To constitute Tribunals inferior to the supreme Court" (Article I, Section 8, clause 9) and to decide what the functions of lower federal courts should be. Although the Constitution describes eleven areas where federal courts shall have jurisdiction (Article III, Section 2, clause 1), it nowhere mentions specifically the most important power of all—judicial review.

Why this incompleteness? It partly stems from the facts that the authors of the Constitution were themselves in disagreement about the judiciary. At one time during their sessions in Philadelphia they debated one of the provisions of the "Virginia Plan" (see p. 90)—that all federal legislation should be examined by a "council of revision," composed of members of the executive department and the judiciary, with a limited power of veto. This idea was rejected, but it opened up the question of judicial review. In the ensuing debate some members took it for granted that the federal courts should have the right to decide on the constitutionality of both state and federal laws; others, including Benjamin Franklin, thought the judiciary had no right to "meddle with legislative business." Unable to agree, the Founding Fathers left the matter for future generations to decide.

Another reason why Article III of the Constitution was left incomplete may have been that some of the members of the Philadelphia Convention did not dare make public just how strong a judiciary they desired. There was apprehension that the federal courts would move into the position formerly held by royal courts, and that the Supreme Court would veto state legislation the way the English Privy Council had disallowed the laws passed by colonial legislatures (see p. 13). Better not to feed these fears, and so hurt the chances of getting the new Constitution ratified.

During the ratification controversy Alexander Hamilton, James Madison, and John Jay wrote the newspaper articles in defense of the Constitution now known collectively as *The Federalist*. Six of the papers, all written by Hamilton, treat the judiciary; they are devoted almost entirely to allaying fears that the federal courts would have too much power. Hamilton argues that the judiciary is "beyond comparison the weakest of the three departments." It lacks the legislature's power over the purse and the executive's power over the sword. All its decisions depend on the willingness of the executive department to carry them out.

When it came to the question of whether the Supreme Court has the right of judicial review Hamilton wobbled. In one place he argued that naturally the judiciary must decide if the legislature has overstepped its powers, but that did not "by any means suppose a superiority of the judicial to the legislative power. It only supposes that the power of the people is superior to both and that where the will of the legislature, declared in its statutes, stands in opposition to that of the people, declared in the Constitution, the judges ought to be governed by the latter rather than the former." Yet elsewhere Hamilton maintained, ". . . there is not a syllable in the plan under consideration which *directly* empowers the national courts to construe the laws according to the spirit of the Constitution," or which gives them any more power to interpret the Constitution than would be enjoyed by the state courts. Fear of judicial encroachment on the powers of Congress and the states, Hamilton maintained, was "in reality a phantom."

Hamilton's fuzziness about the power of the proposed judiciary may reflect a genuine confusion, or it may be that he did not want to show his hand and reveal how strong it might become. But whatever the opinions and intentions of the framers of the new Constitution, it was clearly the job of the first Congress elected under it to set up a judicial system. The Congress was supposed to meet in New York City on March 4, 1789, but not until April 6 did both houses have a quorum. On that day they counted the votes of the electoral college and sent messengers off to inform Washington and John Adams of their election as President and Vice-President. The very next day the Senate appointed a committee to draw up a bill setting up the federal judiciary. Three of the ten members of this committee had been members of the Constitutional Convention, and two were later justices of the Supreme Court. The committee drew up a bill which, after a good deal of debate and some amendment, passed both houses of Congress and was signed by President Washington on September 24, 1789.

The congressional debates over the judiciary bill centered on two major questions. First, what "tribunals inferior to the Supreme Court" should be created? One school of thought, fearful for the rights of the states, argued that the only inferior federal courts should be admiralty courts, whose jurisdiction concerned mostly matters arising on the high seas and so would not infringe on state sovereignty. For the rest, Congress could simply authorize state courts to try federal cases, since all state judges were bound by oath to support the Constitution and to treat it as the "supreme Law of the Land." The Senate committee, supported by majorities in both houses of Congress, decided on the contrary that effective enforcement of federal legislation demanded that the federal government have its own courts. The bill therefore provides for thirteen district courts and three circuit courts.

The second great question was: how much appellate power should be granted to the federal courts, especially to the Supreme Court? On this issue those who feared the extension of federal power argued that the Supreme Court should have the right to hear appeals only from other federal courts. Once allow the right to appeal from state courts to the federal courts, and the latter would "swallow, by degrees, all the State Judiciaries." But the majority of Congress supported the contrary argument that to allow each state judicial system an unrestricted right to interpret the federal Constitution would mean eventual chaos, because ultimately there would be as many systems of interpretation as there were states in the Union. If there was to be uniform application of federal laws, treaties, and the Constitution, if these were in fact to be "the supreme Law of the Land," there must be a right of appeal from both state and federal courts to one final arbiter—the Supreme Court of the United States. So the Judiciary Act of 1789 includes a provision that the Supreme Court has appellate jurisdiction over state courts.

This Judiciary Act of 1789 is one of the most important pieces of legislation ever passed by Congress. It fills in an area left unfinished in the original Constitution and lays out the essential features of the federal judicial system as they have remained ever since.

𝒯o t𝘩e ℛeader

The Judiciary Act of 1789 is long, and filled with technical legal terms. We therefore print here only excerpts dealing with the organization of the federal courts, with the jurisdiction of the Supreme Court, and with the creation of the office of Attorney General of the United States.

The Judiciary Act of 1789

(An Act to Establish The Judicial Courts of the United States)

Section 1. COMPOSITION AND SESSIONS OF THE SUPREME COURT

Be it enacted, That the supreme court of the United States shall consist of a chief justice and five associate justices, any four of whom shall be a quorum, and shall hold annually at the seat of government two sessions, the one commencing the first Monday of February, and the other the first Monday of August.

Section 2. DISTRICTS

That the United States shall be, and they hereby are, divided into thirteen districts, to be limited and called as follows, . . .

Three Levels of Courts

The three ascending levels or pyramid of courts here described have remained an essential feature of the federal judiciary to this day. Over the years, however, there have been many changes. More districts and more circuits have been added, until now there are eleven circuit courts and about a hundred district courts. In addition, Congress has set up some specialized bodies—a Customs Court, a Court of Customs and Patent Appeals, a Court of Claims (to handle claims against the federal government for alleged damages, as when an army bomber hit a skyscraper), and a Tax Court (to handle disputes over federal taxes).

(Continued on p. 167)

Explanatory

Notes **Definitions.** To understand this law, one must know the meaning of various terms. *Jurisdiction* is "the legal power, right, or authority to try cases at law." *Cognizance* is synonymous with jurisdiction. Jurisdiction is of several kinds. A court has *original* jurisdiction if a type of case may be brought before it first. It has *exclusive* jurisdiction if it has the sole right to try a case. It has *concurrent* jurisdiction when another court may try the same kind of case. It has *appellate* jurisdiction when cases are brought to it on appeal from the decisions of lower courts. *Admiralty and maritime* jurisdiction is a specialized branch of law concerning ships and shipping, crimes committed on the high seas, and (formerly) the disposition of prizes (enemy merchant ships) caught by privateers. In *criminal* suits the defendant is accused of an action forbidden by law; in other words, he is suspected of committing a felony, a misdemeanor, or treason. In *civil* suits the plaintiff claims injury, but not because of criminal action. Most civil suits are between private individuals or corporations, but a government may bring a civil action in a case where it maintains it has suffered damages, as when a company furnishing uniforms to the navy fails to live up to agreed standards of quality. A *writ* is a court order. Thus a *writ of mandamus* orders an official to carry out his public duty. A *writ of error* orders a lower court to send the records of a trial to a higher court so that the latter may see whether a mistake in the law has been made.

Section 1. The number of Supereme Court justices has varied from five to nine. Changes in the number were always made for political reasons. For example, in 1801 a Federalist Congress reduced the total membership to five in hope of denying the incoming President, Thomas Jefferson, the power to appoint a Republican to the Court. In 1807 Congress was dominated by the Republicans and they increased the size of the Court to seven so that Jefferson could appoint two of his followers as a counter-weight to the influence of the Federalist Chief Justice John Marshall.

Section 3. DISTRICT COURTS AND DISTRICT JUDGES

That there be a court called a District Court in each of the aforementioned districts, to consist of one judge, who shall reside in the district for which he is appointed, and shall be called a District Judge, and shall hold annually four sessions, . . .

Section 4. CIRCUITS AND CIRCUIT COURTS

That the beforementioned districts, except those of Maine and Kentucky, shall be divided into three circuits, and be called the eastern, the middle, and the southern circuit. . . . and that there shall be held annually in each district of said Circuits two courts which shall be called Circuit Courts, and shall consist of any two justices of the Supreme Court and the district judge of such districts, and two of them shall constitute a quorum. *Provided,* that no district judge shall give a vote in any case of appeal or error from his own decision; but may assign the reasons of such his decision. . . .

Section 9. DISTRICT COURTS' AUTHORITY

That the district courts shall have . . . cognizance of all crimes that shall be cognizable under the authority of the United States, committed within their districts or upon the high seas; where no other punishment than whipping, not exceeding thirty stripes, a fine not exceeding one hundred dollars, or a term of imprisonment not exceeding six months is to be inflicted; and shall also have exclusive original cognizance of all civil cases of admiralty or maritime jurisdiction. . . . And the trial of issues in fact, in the district courts, in all cases except civil and maritime jurisdiction, shall be by jury.

Section 11. JURISDICTION OF CIRCUIT COURTS

That the circuit courts shall have original cognizance, concurrent with the courts of the several States, of all suits of a civil nature at common law or in equity, where the matter in dispute exceeds, exclusive of costs, the sum or value of five hundred dollars, and the United States are plaintiffs or petitioners; or an alien is a party, or the suit is between a citizen of the State where the suit is brought and a citizen of another State. . . . And the circuit courts shall have appellate jurisdiction from the district courts under the rules and restrictions hereinafter provided. . . .

The duties of the judges of the older courts have also become more clearly defined. According to this Judiciary Act of 1789 there were no circuit judges as such, since the circuit courts were manned by district judges and members of the Supreme Court. This arrangement was especially hard on the latter; it forced them to spend a great part of the year away from home engaged in the arduous business of "riding circuit." In the early days it was as necessary for a Supreme Court justice to be a good horseman and in good physical condition as to be learned in the law, because he had to ride as much as 2000 miles a year.

Now the district judges sit only in district courts, and the original jurisdiction of these courts has been greatly extended, so that they deal with the great bulk of cases. The circuit courts, now called Circuit Courts of Appeals, hear most appeals, while retaining original jurisdiction in a few types of cases. The Supreme Court, except for a very occasional interstate dispute, now hears only cases involving the application or interpretation of the Constitution. Contrary to popular misunderstanding, the Supreme Court infrequently deals with the constitutionality of a statute. The cases it accepts are typically those that uphold or disapprove the interpretations of the Constitution rendered in lower courts. (*Continued on p. 169*)

Explanatory Notes Sections 9 and 11. As originally set up, the district courts dealt mostly with rather minor cases, and the circuit courts had a great deal of original jurisdiction.

Section 13. Jurisdiction of the Supreme Court

That the Supreme Court shall have exclusive jurisdiction of all controversies of a civil nature, where a state shall be a party, except between a state and its citizens; and except also between a state and citizens of other states, or aliens, in which case it shall have original but not exclusive jurisdiction. And shall have exclusively all such jurisdiction of suits against ambassadors or other public ministers, or their domestics, or domestic servants, as a court of law can have consistent with the law of nations; . . . The Supreme Court shall also have appellate jurisdiction from the circuit courts and the courts of the several states in the cases hereinafter specially provided for; and shall have power to issue . . . writs of *mandamus* in cases warranted by the principles and usages of law, to any courts appointed, or persons holding office under the authority of the United States.

Section 25. Judicial Review of State Court Decisions

That a final judgment or decree in any suit, in the highest court of law or equity of a State in which a decision in the suit could be had, where is drawn in question the validity of a treaty or statute of, or an authority exercised under, the United States, . . . or where is drawn in question the validity of a statute of, or an authority of any State, on the ground of their being repugnant to the Constitution treaties or laws of the United States . . . may be re-examined, and reversed or affirmed in the Supreme Court of the United States upon a writ of error. . . .

Section 35. Attorney General

. . . . And there shall also be appointed a meet person learned in the law to act as attorney general for the United States, . . . whose duty it shall be to prosecute and conduct all suits in the Supreme Court in which the United States shall be concerned, and to give his advice and opinion upon questions of law when required by the President of the United States, or when requested by the heads of any of the departments, touching any matters that may concern their departments, and shall receive such compensation for his services as shall by law be provided.

Section 25 of the Judiciary Act of 1789 clearly establishes judicial review of the decisions of state courts, by the Supreme Court. By obvious inference this section also gives the Court the right to review state legislation and the actions of state officials which might conflict with the federal Constitution. But one great question was left undecided. Did the Supreme Court have the power of judicial review over the other branches of the federal government? Could it declare laws passed by Congress unconstitutional and so null and void? Could it tell the President of the United States, or his agents, how to act according to the Court's view of the Constitution? Such questions had to be hammered out later.

Explanatory

Notes Section 13. The phrase "consistent with the law of nations" almost destroys the meaning of the statement that the Supreme Court shall have jurisdiction over suits against foreign diplomats. According to the "law of nations" (now usually called "international law") diplomats, and their households as well, are not subject to the laws of the country to which they have been sent. A foreign diplomat could be tried by a United States court only with his own consent and that of his government.

Section 35. Although the office of Attorney General was created by the Judiciary Act of 1789, it does not pertain to the judicial department, but is part of the executive. The Attorney General is a member of the cabinet and is subject to the will of the President. Today the Attorney General has many more tasks than those described here. The Department of Justice, which he heads, contains the law enforcement agencies of the federal government, including the Federal Bureau of Investigation; the Bureau of Prisons; an Anti-Trust Division to prosecute violators of federal laws against monopoly; a Criminal Division to supervise prosecutions of such cases as counterfeiting, post office frauds, and kidnapping. The Department of Justice also includes the Immigration and Naturalization Service.

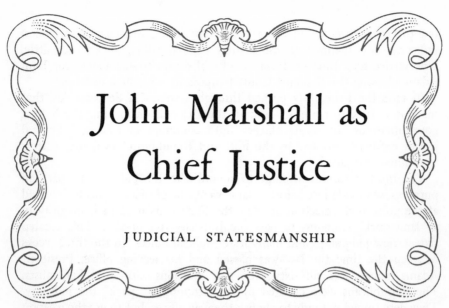

John Marshall as Chief Justice

JUDICIAL STATESMANSHIP

WHEN THE federal government moved to Washington in 1800, the White House was nearly completed, and one wing of the Capitol had been finished. But no place had even been planned for the Supreme Court. It was finally assigned a small basement room in the Capitol.

As this incident suggests, the federal judiciary did not immediately become a strong, independent, third branch of government. Although the first two Presidents, Washington and John Adams, were convinced of the importance of a strong judiciary and tried to staff the federal courts with the ablest legal talent, the judiciary was, as Hamilton had characterized it in *The Federalist*, "beyond comparison the weakest of the three departments."

It did not enhance the dignity of the Supreme Court when Chief Justice John Jay went abroad for nearly a year as a special envoy to Great Britain, and then resigned from the Court after being elected Governor of New York. Washington had great difficulty finding a successor. His first choice, John Rutledge, was rejected by the Senate for partisan reasons. Two other men turned the Chief Justiceship down before Oliver Ellsworth accepted the position.

During the latter part of John Adams' administration, the courts became the sport of party politics. At this time the warfare between the Federalist and Republican parties had reached an extraordinary level of bitterness. The Federalists charged that the Republicans were "filthy Jacobins" ready to throw the Bible into the fire and set up guillotines in city squares. The Republicans called their opponents "boot-licking, servile Tories," aiming to sell out to Great Britain and restore monarchy and aristocracy. The federal judiciary, now manned almost entirely by Federalists, joined the battle. One justice took time off from his official duties to electioneer for John Adams, leaving the Supreme Court temporarily without a quorum.

In 1798 the Federalists pushed through Congress a Sedition Act that made it a crime to write or speak anything calculated to bring the federal government or any of its officers "into contempt or ridicule." Federal judges enforced this law to the hilt, and Republican newspaper editors were fined and jailed.

The most notorious attempt to subordinate the judiciary to partisan purposes was made just before Adams went out of office. Already defeated at the polls in the election of 1800, the Federalists used their majority in a "lame-duck" Congress to pass the Judiciary Act of 1801. This created sixteen new judgeships and many lesser judicial offices. In the three weeks between the time the law was passed and his leaving office, President Adams managed to fill sixty-seven new positions with loyal Federalists. The Republicans were enraged by this attempt to "pack" the judiciary. They determined not only to abolish the new offices, but to use the weapon of impeachment to remove Federalist judges from the bench.

When Oliver Ellsworth resigned as Chief Justice in 1800, Adams at once reappointed John Jay, but Jay refused, saying that the judicial department lacked "the weight and dignity . . . essential to its affording due support to the National Government." Adams then appointed his Secretary of State, John Marshall. The Senate ratified this appointment only after protesting that the new Chief Justice had no judicial experience whatever.

Marshall entered on his duties (without, incidentally, resigning as Secretary of State) on February 4, 1801, just one month before Thomas Jefferson, his arch-enemy and third cousin, was inaugurated President. The two men clashed at every point. Jefferson distrusted courts in general and that headed by John Marshall in particular; Marshall was determined to make the federal judiciary a branch of government coordinate with President and Congress. Jefferson had faith in the popular will; Marshall feared "mobocracy." Jefferson was solicitous for the rights of the states; Marshall was determined to insure the supremacy of the federal government. Jefferson preferred liberty to order, and the pursuit of happiness to property rights; Marshall thought first of protecting the right of a man to get and keep property.

When the struggle began, Marshall seemed at a disadvantage. Jefferson was head of a party triumphant at the polls and in control of both the executive and legislative branches of the federal government. So situated, the Republicans intended to reduce the judiciary to a wholly subordinate position. Yet Marshall won out. He became the most powerful Chief Justice in our history, and the Constitution became the Constitution as he interpreted it. How explain this extraordinary victory?

The most obvious reason why Marshall was able to interpret the Constitution as he saw fit was that he got his fellow justices to agree with him. During most of his thirty-four years as Chief Justice the majority of the Supreme Court were Republicans, often appointed with a view to reducing Marshall's influence. Yet during his entire tenure of office Marshall expressed himself in a minority in only one important case. Usually he spoke for a unanimous Court. Obviously he was a man of extraordinary persuasive ability. Perhaps this stemmed as much from the attractiveness of his personality as from the power of his intellect. He was a friendly, easy-going, convivial man who could make personal friends of political enemies. He stayed at the same boarding house with his fellow justices and dined with them every night. Thus the Supreme Court became a kind of club, and as younger men were brought in they were quietly, almost insensibly, indoctrinated with their leader's attitudes.

During Marshall's years in the Supreme Court several of the lawyers who appeared before it were men of the highest ability, and some of them, like Daniel Webster, were prominent political figures. Thus the arguments before the Court attracted public attention and the ultimate decisions were widely read. Many of the ideas found in Marshall's opinions were not original, but were those presented by lawyers arguing the case.

Although Marshall used the arguments of others—as he had every right to do—he did so with a master hand. He was a magnificent debater. Once admit his premises and you were lost. Jefferson was reported to have said that in conversing with Marshall he never admitted anything: "So great is his sophistry you must never give him an affirmative answer or you will be forced to grant his conclusions. Why, if he were to ask me if it were daylight or not, I'd reply, 'Sir, I don't know, I can't tell.'" Marshall was especially effective in his use of a logical device known as *reductio ad absurdum*—disproof of an opposing argument by showing that when carried to its logical conclusion it is absurd.

Marshall wrote more than half of the opinions the Supreme Court handed down while he was Chief Justice, and they are unusual in legal literature because the layman can easily understand them. They are not burdened with technical terms and precedents. Marshall's critics said that this was because he knew little law; surely his formal legal training—two months at William and Mary College—was scanty. Be that as it may, his opinions were all the more effective because the public could grasp them. His tone was always reasonable and he stuck to the plain, common-sense meaning of the Constitution. The ground is clearly laid out, opposing arguments are given their due before being exploded, and then inexorable logic carries the reader to the inevitable conclusion.

Finally, Marshall succeeded because in the best sense he was a superb politician. He had the ability, which strong-minded men often lack, to know just how far he could go, and to sense when it might be advisable to hedge or retreat. The reader will shortly see how brilliantly he turned a rear-guard action into victory in his opinion in *Marbury v. Madison*. Marshall's opinions are often persuasive as much because of his caution as his boldness, and because he placed limits on federal and judicial power while insisting on their due place. Above all, Marshall never forgot, as he wrote in *McCulloch v. Maryland*, that he was expounding a Constitution, a practical frame of government. He thought constantly in realistic terms—how is this going to work? Essentially what Marshall did was to make the Constitution eminently flexible and therefore *workable*.

To the Reader

As in other documents, the headings used are merely for the convenience of the reader and are not part of the document. In these three decisions by Marshall only excerpts giving the main points are here printed. This enables the reader to get the gist of the decisions, but only the originals can give a sense of the way Marshall seemed to explore every aspect of the cases before him.

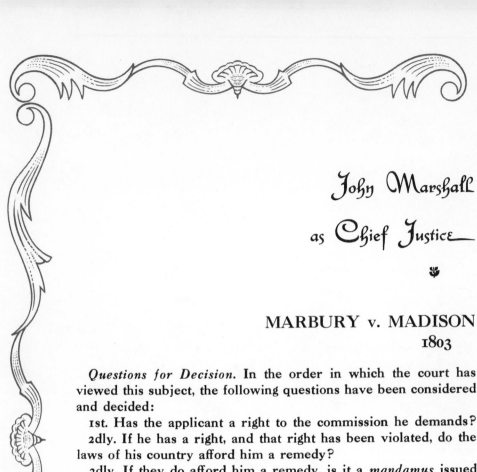

John Marshall

as Chief Justice

❧

MARBURY v. MADISON
1803

Questions for Decision. In the order in which the court has viewed this subject, the following questions have been considered and decided:

1st. Has the applicant a right to the commission he demands?

2dly. If he has a right, and that right has been violated, do the laws of his country afford him a remedy?

3dly. If they do afford him a remedy, is it a *mandamus* issued by this court?

Has Marbury a Right to his Commission? The first object of enquiry is,

Has the applicant a right to the commission he demands? . . .

Mr. Marbury, then, since his commission was signed by the President, and sealed by the secretary of state, was appointed; and as the law creating the office, gave the officer a right to hold for five years, independent of the executive, the appointment was not revocable; but vested in the officer legal rights, which are protected by the laws of his country.

To withhold his commission, therefore, is an act deemed by the court not warranted by law, but violative of a vested legal right.

Judicial Review—Marbury v. Madison

Jefferson and his Republican party were determined to reduce the power of the federal judiciary. What use to win a great victory at the polls if their Federalist opponents could pack the courts and retire into the judiciary as into a fortress? The Republicans furthermore disliked the judicial department because it was not subject to popular control. Unlike the President and Congress, the judges were appointed, not elected, and they held office not for two, four, or six years, but for life. In his First Inaugural Address, Jefferson preached "absolute acquiescence in the decisions of the majority," but the judges might defy the majority by declaring the actions of the elective branches of government unconstitutional. The Republicans therefore denied that the Supreme Court had the final say on constitutionality. Jefferson maintained that each branch of government had a right to interpret the Constitution as it saw fit. Thus when the President came to decide whether to sign or veto a bill passed by Congress, he often became a judge of its constitutionality. This point of view was adopted by several later Presidents, notably Andrew Jackson when he vetoed bills providing federal funds for building roads and for the recharter of the Bank of the United States. *(Continued on p. 179)*

Explanatory

Notes Questions for Decision. In answering the third of these three questions, Marshall decided that the Supreme Court had no jurisdiction in this case. Therefore the first two questions, involving whether or not Marbury had a right to his commission, were superfluous. Hence everything in this opinion up to the point where Marshall discusses whether the Supreme Court had a right to issue writs of *mandamus* must be considered *obiter dicta*—incidental remarks outside the opinion.

Do the Laws Afford Him a Remedy? This brings us to the second enquiry: which is,

If he has a right, and that right has been violated, do the laws of his country afford him a remedy? . . .

The government of the United States has been emphatically termed a government of laws, and not of men. It will certainly cease to deserve this high appellation, if the laws furnish no remedy for the violation of a vested legal right.

By the constitution of the United States, the President is invested with certain important political powers, in the exercise of which he is to use his own discretion, and is accountable only to his country in his political character, and to his own conscience. To aid him in the performance of these duties, he is authorized to appoint certain officers, who act by his authority and in conformity with his orders. . . .

But where a specific duty is assigned by law, and individual rights depend upon the performance of that duty, it seems equally clear that the individual who considers himself injured, has a right to resort to the laws of his country for a remedy. . . .

It is, then, the opinion of the Court,

1st. That by signing the commission of Mr. Marbury, the president of the United States appointed him a justice of peace for the county of Washington in the district of Columbia; . . . and that the appointment conferred on him a legal right to the office for the space of five years.

2dly. That, having this legal title to the office, he has a consequent right to the commission; a refusal to deliver which, is a plain violation of that right, for which the laws of his country afford him a remedy.

Part of Judiciary Act of 1789 Unconstitutional. It remains to be enquired whether,

3dly. He is entitled to the remedy for which he applies. . . .

The act to establish the judicial courts of the United States authorizes the supreme court "to issue writs of *mandamus* in cases warranted by the principles and usages of law, to any courts appointed, or persons holding office under the authority of the United States." . . .

The constitution vests the whole judicial power of the United States in one supreme court, and such inferior courts as congress shall, from time to time, ordain and establish. . . .

A Republican assault on the courts began in 1802 when Congress passed a new Judiciary Act abolishing most of the courts set up by the act of 1801, thus turning out of office the Federalist judges appointed during Adams's last weeks in office. The constitutionality of this new law was highly questionable. The Constitution states that judges "shall hold their Offices during good Behavior," meaning "for life"; if Congress could end a judge's tenure of office simply by abolishing his position, this provision of the Constitution was meaningless.

The triumphant Republicans then turned impeachment into a political weapon against Federalist judges. In 1804 the House impeached John Pickering, a district judge who had lost his sanity; in time the Senate duly found Pickering guilty of "high crimes and misdemeanors" and removed him from office. Then they went after a member of the Supreme Court, Samuel Chase, who had delivered violent anti-Jefferson harangues from the bench. Chase was impeached in 1804, and was given an elaborate trial before the Senate the next year, with Aaron Burr presiding as Vice-President. But two-thirds of the Senate refused to vote that he was guilty and Chase was acquitted. Had he been found guilty, John Marshall would have been the next victim. (Continued on p. 181)

Explanatory

Notes Do the Laws Afford Him a Remedy? The principle expressed in the phrase "a government of laws, and not of men" means that the highest authority in the state is the law, representing the general will, not the officials. Or, to put it another way, the rulers are "public servants," obeying the will of the people as expressed in law. When rulers are not bound by law, despotism results.

Note that Marshall makes it perfectly clear that the President has a right to control his own agents in the executive department who help him to exercise his *political* powers. Thus the Secretary of State or the Attorney General must act as the President directs or run the risk of removal. But Marbury was a judicial officer, his duties defined by act of Congress, and therefore not subject to the executive department.

Part of Judiciary Act of 1789 Unconstitutional. The first quotation is from Section 13 of the Judiciary Act of 1789 (p. 168).

Note the way Marshall shows that if Congress can add to the original jurisdiction of the Supreme Court, the description of its original jurisdiction in the Constitution was meaningless (next page). Here is an example of the *reductio ad absurdum*, mentioned in the discussion of Marshall's abilities as a judge on page 173. The reader will note as he reads on in this decision that Marshall uses this technique again and again to great effect.

179

In the distribution of this power it is declared, that "the supreme court shall have original jurisdiction in all cases affecting ambassadors, other public ministers and consuls, and those in which a state shall be a party. In all other cases, the supreme court shall have appellate jurisdiction." . . .

If congress remains at liberty to give this court appellate jurisdiction, where the constitution has declared their jurisdiction shall be original; and original jurisdiction where the constitution has declared it shall be appellate; the distribution of jurisdiction, made in the constitution, is form without substance. . . .

The authority, therefore, given to the supreme court, by the act establishing the judicial courts of the United States, to issue writs of *mandamus* to public officers, appears not to be warranted by the constitution.

Constitution Superior to Ordinary Laws. That the people have an original right to establish for their future government such principles as, in their opinion, shall most conduce to their own happiness, is the basis on which the whole American fabric has been erected. . . .

This original and supreme will organizes the government, and assigns to different departments their respective powers. It may either stop here or establish certain limits not to be transcended by those departments.

The government of the United States is of the latter description. The powers of the legislature are defined and limited; and that those limits may not be mistaken or forgotten, the constitution is written. To what purpose are powers limited, and to what purpose is that limitation committed to writing, if these limits may, at any time, be passed by those intended to be restrained? . . .

Between these alternatives there is no middle ground. The constitution is either a superior paramount law, unchangeable by ordinary means, or it is on a level with ordinary legislative acts, and, like other acts, is alterable when the legislature shall please to alter it.

If the former part of the alternative be true, then a legislative act contrary to the constitution is not law; if the latter part be true, then written constitutions are absurd attempts, on the part of the people, to limit a power in its own nature illimitable.

The Judges Must be Bound by the Constitution. It is emphatically the province and duty of the judicial department to say what the law is. Those who apply the rule to particular cases must of

Meanwhile a case came before the Supreme Court that gave the Chief Justice an opportunity to fight back. It involved one of forty-two justices of the peace in the District of Columbia whom John Adams appointed on March 2, 1801, the day before he left office. In the hurry of Adams's last few hours in office several of the commissions appointing these men were not delivered. After Jefferson came into power he directed his Secretary of State, James Madison, not to deliver some of the commissions. Jefferson thought Adams' "midnight" appointments to the judiciary were "an outrage on decency" and this was his chance to keep a few Federalists out.

When Madison flatly refused to give him his commission, William Marbury, one of the Adams appointees, sued in the Supreme Court for a writ of *mandamus* ordering the Secretary of State to seal and deliver the commissions. The Court took up the case in February, 1803. It offered Marshall an embarrassing choice—if the Supreme Court issued the writ, Madison would certainly ignore it, and the Court would be publicly humiliated. If, on the other hand, the Court refused to insist that Madison grant Marbury his commission, Marshall would be giving aid and comfort to his dearest enemy, Thomas Jefferson.

Marshall found an adroit way out of this dilemma by holding that the portion of the Judiciary Act of 1789 empowering the Supreme Court to issue writs of *mandamus* (see Section 13, p. 168) was unconstitutional. The great beauty of this was that Marshall avoided the humiliation of having the writ ignored and at the same time solemnly asserted that it was the power of the Supreme Court to declare laws unconstitutional.

Usually when a court declares that it lacks jurisdiction in a case, the matter stops there. But Marshall could not resist the opportunity to denounce Madison, and by obvious inference Madison's superior, President Jefferson. He therefore so organized his opinion that he took up the question of the constitutionality of the Judiciary Act of 1789 last. He set up three questions: Did Marbury have a right to his commission? If he had such a right, had he a legal remedy? Was a writ of *mandamus* from the Supreme Court the proper remedy? In answering the first question Marshall declared Madison's actions totally illegal. In answering the second question, Marshall declared that the courts had a right to judge such illegal acts of the executive department and to protect their victims. But alas, said Marshall in answering the third question, Marbury came to the wrong court. It was all wonderfully ingenious and was designed to infuriate the Republicans, as it did. *(Continued on p. 183)*

𝓔xplanatory

𝓝otes○ **The Judges Must be Bound by the Constitution.** Note how Marshall points up the absurdity of opposing arguments by a series of rhetorical questions.

necessity expound and interpret that rule. If two laws conflict with each other, the courts must decide on the operation of each.

So if a law be in opposition to the constitution; if both the law and the constitution apply to a particular case, so that the court must either decide that case conformably to the law, disregarding the constitution, or conformably to the constitution, disregarding the law, the court must determine which of these conflicting rules governs the case. This is of the very essence of judicial duty.

The judicial power of the United States is extended to all cases arising under the constitution.

Could it be the intention of those who gave this power to say that in using it the constitution should not be looked into? That a case arising under the constitution should be decided without examining the instrument under which it arises?

This is too extravagant to be maintained.

In some cases, then, the constitution must be looked into by the judges. And if they can open it at all, what part of it are they forbidden to read or to obey? . . .

From these, and many other selections which might be made, it is apparent that the framers of the constitution contemplated that instrument as a rule for the government of *courts,* as well as of the legislature. Why otherwise does it direct the judges to take an oath to support it? This oath certainly applies in an especial manner to their conduct in their official character. How immoral to impose it on them if they were to be used as the instruments, and the knowing instruments, for violating what they swear to support! . . .

Conclusion. It is also not entirely unworthy of observation, that in declaring what shall be the *supreme* law of the land, the constitution itself is first mentioned, and not the laws of the United States generally, but those only which shall be made in *pursuance* of the constitution, have that rank.

Thus, the particular phraseology of the constitution of the United States confirms and strengthens the principle, supposed to be essential to all written constitutions, that a law repugnant to the constitution is void, and that courts, as well as other departments, are bound by that instrument.

[*Mandamus* denied.]

At the time it was tried, then, the case of *Marbury v. Madison* was seen as a maneuver in the partisan struggle between the Federalist judiciary and the Jefferson administration. Nor was the matter under consideration one of any great importance. The office of justice of the peace is not an important one, and had Marbury been granted the position, his commission would have had only two more years to run. But in the long perspective of history, *Marbury v. Madison* has been called "the most important decision in all Supreme Court history." Its importance stems not so much from the fact that the Court decided on the constitutionality of a federal law—it had done that at least once before—but that Marshall, in the closing section of the opinion, gave a magnificent statement of why it was not only the right but the duty of the judiciary to judge whether or not laws are in agreement with the Constitution. The precedent set by *Marbury v. Madison* was of little immediate significance, and not for over half a century did the Supreme Court declare another federal law unconstitutional (in the Dred Scott case). But the relentless logic with which Marshall showed that the federal courts *must* interpret the Constitution in order to obey it impressed itself deep in men's minds, and the courts' power of judicial review eventually became as much a fact as the President's veto power.

Explanatory Notes Conclusion. To understand the meaning of the first sentence here, reread the "Supreme Law of the Land" clause (Article VI, Section 2, p. 132).

McCULLOCH v. MARYLAND
1819

. . . . The first question made in this cause is, has Congress power to incorporate a bank?

States' Rights Theory of Constitution. In discussing this question, the counsel for the State of Maryland have deemed it of some importance, in the construction of the constitution, to consider that instrument not as emanating from the people, but as the act of sovereign and independent States. The powers of the general government, it has been said, are delegated by the States, who alone are truly sovereign; and must be exercised in subordination to the States, who alone possess supreme dominion.

Constitution Created by the People. It would be difficult to sustain this proposition. The convention which framed the constitution was, indeed, elected by the State legislatures. But the instrument, when it came from their hands, was a mere proposal, without obligation, or pretensions to it. It was reported to the then existing Congress of the United States, with a request that it might "be submitted to a convention of Delegates, chosen in each State, by the people thereof, under the recommendation of its legislature, for their assent and ratification." This mode of proceeding was adopted; and by the Convention, by Congress, and by the State Legislatures, the instrument was submitted to the people. They acted upon it, in the only manner in which they can act safely, effectively, and wisely, on such a subject, by assembling in Convention. It is true, they assembled in their several States; and where else should they have assembled? . . .

From these Conventions the constitution derives its whole authority. The government proceeds directly from the people; is "ordained and established" in the name of the people; . . .

. . . . The government of the Union, then . . . is emphatically and truly a government of the people. In form and in substance it emanates from them, its powers are granted by them, and are to be exercised directly on them, and for their benefit.

National Supremacy and Implied Powers—McCulloch v. Maryland

During the decade following the War of 1812 John Marshall reached the height of his influence. The Supreme Court could no longer be fairly regarded as simply an agency of the Federalist party because Republican justices were now in a majority and the Federalist party itself had disintegrated. During the "Era of Good Feeling" following the war there was a new feeling of nationalism, and Marshall's repeated assertion of the power of the federal government accorded with the dominant mood of the time.

Marshall's conduct of his office helped to increase the dignity and influence of the Court. He introduced the practice of having a single judge speak for the whole Court in a unanimous decision, and for the majority if divided. This gave opinions far greater weight, especially since most of them were unanimous. The Chief Justice wrote the majority of opinions himself. As the years went on, wrote a later admirer, "the Constitution seemed not so much to rise under his name to full stature, as to be gradually unveiled by him until it stood revealed in the harmonious perfection of the form which its framers had designed." Marshall's great adversary had another opinion: "The great object of my fear," wrote Jefferson in 1821, "is the Federal Judiciary. That body, like gravity, ever acting, with noiseless foot, and unalarming advance . . . is engulphing insidiously the special governments (i.e. the states) into the jaws of that which feeds them."

(Continued on p. 187)

Explanatory Notes

Constitution Created by the People. Marshall was venturing here into disputed territory. The ratifying conventions of 1787–1788 were not mere convenient places to ascertain the will of all the people (like polling booths in a presidential election), but were assemblies where each state individually decided whether or not to join the federal Union. But—as James Madison asserted in his old age at the height of the states' rights controversy—it was not state governments that formed the Constitution, but "the people of the states." And in 1802 Thomas Jefferson spoke of the First Amendment as a "solemn act of the whole people." In any case, as the United States grew into an industrial nation spanning a continent, state loyalties diminished and loyalty to the nation vastly increased, so that the federal government did become the government of all the people. So it can be said that Marshall may not have been entirely right about the past, but he nevertheless rightly predicted the future.

Limited Federal Government, Supreme within its Sphere. If any one proposition could command the universal assent of mankind, we might expect it would be this: that the government of the Union, though limited in its powers, is supreme within its sphere of action. This would seem to result necessarily from its nature. It is the government of all; its powers are delegated by all; it represents all, and acts for all. . . . But this question is not left to mere reason: the people have, in express terms, decided it, by saying, "this constitution, and the laws of the United States, which shall be made in pursuance thereof," "shall be the supreme law of the land," and by requiring that the members of the State legislatures, and the officers of the executive and judicial departments of the States, shall take the oath of fidelity to it.

The government of the United States, then, though limited in its powers, is supreme; and its laws, when made in pursuance of the constitution, form the supreme law of the land, "anything in the constitution or laws of any State, to the contrary, notwithstanding." . . .

Is the Right to Incorporate a Bank an Implied Power of Congress? Among the enumerated powers, we do not find that of establishing a bank or creating a corporation. But there is no phrase in the instrument which, like the articles of confederation, excludes incidental or implied powers; and which requires that everything granted shall be expressly and minutely described. . . . In considering this question, . . . we must never forget, that it is *a constitution* we are expounding.

Perhaps the most far-reaching of the many decisions in which Marshall limited the powers of the states and expanded that of the federal government was *McCulloch v. Maryland*. This case concerned the right of the state of Maryland to tax a branch of the Bank of the United States.

The B.U.S., as it was called, was a corporation chartered by Congress in 1816; it acted both as a federal agency and a private bank. Four-fifths of its stock was owned by private individuals. Throughout the twenty years it existed the Bank attracted widespread hostility. In the years 1816–1819 dislike of the "monster" was reflected in state laws forbidding the establishment of branches of the B.U.S. or levying heavy taxes on them. *McCulloch v. Maryland* concerned a stamp tax levied by that state on notes circulated by the Baltimore branch of the B.U.S. Recognized as a test case, it was argued before the Court for nine days by six of the most brilliant lawyers in the country. Marshall's opinion, speaking for a unanimous Court, owes its great influence to the way he explored the origin of the Constitution and the question of implied powers. It is marked by clear organization and simple, non-lawyer-like language.

Marshall opened his argument by looking at the creation of the Constitution. He found that it had been made by "the people," acting collectively. The federal government, he wrote, "is the government of all; its powers are delegated by all; it represents all, and acts for all." Its powers are limited, to be sure, but it is in no way subordinate to the states and is "supreme within its sphere." Here Marshall was consciously and directly refuting the states' rights theory, especially as presented by Jefferson in the Kentucky Resolutions of 1798 and 1799. Jefferson maintained that the Constitution was a "compact" (meaning "contract") between sovereign states agreeing to set up the federal government as their "agent" for certain special purposes. It was the duty of the states to protect their citizens should the federal government overstep its powers, as when the Sedition Act of 1798 inhibited the freedom of speech and press.

(Continued on p. 189)

Explanatory

Notes Is the Right to Incorporate a Bank an Implied Power of Congress?
When Marshall remarks that "we must never forget, that it is *a constitution* we are expounding," he means that it is wholly impractical to set up minute rules for how a government should act in all future circumstances. A frame of government must be flexible enough to allow men to meet changing circumstances.

But the constitution of the United States has not left the right of Congress to employ the necessary means, for the execution of the powers conferred on the government, to general reasoning. To its enumeration of powers is added that of making "all laws which shall be necessary and proper, for carrying into execution the foregoing powers, and all other powers vested by this constitution, in the government of the United States, or in any department thereof."

The counsel for the State of Maryland have urged various arguments, to prove that this clause, though in terms a grant of power, is not so in effect; but is really restrictive of the general right, which might otherwise be implied, of selecting means of executing the enumerated powers. . . .

But the argument on which most reliance is placed, is drawn from the peculiar language of this clause. Congress is not empowered by it to make all laws, which may have relation to the powers conferred on the government, but such only as may be *"necessary and proper"* for carrying them into execution. The word *"necessary"* is considered as controlling the whole sentence, and as limiting the right to pass laws for the execution of the granted powers, to such as are indispensable, and without which the power would be nugatory. . . .

Is it true, that this is the sense in which the word "necessary" is always used? If reference be had to its use, in the common affairs of the world, or in approved authors, we find that it frequently imports no more than that one thing is convenient, or useful, or essential to another. . . .

Let the end be legitimate, let it be within the scope of the constitution, and all means which are appropriate, which are plainly adapted to that end, which are not prohibited, but consist with the letter and spirit of the constitution, are constitutional. . . .

After the most deliberate consideration, it is the unanimous and decided opinion of this court, that the act to incorporate the Bank of the United States is a law made in pursuance of the constitution, and is a part of the supreme law of the land. . . .

The constitutional background of the War Between the States is in these conflicting opinions. On the one hand Calhoun, and other southern political theorists, carried Jefferson's compact theory to its logical conclusion: that a state in the exercise of its sovereignty had the right not only to nullify federal laws, but ultimately even to secede from the federal Union. On the other hand, Marshall's argument that the Union was created by all the people gradually became much more than a mere legal theory. In his great oration, the "second Reply to Hayne," in 1830, Daniel Webster gave the theory warmth and color, and Webster's words were repeated thousands of times in thousands of schoolhouses and at thousands of Fourth of July celebrations. When the Confederacy seceded in 1861, it was devotion to the Union, as representing "government of the people, by the people, and for the people," that made Northerners willing to bear the sacrifices of a long and bitter war.

The federal government was supreme within its sphere, but what was its sphere? Was it strictly limited to those particular powers enumerated in the Constitution, or might it exercise implied powers as well? Marshall's answer to these questions is a classic statement of loose construction (see p. 113). It is based directly on Hamilton's defense of the constitutionality of the first Bank of the United States in a letter to President Washington. According to Marshall (paraphrasing Hamilton), the enumerated powers granted to Congress by the Constitution state the *purposes* of the federal government, leaving Congress free to choose the *means* of putting them into execution. The "elastic clause" (Article I, Section 8, clause 18), giving Congress the right "To make all Laws which shall be necessary and proper" for carrying out its other powers, was designed not to restrict but to enlarge congressional choice of action. A proper synonym for "necessary and proper" was "convenient." A central bank was an obvious means of aiding the federal government to collect taxes, borrow money, regulate commerce, and control currency. Hence it was "within the scope of the constitution." (Continued on p. 191)

Has Maryland a Right to Tax the Bank? It being the opinion of the Court, that the act incorporating the bank is constitutional; and that the power of establishing a branch in the State of Maryland might be properly exercised by the bank itself, we proceed to inquire—

2. Whether the State of Maryland may, without violating the constitution, tax that branch? . . .

The power of Congress to create, and of course to continue, the bank, was the subject of the preceding part of this opinion; and is no longer to be considered as questionable.

. . . . That the power to tax involves the power to destroy; that the power to destroy may defeat and render useless the power to create; . . . are propositions not to be denied.

If the States may tax one instrument, employed by the government in the execution of its powers, they may tax any and every other instrument. They may tax the mail; they may tax the mint; they may tax patent rights; they may tax the papers of the custom-house; they may tax judicial process; they may tax all the means employed by the government, to an excess which would defeat all the ends of government. This was not intended by the American people. They did not design to make their government dependent on the States. . . .

The question is, in truth, a question of supremacy; and if the right of the States to tax the means employed by the general government be conceded, the declaration that the constitution, and the laws made in pursuance thereof, shall be the supreme law of the land, is empty and unmeaning declamation. . . .

The Court has bestowed on this subject its most deliberate consideration. The result is a conviction that the States have no power, by taxation or otherwise, to retard, impede, burden, or in any manner control, the operations of the constitutional laws enacted by Congress to carry into execution the powers vested in the general government. This is, we think, the unavoidable consequence of that supremacy which the constitution has declared. We are unanimously of opinion, that the law passed by the legislature of Maryland, imposing a tax on the Bank of the United States, is unconstitutional and void. . . .

Judgment Reversed.

Having established the constitutionality of the B.U.S., the Chief Justice finally asks whether Maryland has the right to tax its operations. Here Marshall's opinion is based on weaker grounds than in his treatment of the other questions. His comparison of the B.U.S. with the Post Office and the Mint is not quite accurate. The latter are part of the executive department run as public services. The B.U.S. was an incorporated business concern, 80 per cent privately owned, and paying fat dividends to its stock holders. Were not its profits a legitimate object of taxation, like any other private wealth? The statement, "The power to tax involves the power to destroy," hides pitfalls too. Carried to a logical extreme, it would mean the end of all taxation, and so of all government. The true issue was not the *fact* that Maryland taxed a profit-making corporation, but the *degree*—was the Maryland tax so unreasonably high as to put the Baltimore branch of the B.U.S. out of business?

Until the twentieth century, Marshall's decision in *McCulloch v. Maryland* put both state and federal agencies of any kind, as well as official salaries, beyond the power of taxation. In the past generation, however, this immunity of governmental agencies has been broken down. Thus, to take a specific instance, the salaries of federal judges are subject to both state and federal income taxes. Some immunities are left, however; for instance note that the income from certain United States and municipal bonds is free of taxation.

Marshall's decision in *McCulloch v. Maryland* was the occasion for bitter controversy. It was widely applauded especially in the more conservative East, but in the West, where feeling against the "octopus" was strong, the Supreme Court met defiance. The state of Ohio levied a tax of over $100,000 on the Bank, and when its officers refused to pay, state agents simply took the money from the vaults. Only after five years of dispute, during the course of which state officials were jailed for contempt, did the state give in. Later, Andrew Jackson carried on war against the Bank, partly on the ground that it was unconstitutional, and eventually "killed" it by withdrawing government deposits.

Yet here again, as in the *Marbury v. Madison* case, Marshall lost the immediate battle, but won the campaign. The squabbles over the B.U.S. have long since been swept into the dust-bin of history, but Marshall's view on the nature and powers of the federal Union has largely prevailed.

Explanatory

Notes Has Maryland a Right to Tax the Bank? When at the very end Marshall declares the "Judgment Reversed," he was overruling a decision by the Maryland Court of Appeals.

GIBBONS v. OGDEN
1824

Basis of Gibbons' Appeal. The appellant contends that this decree is erroneous because the laws which purport to give the exclusive privilege it sustains are repugnant to the constitution and laws of the United States. They are said to be repugnant—1st. To that clause in the constitution which authorizes congress to regulate commerce. 2d. To that which authorizes congress to promote the progress of science and useful arts.

No Common Sense Basis for Strict Construction. This instrument contains an enumeration of powers expressly granted by the people to their government. It has been said that these powers ought to be construed strictly. . . . What do gentlemen mean by a strict construction? . . . If they contend for that narrow construction which, in support of some theory not to be found in the constitution, would deny to the government those powers which the words of the grant, as usually understood, import, and which are consistent with the general views and objects of the instrument; for that narrow construction, which would cripple the government, and render it unequal to the objects for which it is declared to be instituted, . . . then we cannot perceive the propriety of this strict construction, nor adopt it as the rule by which the constitution is to be expounded. . . .

Definition of "Commerce." The words are: "congress shall have power to regulate commerce with foreign nations, and among the several states, and with the Indian tribes." The subject to be regulated is commerce; and our constitution being, as was aptly said at the bar, one of enumeration, and not of definition, to ascertain the extent of the power, it becomes necessary to settle the meaning of the word. . . .

Regulation of Interstate Commerce—
Gibbons v. Ogden

Most of the immense increase in the power of the Supreme Court during John Marshall's thirty-four years as Chief Justice came from its power to overrule state courts and to veto state laws as unconstitutional. This power was granted the Court by Section 25 of the Judiciary Act of 1789 (see p. 168).

The Marshall Court was especially strict in scrutinizing state laws that in any way invaded property rights. The legal right to property depends on strict enforcement of agreements. Marshall therefore paid particular attention to that portion of Article I, Section 10, clause 1 that forbids the states to pass any law "impairing the Obligations of Contracts."

The Founding Fathers intended this phrase to prevent states from forcing creditors to accept depreciated paper currency. But Marshall greatly extended its meaning. In the case of *Sturges v. Crowninshield* (1819), the Supreme Court held a New York State bankruptcy law unconstitutional because it allowed a debtor to evade his promise to pay his creditor. In *Fletcher v. Peck* (1809), grants of land made by a bribed Georgia legislature were declared "contracts," and the action of a later legislature in withdrawing the grants was therefore illegal. In *Dartmouth College v. Woodward* (1819) Marshall stated that the Dartmouth College charter granted by George III in 1769 was a contract and therefore could not be altered by the New Hampshire legislature. The total effect of these decisions was both to protect property holders, and to free businessmen from interference by state laws. The Dartmouth College case also promoted the corporation as a form of business organization. (Continued on p. 195)

Explanatory

Notes Basis of Gibbons' Appeal. Although Marshall here sets up two questions to be decided, he based his support of Gibbons' appeal entirely on the commerce clause and did not bother to debate the question whether the federal power to issue patents was invaded by the exclusive steamboat franchise granted to Fulton and Livingston.

Definitions of "Commerce." In the words "our constitution being, as was aptly said at the bar, one of enumeration, and not of definition. . . ." Marshall pays tribute to Daniel Webster, who argued the case for Gibbons and supplied the Chief Justice with many of the arguments used in this decision. Webster meant by the phrase that the major purpose of the Constitution was to grant the federal government powers so that it could act effectively, not to limit its scope.

If commerce does not include navigation, the government of the Union has no direct power over that subject, and can make no law prescribing what shall constitute American vessels, or requiring that they shall be navigated by American seamen. Yet this power has been exercised from the commencement of the government, has been exercised with the consent of all, and has been understood by all to be a commercial regulation. All America understands, and has uniformly understood, the word "commerce," to comprehend navigation. It was so understood, and must have been so understood, when the constitution was framed. The power over commerce, including navigation, was one of the primary objects for which the people of America adopted their government, and must have been contemplated in forming it. The convention must have used the word in that sense, because all have understood it in that sense; and the attempt to restrict it comes too late. . . .

Distinction between Intrastate Commerce and Interstate Commerce. The subject to which the power is next applied, is to commerce, "among the several states." The word "among" means intermingled with. A thing which is among others, is intermingled with them. Commerce among the states, cannot stop at the external boundary line of each state, but may be introduced into the interior. It is not intended to say, that these words comprehend that commerce, which is completely internal, which is carried on between man and man in a state, or between different parts of the same state, and which does not extend to or affect other states. Such a power would be inconvenient, and is certainly unnecessary. Comprehensive as the word "among" is, it may very properly be restricted to that commerce which concerns more states than one. . . . The genius and character of the whole government seem to be, that its action is to be applied to all the external concerns of the nation, and to those internal concerns which affect the states generally; but not to those which are completely within a particular state, which do not affect other states, and with which it is not necessary to interfere, for the purpose of executing some of the general powers of the government. The completely internal commerce of a state, then, may be considered as reserved for the state itself.

These and other decisions drew violent criticism. The Court, it was said, was undermining state sovereignty. It was interfering with the right of the people, acting through their state legislatures, to right wrongs and to unfasten "the clutch of the dead hand of past generations." There were demands that Marshall be impeached, that Article 25 of the Judiciary Act be repealed, that Supreme Court justices be limited to six-year non-renewable terms, and that the Court be "packed" by adding new justices. But in the long run the country came to agree with James Madison, no friend of Marshall, who wrote that the right of the federal judiciary to review state laws was "the only defensive armor of the Federal Government, or rather for the Constitution and laws of the United States." "Strip it of that armor," wrote Madison, "and the door is open for nullification, anarchy, and convulsion."

No case better illustrated the need for granting the Supreme Court the right to oversee state legislation than that of *Gibbons v. Ogden* (1824). This involved the action of the state of New York in granting a monopoly over steamship navigation to Robert Fulton and a partner, Robert Livingston. Any steamboat plying New York State waters without a license from Fulton and Livingston was liable to confiscation. In retaliation New Jersey, Connecticut, and Ohio passed laws barring New York boats from their waters. To make matters worse, several other states followed New York in granting exclusive steamship franchises.

The suit was appealed to the Supreme Court by one Thomas Gibbons, who operated a steamship to New York City under a license from the federal government, versus Aaron Ogden, who had a license from the Fulton-Livingston monopoly. Ogden had obtained an injunction from a New York court ordering Gibbons not to enter the Hudson River. The highest court of New York sustained the injunction, holding that the Fulton-Livingston franchise was a property right and that not to enforce it would be to violate the constitutional prohibition against "impairing the Obligations of Contracts." One might suppose that this line of reasoning would appeal to Marshall, but other considerations made him declare the New York State law unconstitutional. It was clearly a case where state legislation conflicted with the right of Congress to grant patents (Article I, Section 8, clause 8). A more important question was whether the New York steamship monopoly was an interference with the power of Congress over interstate commerce. (*Continued on p. 197*)

Explanatory

Notes⌐ **Distinction between Intrastate Commerce and Interstate Commerce.** The latter part of the paragraph with Marshall's summary of the division of power between the federal government and the states should be noted.

Federal Powers over Commerce Must be Exercised within State Boundaries. But, in regulating commerce with foreign nations, the power of congress does not stop at the jurisdictional lines of the several states. It would be a very useless power, if it could not pass those lines. The commerce of the United States with foreign nations is that of the whole United States; every district has a right to participate in it. The deep streams which penetrate our country in every direction pass through the interior of almost every state in the Union, and furnish the means of exercising this right. If congress has the power to regulate it, that power must be exercised whenever the subject exists. If it exists within the states, if a foreign voyage may commence or terminate at a port within a state, then the power of congress may be exercised within a state.

This principle is, if possible, still more clear, when applied to commerce "among the several states." They either join each other, in which case they are separated by a mathematical line, or they are remote from each other, in which case other states lie between them. What is commerce "among" them; and how is it to be conducted? Can a trading expedition between two adjoining states, commence and terminate outside of each? And if the trading intercourse be between two states remote from each other, must it not commence in one, terminate in the other, and probably pass through a third? . . . The power of Congress, then, whatever it may be, must be exercised within the territorial jurisdiction of the several States.

The Power to Regulate. We are now arrived at the inquiry—What is this power?

It is the power to regulate; that is to prescribe the rule by which commerce is to be governed. This power, like all others vested in Congress, is complete in itself, may be exercised to its utmost extent, and acknowledges no limits other than are prescribed in the constitution. . . .

Just what does the Constitution mean when it states that Congress has power "To regulate Commerce . . . among the several States" (Article I, Section 8, clause 3)? In answering this question Marshall defined the key words in reverse order: "Commerce," "among," and "To regulate."

The lawyers for the Fulton-Livingston monopoly claimed that "Commerce" meant mere exchange of goods and did not include navigation. Marshall easily demolished this argument by showing that from the first the federal government had passed laws controlling shipping. He went on to define commerce in the broadest possible terms: it was any form of intercourse between states, including means of transportation.

On the definition of the word "among" depended the distinction between *intra*state and *inter*state commerce. Those arguing for a narrow definition insisted that interstate commerce took place only when state lines were crossed. Marshall pointed out that interstate commerce of necessity must be carried on within states. A boat steaming from Albany, New York, to Hoboken, New Jersey, operates first inside New York State and then inside New Jersey. What distinguishes interstate commerce from intrastate commerce, then, is the ultimate destination. So, says Marshall, interstate commerce is "intermingled with" intrastate commerce.

Finally, what does "To regulate" mean? Here Marshall simply insisted that the federal power to legislate is supreme and any state law conflicting with a federal law is unconstitutional. This portion of the decision left room for later judges to explore the "twilight zone" where there is conflict between the federal government's power to regulate interstate commerce and the states' "police" power over the morals, health, and security of their citizens (see pp. 250–257). A typical example of this conflict is when a state attempts to build a bridge or a dam over a navigable stream.

(Continued on p. 199)

Explanatory

Notes The Power to Regulate. Although Marshall clearly insists on the supremacy of federal power over interstate commerce when Congress chooses to legislate, he does not in this decision go deeply either into the question whether the states have power to legislate when Congress does not choose to do so, or into the question of the extent of the "police powers" of the states. Justice William Johnson, who wrote a separate concurring opinion, went farther than Marshall and claimed that the power of Congress to regulate commerce was "exclusive, leaving nothing for the state to act upon."

When State and Federal Powers Conflict Former Must Give Way. Since, however, in exercising the power of regulating their own purely internal affairs, whether of trading or police, the states may sometimes enact laws the validity of which depends on their interfering with, and being contrary to, an act of congress passed in pursuance of the constitution, the court will enter upon the inquiry, whether the laws of New York, as expounded by the highest tribunal of that state, have, in their application to this case, come into collision with an act of congress, and deprived a citizen of a right to which that act entitles him. Should this collision exist, it will be immaterial whether those laws were passed in virtue of a concurrent power "to regulate commerce with foreign nations and among the several states," or in virtue of a power to regulate their domestic trade and police. In one case and the other the acts of New York must yield to the law of congress; . . . the constitution is supreme law. . . . In every such case the act of congress, or treaty, is supreme; and the law of the state, though enacted in the exercise of powers not controverted, must yield to it. . . .

As this decides the cause, it is unnecessary to enter into an examination of that part of the constitution which empowers congress to promote the progress of science and the useful arts.

Decree of Court of New York reversed and annulled and bill of Aaron Ogden dismissed.

Gibbons v. Ogden was the only decision that John Marshall ever wrote that received popular applause. The breaking of the New York steamship monopoly was received with public celebrations, and it had immediate effects. Within a year the number of steamships sailing from New York rapidly increased from six to forty-three; this great growth of commerce helped to make the city the largest port in the United States. *Gibbons v. Ogden* has been called "the emancipation proclamation of American commerce" because it prevented state regulations from clogging the channels of trade.

Marshall's broad definition of "commerce among the several states" today enables Congress to pass laws protecting migratory birds and making kidnapping a federal offense. It also provides the constitutional basis for the great federal regulatory agencies such as the Interstate Commerce Commission. Because radio waves are "interstate commerce," the Federal Communications Commission decides who may operate a TV station and how much of its time may be devoted to commercials. Because goods produced in factories cross state lines, the National Labor Relations Board decides whether shop foremen may join a union or whether workers discharged for union activity may get back pay (see pp. 258–265). Thus *Gibbons v. Ogden* still affects our daily lives.

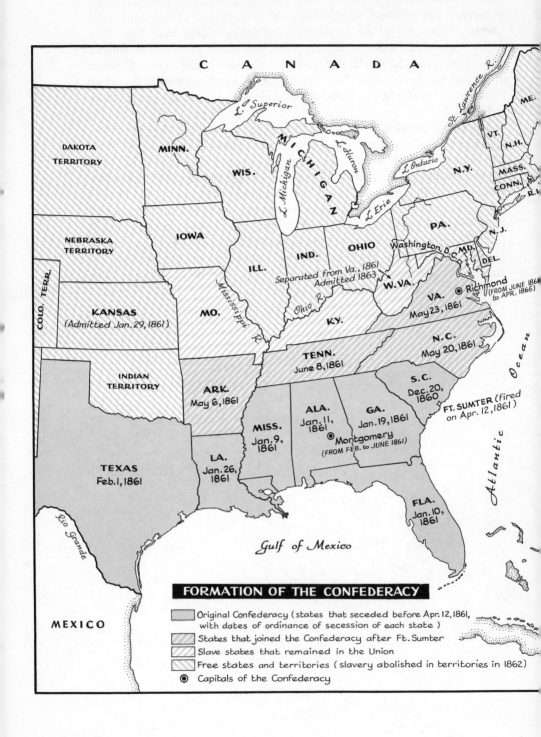

FORMATION OF THE CONFEDERACY

- Original Confederacy (states that seceded before Apr. 12, 1861, with dates of ordinance of secession of each state)
- States that joined the Confederacy after Ft. Sumter
- Slave states that remained in the Union
- Free states and territories (slavery abolished in territories in 1862)
- ◉ Capitals of the Confederacy

The Confederate
Constitution

TRYING TO IMPROVE THE ORIGINAL

T HE CONSTITUTIONAL doctrines expounded by John Marshall accorded well with the growing national patriotism that developed as the United States expanded in population, wealth, and territory during the nineteenth century. But at the same time there also grew up a wholly contrary constitutional philosophy, associated above all with the name of John C. Calhoun of South Carolina.

When he entered politics on the eve of the War of 1812, Calhoun was an uncompromising nationalist who said that discussion of constitutional checks on federal power was "a useless consumption of time." But by 1828 he had made a complete political somersault. In that year he wrote a paper defending states' rights in terms far more extreme than any used by Jefferson and Madison in the Kentucky and Virginia Resolutions (see p. 187); published anonymously by the legislature of South Carolina, it was called the *South Carolina Exposition and Protest*. This document was aimed at the "Tariff of Abominations" which had been passed in May, 1828, and which had raised duties on imported manufactured goods to unprecedented heights. Throughout the South, and especially in South Carolina, there was strong feeling that a high protective tariff was a subsidy to northern manufacturers at the expense of southern cotton and tobacco planters.

In the *Exposition and Protest* Calhoun argued that the taxing power of Congress (Article I, Section 8, clause 1, p. 110) is limited by the provisions that taxes shall "provide for the . . . general Welfare of the United States; . . . and . . . shall be uniform throughout the United States." According to Calhoun, the protective tariff was designed not to promote the welfare of the whole country, but the particular welfare of northern manufacturers. Nor was such a tax "uniform" because the South as an agrarian section naturally imported more foreign goods in exchange for its exports of cotton and tobacco and therefore paid more than its share of tariff duties.

If Congress exceeded its powers, what was the remedy? Calhoun found it in "nullification," suggested by Jefferson in the Second Kentucky Resolution of 1799. In the *Exposition and Protest*, and in later writings as well, Calhoun carried this theory to a logical conclusion. In doing so, he contradicted the ideas propounded by John Marshall at every point. Where Marshall found the Constitution to be created by the "People of the United States" acting collectively, Calhoun insisted that it had been created by the states acting in their individual and sovereign capacities. Marshall saw the Constitution as creating a national government, limited in powers but supreme within its sphere; Calhoun saw it as a sort of treaty—a mutual "compact" (contract) between sovereign states whereby they agreed to set up the federal government as their agent for narrowly specified purposes. Where Marshall said it was for the federal judiciary to determine the constitutionality of federal laws, Calhoun insisted that this was the right of each individual state. When the citizens of a state thought a particular law was an over-expansion of federal power, they could call for a state convention to consider the question. If this convention decided that the federal government had in fact overstepped its prescribed bounds, it had the right to declare the offending law "null, void, and of no effect." Nullification would continue in operation unless three-quarters of the states—enough to amend the Constitution—decided the law in question to be constitutional.

South Carolina limited itself to protesting the Tariff of 1828, but in 1832 Congress passed another tariff law, with somewhat lower duties but still protective. South Carolina thereupon put the Calhoun theory into practice. It called a state convention in November, 1832, and that body declared the tariff acts of 1828 and 1832 "unauthorized by the Constitution," and therefore "null, void and no law, nor binding upon this state, its officers, or citizens." No appeal from any case arising under the ordinance should be made to the Supreme Court of the United States. The federal government was solemnly warned that the use of force to compel obedience to the tariff laws would justify the people of South Carolina in withdrawing from the Union and setting up an independent government.

Andrew Jackson answered the South Carolina convention by a proclamation denouncing nullification as "incompatible with the existence of the Union." He asked Congress for power to use the army and navy against South Carolina if need be. But a compromise prevented armed conflict. Congress in March, 1833, passed the Force Bill and at the same time a bill providing for gradual lowering of the tariff. The South Carolina convention thereupon withdrew its Ordinance of Nullification, but in a last defiant gesture it nullified the Force Bill.

Andrew Jackson always regretted the Compromise of 1833. Better for the ultimate fate of the Union, he thought, if the South Carolina nullification movement had been crushed. He remarked that the next step would be the secession of the South, and the issue would be slavery. It was an unhappy but astute prediction.

Opinion in both North and South was hardening on slavery. In the North the growing abolition movement was spreading the idea that slavery was a criminal denial of the principles upon which the United States was founded. Southerners increasingly defended their "peculiar institution" as a "positive good."

Conflict between the opposing viewpoints came to a crisis in 1849–1850. As a result of the Mexican War, the United States had acquired a vast area stretching west from Texas to the Pacific. What should be the status of slavery therein? Northern opinion was overwhelmingly in favor of closing the newly acquired lands to slavery on the precedents of the Northwest Ordinance and the Missouri Compromise. The southern states regarded such action as a flat denial of the equal right of their citizens to take property into the territories. The issue was forced by California's application to enter the Union as a free state. When Congress met in December, 1849, feelings were so bitter that it took over sixty ballots to elect a Speaker of the House, and Congressmen went to the Capitol armed with bowie knives and pistols. In March, 1850, Calhoun, in his last speech to the Senate, said that unless the North stopped attacking slavery, the South had no choice but submission or secession. In the summer of 1850, delegates from nine southern states met at Nashville, Tennessee, to consider disunion. Intersectional strife was finally avoided, however, by the Compromise of 1850, of which Henry Clay and Daniel Webster were the principal architects. This Compromise was embodied in a series of laws that neatly balanced northern and southern demands. California was admitted as a free state, but nearly all the rest of the Mexican Cession outside of Texas was opened to slavery if the inhabitants so desired. The slave trade was abolished in the District of Columbia, but a more stringent Fugitive Slave Law was designed to make it easier to recapture runaway slaves. Texas, recently admitted to the Union as a slave state, was cut down in size, but the debts of the state were taken over by the federal government.

The Compromise of 1850 only postponed secession. During the decade of the 1850's a series of events too complex to detail here inflamed opinion in both North and South. The principal machinery of compromise was shattered when the two great national parties broke into pieces, the Whigs in the years 1854–1856, and the Democrats in 1860. Before the presidential election of 1860 four presidential candidates were nominated. Abraham Lincoln was the candidate of the Republican party that sought to bar slavery from the territories. John C. Breckinridge represented the extreme pro-slavery southern Democrats known as "fire-eaters." Stephen A. Douglas, candidate of the northern Democrats, and John Bell, representing the Constitutional Union party (a remnant of the old Whigs), both sought to find compromise solutions to the slavery question. In the election, Breckinridge carried the Gulf states, plus South Carolina, North Carolina, Georgia, Arkansas, and Tennessee; Douglas and Bell divided the border states; and Lincoln gained all but three of the electoral votes of the free states. Lincoln polled only about 40 percent of the popular vote, but his support was so largely concentrated in the populous North that he won a clear majority in the electoral college.

The election of a totally sectional candidate for the Presidency was the signal for the states of the deep South to secede. According to the Calhoun theory of the Constitution, a sovereign state might withdraw from the Union by the same method through which it had originally joined—a convention elected by the people. This might be called a process of de-ratification. On December 20, 1860, such a convention met in South Carolina and passed a solemn Ordinance of Secession by a unanimous vote. South Carolina was soon followed out of the Union by the other states of the deep South.

On February 4, 1861, delegates from South Carolina, Georgia, Florida, Alabama, Mississippi, and Louisiana met at Montgomery, Alabama, to draw up plans for a new union. They were later joined by Texas. Anxious to present Lincoln with a set of accomplished facts before he took office in March, the convention worked fast. It drew up a temporary Constitution in four days, elected and inaugurated Jefferson Davis as temporary President within a fortnight, and produced a permanent Constitution for the Confederate States of America in just over a month.

The members of the Montgomery Convention did not regard themselves as rebels. According to one of their number, they were "not such men as revolutions or civil commotions usually bring to the surface," but "men of substance, as well as of solid character . . . well versed in the principles of Government." No less than forty-two of the forty-eight who signed the Confederate Constitution had been trained as lawyers; half of them had been members of Congress; one, John Tyler, was a former President of the United States.

To be sure, they were also men who were suffering from delusions. They were deaf to the world-wide condemnation of slavery; they had convinced themselves that the South could withdraw from the Union peaceably; in the unlikely event of war, they regarded a southern victory as certain.

Although blind to the realities of the moment, the authors of the Confederate Constitution had a sense of the past. They believed their task to be one of restoration; they were going back, they thought, to the original purposes of the Founding Fathers of 1787. According to Alexander H. Stephens, Vice-President of the Confederacy, "We quit the Union, but we rescued the Constitution."

From the very first Southerners had played a role in American politics far beyond their numbers. A Southerner, Thomas Jefferson, was the author of the Declaration of Independence; his fellow Virginian, James Madison, was the principal author and expounder of the United States Constitution. For forty-nine of the seventy-two years between Washington's Inauguration in 1789 and Lincoln's in 1861, Southerners had held the office of President. Twelve of the twenty-three Speakers of the House during that time had been from the South as had eighteen of the twenty-nine justices, including the great Chief Justices John Marshall and Roger B. Taney.

Southerners thus naturally regarded themselves as particularly qualified to defend their "peculiar institution"—slavery—on constitutional grounds. Whatever the moral, economic, social, or political arguments that might be made against the existence of human slavery in a country founded on the principle that God endowed all men with equal rights, Southerners generally had the better of the argument as to their legal rights as slaveholders under the United States Constitution.

Thus when the members of the Montgomery Convention came to write a Constitution they had to live up to their tradition in a number of ways:

1. The Confederate Constitution must be based on the theory of the nature of the federal Union found in the Articles of Confederation—a free compact among sovereign states, with the central government clearly limited in its functions.

2. The new Constitution must protect slavery along the lines Southerners had long maintained. Specifically, the right of slaveholders to take their human property into the territories must be guaranteed, and provision made to enforce an effective fugitive slave law.

3. The new central government should be made more efficient, more economical, and less the sport of party politics than the old.

4. The new document must be neater in its structure; it was particularly important that the limitations on national power in the Bill of Rights be incorporated into the body of the text and not tacked on at the end.

The Confederate Constitution was thus not a new document. Only nineteen of the eighty-five clauses of the original Constitution plus the first twelve amendments suffered significant change, and only six new clauses were added. This suggests that the members of the Montgomery Convention thought that on the whole the work of the Founding Fathers had stood the test of time. Those changes or additions not motivated by the desire to protect slavery, however, reflect considered criticism and proposals for improvement in the light of seventy years of experience. Despite the short and disastrous career of the government it established, the Constitution of the Confederate States of America deserves serious study. Such study may prove not only an interesting exercise in political science; it may also cast light on the way the American people had kept their Constitution dynamic, molding and modifying it to changing conditions.

To the Reader

Note that in these selections from the Confederate Constitution:

1. Language taken directly from the United States Constitution is in standard bold type, for example see next page:

". . . **and secure the blessings of liberty to ourselves and our posterity. . . .**"

2. Any words added or substituted are printed in bold type and underlined, for example:

". . . **each State acting in its sovereign and independent character, . . .**"

3. Words and phrases from the United States Constitution omitted from the Confederate Constitution are in brackets and in light-face thus:

". . . [promote the General Welfare]. . . ."

The authors of the Confederate Constitution changed the capitalization and spelling of the original document to conform to later usage. These changes are not shown.

As in other documents reprinted in this book, the descriptive headings and subheadings have been added by the authors. In these subheadings, the words "similar" and "identical" are used to compare clauses found in the two documents. "Similar" means that the clauses are different in only minor points. "Identical" means the clauses are exactly alike.

Only those portions of the Confederate Constitution that contain significant changes are here printed in full. The contents and the location of the clauses taken from the original document are indicated, with page references. Thus by going back to the text of the United States Constitution printed on pages 96–158 whenever a passage is not reproduced here, the student can reconstruct the Confederate Constitution except for a few verbal changes, most of them being the substitution of "Confederate" for "United" as is done in the preamble.

Constitution

of the

Confederate States

of America

PREAMBLE

WE, THE PEOPLE of the Confederate States, each State acting in its sovereign and independent character, in order to form a permanent federal government, establish justice, insure domestic tranquillity, [provide for the common defence, promote the General Welfare,] and secure the blessings of liberty to ourselves and our posterity—invoking the favor and guidance of Almighty God—do ordain and establish this Constitution for the Confederate States of America.

Preamble

The founders of the Confederacy repudiated the idea presented by John Marshall in *McCulloch v. Maryland* (see pp. 184–191) that the people of the United States collectively created the Constitution. Instead, they insisted that it had been made by "a number of separate and distinct peoples, known as States." The preamble of the Confederate Constitution therefore declares that each state is acting "in its sovereign and independent character."

The principle of states' rights inspired nearly as much devotion in the South as the almost religious feeling for the Union in the North. When the secession movement began, and above all when war followed, Southerners had to decide whether or not to stand by the Union. Faced with this hard decision, most of them, like Robert E. Lee, felt that their states had first claim on their loyalty. The states' rights theory explains why Southerners have insisted on the term "War Between the States." According to Alexander H. Stephens:

> The war . . . was no Insurrection or Rebellion, or even Civil War in any proper sense of these terms. A Rebellion or Insurrection is resistance to the Sovereign Power of any Society, Commonwealth, or State by those owing it allegiance. . . . A Civil War is but another name for the same sort of resistance, where it assumes so formidable a magnitude as to divide the members of the same Society or Commonwealth into two great Parties. . . .
>
> But this war . . . was not of this character at all. For . . . the people of the United States never did form or constitute *one Political Society*. . . . The States held no such relation to the Union as Counties and Districts do to a State, as maintained by Mr. Lincoln. The citizens of each State owed allegiance to their own separate States.
>
> The war, therefore, was a war between States separately organized into two separate Federal Republics. Eleven States on the one side, under the name and style of "Confederate States of America," and twenty-two States on the other side, under the like name and style of "The United States of America."

Explanatory

Notes **Preamble.** Observe the omission of "provide for the common defence" and "promote the General Welfare." The members of the convention had every desire to leave the Union peaceably. They saw no occasion for war and did not expect it. The first Confederate Secretary of War promised to wipe up with his handkerchief every drop of blood spilled as a result of the secession of the southern states. The phrase "general Welfare" was omitted here and also from Article I, Section 8, clause 1 (the taxing power) because it was too "elastic" and could be used to justify almost any conceivable expansion of federal power.

Article I. LEGISLATIVE DEPARTMENT

Section 1. CONGRESS

The Two Houses of Congress. All legislative powers herein delegated shall be vested in a Congress of the Confederate States, which shall consist of a Senate and House of Representatives.

Section 2. HOUSE OF REPRESENTATIVES

1. *House Members Elected by the People.* The House of Representatives shall be composed of members chosen every second year by the people of the several States; and the electors in each State shall be citizens of the Confederate States, and have the qualifications requisite for electors of the most numerous branch of the State Legislature; but no person of foreign birth, not a citizen of the Confederate States, shall be allowed to vote for any officer, civil or political, State or Federal.

2. *Qualifications of Representatives.* No person shall be a Representative who shall not have attained the age of twenty-five years, and [been seven Years] a citizen of the Confederate States, and who shall not, when elected, be an inhabitant of that State in which he shall be chosen.

3. *House Membership Based on State Populations.* Representatives and direct taxes shall be apportioned among the several States, which may be included within this Confederacy, according to their respective numbers, which shall be determined, by adding to the whole number of free persons, including those bound to service for a term of years, and excluding Indians not taxed, three-fifths of all slaves. The actual enumeration shall be made within three years after the first meeting of the Congress of the Confederate States, and within every subsequent term of ten years, in such manner as they shall by law direct. The number of Representatives shall not exceed one for every fifty thousand, but each State shall have at least one Representative; and until such enumeration shall be made, the State of South Carolina shall be entitled to choose six; the State of Georgia ten; the State of Alabama nine; the State of Florida two; the State of Mississippi seven; the State of Louisiana six; and the State of Texas six.

4. *Election for Vacancies in the House.* [IDENTICAL WITH ARTICLE I, SECTION 2, CLAUSE 4, P. 98.]

The Confederate Congress

The way the Montgomery Convention accepted most of the essential features of the Constitution of 1787 is strikingly illustrated by the first seven sections of Article I, which detail the way the Confederate Congress is chosen, organized, and does business. No important feature is altered. Here again appears a bicameral legislature, with equal representation of the states in the Senate and representation on the basis of population in the House. Here are many of the same qualifications for membership, the same method of election, the same special functions of each house, the same privileges and restraints on members. In the twenty-four clauses of these seven sections there are only four changes of any importance. Two of these were designed to reenforce states' rights, and two to give the President more power to influence legislation.

The first clause of the Constitution of the United States states that all legislative powers are *"granted"* to Congress. Here they are *"delegated."* The verb "to grant" may mean to make an irrevocable gift; it may imply that Congress has a "right" to legislate for the country as a whole. In other words, the original clause might imply that the states had permanently given over a share of their sovereignty to the federal government. This was the meaning given it by John Marshall in *McCulloch v. Maryland* when he wrote, "the government of the Union, though limited in its powers, is supreme within its sphere of action" (see p. 186). The verb "to delegate," on the other hand, implies "to depute," to appoint someone to act in your behalf. This emphasized the theory that the federal government is simply the agent of the sovereign states. (Continued on p. 213)

Explanatory

Notes⌒ Article I, Section 2, clause 3. ". . . three-fifths of all slaves . . . ." The original Constitution here uses the circumlocution "other Persons." The Founding Fathers considered slavery to be an evil and were ashamed of its existence in the United States; the leaders of the Confederacy, on the other hand, defended their "peculiar institution" as "a positive good."

". . . South Carolina shall be entitled to choose six; the State of Georgia ten; etc. . . ." To start with, each state was given its former representation in the Congress of the United States.

5. *Election of the Speaker of the House; Impeachment.* The House of Representatives shall choose their Speaker and other officers; and shall have the sole power of impeachment; except that any judicial or other Federal officer resident and acting solely within the limits of any State, may be impeached by a vote of two-thirds of both branches of the Legislature thereof.

Section 3. SENATE

1. *Number of Senators, Election, Term of Office.* The Senate of the <u>Confederate</u> States shall be composed of two Senators from each State, chosen for six years by the Legislature thereof, at the regular session next immediately preceding the commencement of the term of service; and each Senator shall have one vote.

2. *One-Third Senate Chosen Every Two Years.* [IDENTICAL WITH ARTICLE I, SECTION 3, CLAUSE 2, P. 100.]

3. *Qualifications of Senators.* No person shall be a Senator who shall not have attained the age of thirty years, and [been nine Years] a citizen of the <u>Confederate</u> States; and who shall not, when elected, be an inhabitant of the State for which he shall be chosen.

4. *Vice-President Presides over Senate.* [SIMILAR TO ARTICLE I, SECTION 3, CLAUSE 4.]

5. *Other Officers.* [SIMILAR TO ARTICLE I, SECTION 3, CLAUSE 5.]

6. *Senate a Court in Cases of Impeachment.* [SIMILAR TO ARTICLE I, SECTION 3, CLAUSE 6.]

7. *Punishment for Officials Convicted in Cases of Impeachment.* [SIMILAR TO ARTICLE I, SECTION 3, CLAUSE 7.]

Section 4. ELECTIONS AND MEETINGS OF CONGRESS

1. *Regulation of Elections.* [SIMILAR TO ARTICLE I, SECTION 4, CLAUSE I, P. 102.]

2. *Sessions of Congress.* [IDENTICAL WITH ARTICLE I, SECTION 4, CLAUSE 2.]

Section 5. ORGANIZATION AND RULES OF EACH HOUSE

1. *Power over Membership and Sittings.* [IDENTICAL WITH ARTICLE I, SECTION 5, CLAUSE I, P. 104.]

2. *Power over Rules and Behavior.* [SIMILAR TO ARTICLE I, SECTION 5, CLAUSE 2.]

3. *Keeping a Record of Proceedings.* [IDENTICAL WITH ARTICLE I, SECTION 5, CLAUSE 3.]

4. *Adjournment.* [IDENTICAL WITH ARTICLE I, SECTION 5, CLAUSE 4.]

Section 2, clause 5, states that federal officers, including judges, whose jurisdiction lay entirely within a state could be impeached by a two-thirds vote of the legislature. This provision was one of the few in the entire Confederate Constitution that carried the theory of state rights to a logical extreme. It gave state legislatures, in effect, the power to practically nullify judicial decisions and the administration of federal laws. The exercise of such a power could have dissolved the Confederacy, because it would have been only a step from nullification to secession. In fact, no Confederate state legislature ever exercised its power under this clause, although there were threats to impeach officials sent from Richmond to conscript troops and requisition food.

One is apt to associate belief in states' rights with distrust of strong executive power. Yet the President of the Confederacy was granted greater power over legislation than the President of the United States. Members of his cabinet were authorized to sit in Congress and join debates and his power of veto was increased. The authors of the Confederate Constitution were more afraid of an irresponsible Congress and of legislation in favor of special interests than of a strong President. *(Continued on p. 215)*

Explanatory

Notes Article I, Section 5. **Organization and Rules of Each House.** Since there was no time to build a Capitol, the Confederate Congress met in the Virginia State House, which had been designed by Thomas Jefferson, sharing the building with the Virginia legislature.

Neither house of the Confederate Congress published a full record of its proceedings, the Senate because it was unable to find an efficient stenographer, and the House because it found that printing costs would be exorbitant.

The Confederate Congress came under attack because it frequently voted to hold secret sessions in order to prevent military information from leaking out.

Section 6. CONGRESSIONAL PRIVILEGES AND RESTRAINTS

1. *Payment and Privileges.* [SIMILAR TO ARTICLE I, SECTION 6, CLAUSE I, P. 106.]

2. *Congressmen not to Hold Other Federal Offices; Cabinet May Sit in the Congress.* No Senator or Representative shall, during the time for which he was elected, be appointed to any civil office under the authority of the Confederate States, which shall have been created, or the emoluments whereof shall have been increased during such time; and no person holding any office under the Confederate States shall be a member of either House during his continuance in office. But Congress may, by law, grant to the principal officer in each of the Executive Departments a seat upon the floor of either House, with the privilege of discussing any measure appertaining to his department.

Section 7. HOW BILLS BECOME LAWS

1. *Revenue Bills.* [SIMILAR TO ARTICLE I, SECTION 7, CLAUSE I, P. 108.]

2. *President's Veto.* Every bill which shall have passed both Houses, shall, before it becomes a law, be presented to the President of the Confederate States; if he approve, he shall sign it; but if not, he shall return it, with his objections, to that House in which it shall have originated, who shall enter the objections at large on their journal, and proceed to reconsider it. If, after such reconsideration, two-thirds of that House shall agree to pass the bill, it shall be sent, together with the objections, to the other House, by which it shall likewise be reconsidered, and if approved by two-thirds of that House, it shall become a law. But in all such cases, the votes of both Houses shall be determined by yeas and nays, and the names of the persons voting for and against the bill shall be entered on the journal of each House respectively. If any bill shall not be returned by the President within ten days (Sundays excepted) after it shall have been presented to him, the same shall be a law, in like manner as if he had signed it, unless the Congress, by their adjournment, prevent its return; in which case it shall not be a law. The President may approve any appropriation and disapprove any other appropriation in the same bill.

In Section 6, clause 2, Congress is permitted to allow cabinet members non-voting seats "upon the floor of either House." This is an extraordinary provision because it strikes at the principle of separation of powers (see pp. 105–107). It would allow a cabinet member of strong personality and persuasive powers such as, say, Alexander Hamilton, to dominate Congress. Carried to a logical extreme, this permission for allowing all the major executive officers, except the President and Vice-President, to sit in either house might have resulted in something like the English House of Commons where the cabinet dominates the legislative process. It was for just this reason that young Woodrow Wilson, a great admirer of the British system of government and also a loyal Southerner, later argued that this provision of the Confederate Constitution should be adopted by the government of the United States. In an article entitled "Cabinet Government," published in 1879, Wilson insisted that granting cabinet members the right to sit in Congress would bring it close to the British system. He thought this change would result in coherent legislation for the benefit of the whole people instead of "piecemeal" legislation on behalf of special interests.

In Section 7, clause 2, the President of the Confederacy is granted the "item veto"—the power, that is, to strike out particular clauses of appropriation bills submitted to him, rather than to have to accept or reject bills as a whole. As it was—and is—under the original Constitution, the President may be forced to accept certain items of a bill, even though he disapproves of them, in order to get any law at all. The trouble with much congressional legislation has always been that it is apt to contain too many favors to special or local interests. Let us say, for instance, that the Department of Defense, in the interest of economy and efficiency, persuades the President to propose the closing down of several navy yards, army camps, or air fields. Immediately, people in the localities affected appeal to their Congressmen representing them because the abandonment of these military posts will mean a loss of income. By the familiar process of bargain and "log-rolling," the Congressmen representing these localities thereupon support each other in obtaining legislation to keep the posts going and money appropriated for their upkeep. These provisions are then written into a general military appropriation bill, which duly passes both houses of Congress and is laid on the President's desk. The President then has a painful choice. He may stand by his original purposes and veto the bill, in which case there may be no funds for vital military purposes; or he may swallow his pride and sign it, thereby allowing the people's money to be wasted and the efficiency of the armed forces to be reduced. In either case the country as a whole is the loser. With the item veto, all this could be avoided. (Continued on p. 217)

In such case he shall, in signing the bill, designate the appropriations disapproved; and shall return a copy of such appropriations, with his objections, to the House in which the bill shall have originated; and the same proceedings shall then be had as in case of other bills disapproved by the President.

3. *Veto Power Extended to Resolutions.* [SIMILAR TO ARTICLE I, SECTION 7, CLAUSE 3.]

Along the same lines as the item veto, the Confederate Constitution prohibits "riders." A "rider" is an extra provision tacked on to a bill, often having very little to do with the subject at hand. Thus the Platt Amendment that made Cuba a protectorate of the United States in 1901 was originally a rider on an army appropriation bill. Article I, Section 9, clause 20 of the Confederate Constitution is designed to prevent this practice by specifying that every bill shall relate to a single subject, clearly defined.

The item veto, combined with the prohibition on riders, finds strong support among authorities on government today as a means of promoting economical and responsible government. In a widely read book, *The Need for Constitutional Reform*, William Yandell Elliott argues that the President of the United States should be given the powers accorded to the President of the Confederacy:

> Armed with an item veto on appropriations, and such a protection against attaching to a bill, which he must accept, measures which, taken separately, he would reject, the President could really represent the national will as against group and sectional raids on the treasury.

All Presidents in the twentieth century, regardless of party, have declared their desire for the power of "item veto."

Section 8. Powers Granted Congress

1. *Taxation.* The Congress shall have power—To lay and collect taxes, duties, imposts, and excises, <u>for revenue necessary</u> to pay the debts, provide for the common defence [and General Welfare of the United States] <u>and carry on the Government of the Confederate States; but no bounties shall be granted from the treasury; nor shall any duties or taxes on importations from foreign nations be laid to promote or foster any branch of industry; and</u> all duties, imposts, and excises shall be uniform throughout the <u>Confederate</u> States:

2. *Borrowing.* [IDENTICAL WITH ARTICLE I, SECTION 8, CLAUSE 2, P. 110.]

3. *Regulation of Commerce.* To regulate commerce with foreign nations, and among the several States: and with the Indian tribes; <u>but neither this, nor any other clause contained in the Constitution, shall ever be construed to delegate the power to Congress to appropriate money for any internal improvement intended to facilitate commerce; except for the purpose of furnishing lights, beacons, and buoys, and other aids to navigation upon the coasts, and the improvement of harbors, and the removing of obstructions in river navigation, in all which cases, such duties shall be laid on the navigation facilitated thereby, as may be necessary to pay the costs and expenses thereof:</u>

4. *Naturalization and Bankruptcies.* To establish uniform <u>laws</u> of naturalization, and uniform laws on the subject of bankruptcies throughout the <u>Confederate</u> States, <u>but no law of Congress shall discharge any debt contracted before the passage of the same:</u>

5. *Coinage.* [IDENTICAL WITH ARTICLE I, SECTION 8, CLAUSE 5.]

6. *Punishing Counterfeiters.* [IDENTICAL WITH ARTICLE I, SECTION 8, CLAUSE 6.]

The Confederacy a National Government

As their distrust of centralized government would lead one to expect, the designers of the Confederate Constitution restricted the powers of Congress. They cut out the loose phrase that permitted appropriations of money to "provide for the . . . general Welfare." They forbade protective tariffs and federal spending for internal improvements such as roads and canals. The Post Office was expected to pay its own way.

Yet what strikes one about this Article I, Section 8, is how little the powers of Congress have actually been contracted. All but four remained untouched. It is particularly surprising to find the "elastic clause" reproduced almost exactly. It was "loose construction" of this provision that had permitted the federal government to acquire many "implied powers" not written into the Constitution (see pp. 113, 189, and 248).

During the short life of the Confederate government it, too, acquired through liberal interpretation of the elastic clause new powers that its creators never anticipated. The power to tax was expanded to include the right to seize ten per cent of all crops at a price set by the authorities at Richmond. The commerce power was held to justify efforts to fix prices and wages. Above all, the war powers of Congress were expanded. In spite of the explicit prohibition on appropriations for internal improvements, the Confederate Congress voted funds to build railroads needed to carry troops and supplies. It also made ventures into "state socialism," empowering the central government to take over all telegraph lines and establish factories to make shoes and uniforms. An almost fantastic exercise of

(Continued on p. 221)

Explanatory

Notes Article I, Section 8, clause 1. The prohibition of a protective tariff gave evidence that many Southerners regarded protection as a means whereby northern industry gained bounties at the expense of southern agriculture.

Article I, Section 8, clause 3. The ban on internal improvements, like the prohibition of protective tariffs, reflects a long-standing controversy in which the South found itself opposed to the North. Generally speaking, the Northwest and East favored the use of federal funds for roads and canals. The South was opposed. Clay's "American System" had associated internal improvements with a protective tariff; also, with a magnificent river system the South had less need for roads and canals than other sections.

In forbidding protective tariffs and internal improvements at federal expense, the authors of the Confederate Constitution were simply making explicit their regional view of the meaning of the original document.

219

7. *Postal Service.* To establish post-offices and post-routes; but the expenses of the Post-office Department, after the first day of March, in the year of our Lord eighteen hundred and sixty-three, shall be paid out of its own revenues:

8. *Copyrights and Patents.* [IDENTICAL WITH ARTICLE I, SECTION 8, CLAUSE 8.]

9. *Lower Courts.* [IDENTICAL WITH ARTICLE I, SECTION 8, CLAUSE 9.]

10. *Punishing Piracy.* [IDENTICAL WITH ARTICLE I, SECTION 8, CLAUSE 10.]

11. *Declaring War.* [IDENTICAL WITH ARTICLE I, SECTION 8, CLAUSE 11.]

12. *Army.* [IDENTICAL WITH ARTICLE I, SECTION 8, CLAUSE 12.]

13. *Navy.* [IDENTICAL WITH ARTICLE I, SECTION 8, CLAUSE 13.]

14. *Regulating the Armed Forces.* [IDENTICAL WITH ARTICLE I, SECTION 8, CLAUSE 14.]

15. *Calling Out Militia.* [SIMILAR TO ARTICLE I, SECTION 8, CLAUSE 15.]

16. *Regulating Militia.* [SIMILAR TO ARTICLE I, SECTION 8, CLAUSE 16.]

17. *Areas under Exclusive Control of Congress.* [SIMILAR TO ARTICLE I, SECTION 8, CLAUSE 17.]

18. *The "Elastic Clause."* [SIMILAR TO ARTICLE I, SECTION 8, CLAUSE 18.]

implied powers occurred at the very end of the war when southern reserves of manpower were close to exhaustion. With the strong support of General Lee, the Congress empowered the Confederate War Department to enlist 300,000 Negroes in the army, offering them freedom as a reward, and this in spite of the prohibition on legislation "denying or impairing the right of property in negro slaves" in Article I, Section 9, clause 4.

The name "Confederate States of America" suggested, as it was intended to, that the new union was a league of sovereign and independent states like the former Confederation. Yet this Article I, Section 8,—especially as put into practice—indicates that the Confederacy was much more than a league. Look ahead to Article VI, clauses 3 and 4, and you will find reproduced the provisions that make the Constitution the "supreme law of the land," and that require all federal and state officials to support it on oath. In truth, it could be said of the Confederate Constitution, as Madison said of the Constitution he helped to write, that it was neither a confederation nor a nation, but "a composition of both."

This dual character of the Confederate government accorded with larger realities. In spite of loyalty to individual states and the cult of states' rights, the Confederacy had many of the aspects of a nation. Its national flag, the "stars and bars," and its songs, "Dixie" and "The Bonnie Blue Flag," inspired national patriotism. Its people sang that they were "a band of brothers" fighting to uphold "southern rights." The "lost cause" was only officially based on the legal abstraction of state sovereignty; in fact, it was the cause of a nation struggling to be born.

Explanatory

Notes Article I, Section 8, clause 7. The United States Post Office Department had been running a heavy deficit. Southerners were of the opinion that carrying mail for less than cost was a subsidy to businessmen who used the mails for advertising. Hence the provision that the Confederate Post Office should pay its way. John H. Reagan, Postmaster General of the Confederacy, obeyed this instruction to the letter, but his efforts to make his department break even were unpopular because he had to charge high rates and reduce services.

Article I, Section 8, clause 17. "**The seat of government of the Confederate States. . . .**" The Confederate Congress was offered several sites for building a new capital, but never accepted any of them. Montgomery, Alabama, was the capital of the Confederacy from February until June, 1861. Then the Confederate government moved to Richmond, Virginia, remaining there until just before Grant took the city early in April, 1865. For a few weeks after the flight from Richmond, Jefferson Davis attempted to direct the crumbling Confederacy from Danville, Virginia.

Section 9. POWERS DENIED THE CONFEDERATE CONGRESS

1. *Foreign Slave Trade Prohibited.* <u>The importation of negroes of the African race, from any foreign country, other than the slaveholding States or Territories of the United States of America, is hereby forbidden; and Congress is required to pass such laws as shall effectually prevent the same.</u>

2. *Slave Trade with non-Confederate States and Territories may be Prohibited.* <u>Congress shall also have power to prohibit the introduction of slaves from any State not a member of, or Territory not belonging to, this Confederacy.</u>

3. *May not Suspend* Habeas Corpus *Except in Crisis.* [IDENTICAL WITH ARTICLE I, SECTION 9, CLAUSE 2, P. 112.]

4. *May not Pass Bills of Attainder,* Ex Post Facto *Laws, or Laws Depriving Slave Owners.* No bill of attainder, or *ex post facto* law, or <u>law denying or impairing the right of property in negro slaves</u> shall be passed.

5. *May Not Levy Taxes Except in Proportion to Population.* [IDENTICAL WITH ARTICLE I, SECTION 9, CLAUSE 4.]

6. *Restriction on Export Taxes.* No tax or duty shall be laid on articles exported from any State, <u>except by a vote of two-thirds of both Houses.</u>

Limitations on Congressional Power

One might expect that a Constitution based on the theory of states' rights would impose new limitations on federal power. At first sight these expectations seem to be fulfilled, since the Confederate Article I, Section 9, detailing restrictions on the powers of Congress, contains twenty clauses rather than eight. In fact, however, most of the new restrictions are not actually new at all. Clauses 12 through 19 of this section are simply Amendments I through VIII, of the Constitution of the United States. It is surely more logical to put these provisions of the Bill of Rights here rather than at the end of the document, because it makes clear that these are restrictions on Congress, but it does not make them more effective legally.

One of the Confederate restrictions on Congress deals with the slave trade. Article I, Section 9, clause 1, of the United States Constitution forbids Congress to limit the importation of slaves for twenty years; rather surprisingly its replacement in the Confederate Constitution requires Congress to *prohibit* the foreign slave trade. Some Southerners favored a reopening of this traffic, pointing out that the demand for slaves exceeded the supply, and arguing that it was an act of kindness to transport Negroes from the pagan barbarism of their homeland to the Christian civilization of America. In fact, however, the African slave trade was so odious an example of "man's inhumanity to man" that the great majority of the delegates to the Montgomery Convention refused to consider resuming it. Furthermore, the Confederacy counted on the friendship of Great Britain; resumption of the slave trade would have been a slap in the face at British public opinion.

The second clause of Section 9 is not a restriction on Congress, but rather the grant of power to forbid the importation of slaves from the United States. This may have been designed as a lever to induce the rest of the slave states to join the Confederacy, because these "border states" derived income from selling slaves to the deep South. *(Continued on p. 225)*

Explanatory

Notes Article I, Section 9, clause 3. At the recommendation of President Davis, the Confederate Congress three times voted to suspend the writ of *habeas corpus*. Davis argued that he needed to jail suspects without trial in order to enforce the conscription laws and to catch spies. This action was bitterly attacked. A Georgia newspaper announced the suspension of the writ in a paper bordered with black; some state judges declared the suspension unconstitutional and granted the writ anyway; the Georgia legislature passed a condemnatory resolution; and North Carolina passed a law nullifying the suspension.

7. *May not Favor One Port over Another.* No preference shall be given by any regulation of commerce or revenue to the ports of one State over those of another. [nor shall Vessels bound to, or from, one State, be obliged to enter, clear, or pay Duties in another.]

8. *May not Spend Money without Appropriations or Maintain Secrecy in Finances.* [IDENTICAL WITH ARTICLE I, SECTION 9, CLAUSE 7.]

9. *Executive Budget.* Congress shall appropriate no money from the treasury except by a vote of two-thirds of both Houses, taken by yeas and nays, unless it be asked and estimated for by some one of the heads of departments, and submitted to Congress by the President; or for the purpose of paying its own expenses and contingencies; or for the payment of claims against the Confederate States, the justice of which shall have been judicially declared by a tribunal for the investigation of claims against the Government, which it is hereby made the duty of Congress to establish.

10. *Restrictions on Appropriations.* All bills appropriating money shall specify in federal currency the exact amount of each appropriation and the purposes for which it is made; and Congress shall grant no extra compensation to any public contractor, officer, agent or servant, after such contract shall have been made or such service rendered.

11. *May not Grant Titles of Nobility.* [SIMILAR TO ARTICLE I, SECTION 9, CLAUSE 8.]

12. *Religion, Speech, Press, Petition.* [IDENTICAL WITH AMENDMENT I, P. 138.]

13. *States Retain Militia.* [IDENTICAL WITH AMENDMENT II, P. 138.]

14. *No Soldiers in Private Homes in Peace Time.* [IDENTICAL WITH AMENDMENT III, P. 138.]

15. *No General Search Warrants.* [IDENTICAL WITH AMENDMENT IV, P. 138.]

16. *Protection of Individual Rights in Criminal Prosecutions.* [IDENTICAL WITH AMENDMENT V, P. 140.]

17. *Conduct of Trials.* [IDENTICAL WITH AMENDMENT VI, P. 142.]

18. *Right to Trial by Jury.* [IDENTICAL WITH AMENDMENT VII, P. 142.]

19. *Moderation in Bails, Fines, Punishments.* [IDENTICAL WITH AMENDMENT VIII, P. 142.]

20. *No "Riders."* Every law, or resolution having the force of law, shall relate to but one subject, and that shall be expressed in the title.

Three of the added restrictions in Article I, Section 9, are designed to promote coherent and economical legislation, like the item veto in Article I, Section 7, clause 2, already discussed. Clause 9, by requiring a two-thirds vote for nearly all appropriations not recommended by the executive departments, makes budget-making an executive prerogative. This is intended to prevent "pork-barrel" legislation in which Congressmen strive to see that the federal government spends money in their districts. Clauses 10 and 20, further controlling appropriations and prohibiting "riders," are along the same lines.

Article I, Section 9, increased the taxing power. Clause 5 of this Section in the United States Constitution flatly forbids export taxes. The corresponding provision of the Confederate Constitution, clause 6, permits Congress to vote them by a two-thirds majority.

To summarize: eight of the new clauses in Article I, Section 9, are simply parts of the Bill of Rights more logically placed; one clause forbids the foreign slave trade; three are designed to make Congress legislate more responsibly; two actually grant Congress new powers. In the whole Section there is not one single new limitation on federal power of any consequence. All of which bears out the point made in discussing Article I, Section 8: that the stated powers of the Confederate Government were not much less than those of the federal government it replaced.

Explanatory

Notes⊃ Article I, Section 9, clause 7. The latter portion of this clause as it appears in the United States Constitution is omitted since it logically belongs in Article I, Section 10, as a restriction on the states.

Article I, Section 9, clause 20. The meaning and importance of this clause are treated in the discussion of the Confederate President's item veto on p. 215.

Section 10. POWERS DENIED THE STATES

1. *Various Actions Forbidden to the States.* No State shall enter into any treaty, alliance, or confederation; grant letters of marque and reprisal; coin money [emit Bills of Credit]; make anything but gold and silver coin a tender in payment of debts; pass any bill of attainder, or *ex post facto* law, or law impairing the obligation of contracts; or grant any title of nobility.

2. *May not Levy Import or Export Duties.* [SIMILAR TO ARTICLE I, SECTION 10, CLAUSE 2, P. 114.]

3. *May Improve Rivers and Harbors, May not Wage War.* No State shall, without the consent of Congress, lay any duty on tonnage, except on sea-going vessels, for the improvement of its rivers and harbors navigated by the said vessel; but such duties shall not conflict with any treaties of the Confederate States with foreign nations; and any surplus revenue, thus derived, shall, after making such improvement, be paid into the common treasury. Nor shall any State keep troops or ships of war in time of peace, enter into any agreement or compact with another State, or with a foreign power, or engage in war, unless actually invaded, or in such imminent danger as will not admit of delay. But when any river divides or flows through two or more States, they may enter into compacts with each other to improve the navigation thereof.

Limitations on State Action

We might expect a Constitution based on the principle of state sovereignty to reduce the limitations on the powers of the states. Yet the new Article I, Section 10, makes only three concessions in the direction of enlarging the sphere of state action. States are permitted to emit bills of credit, levy duties on shipping in order to pay for river and harbor improvements, and make pacts with other states concerning river navigation.

Article II. EXECUTIVE DEPARTMENT

Section 1. PRESIDENT AND VICE-PRESIDENT

1. *Term of Office.* The Executive power shall be vested in a President of the Confederate States of America. <u>He and the Vice-President shall hold their offices for the term of six years; but the President shall not be reëligible. The President and Vice-President shall</u> be elected as follows:

2. *Number of Electors.* [SIMILAR TO ARTICLE II, SECTION I, CLAUSE 2, P. 116.]

3, 4, 5. *Election of President and Vice-President.* [SIMILAR TO AMENDMENT XII EXCEPT BROKEN UP INTO THREE HEADINGS, P. 144.]

6. *Time for Choosing Electors.* [SIMILAR TO ARTICLE II, SECTION I, CLAUSE 4, P. 116.]

7. *Qualifications for President.* [SIMILAR TO ARTICLE II, SECTION I, CLAUSE 5, P. 118.]

8. *Presidential Succession in Case of Vacancy.* [IDENTICAL WITH ARTICLE II, SECTION I, CLAUSE 6.]

9. *Presidential Salary.* [SIMILAR TO ARTICLE II, SECTION I, CLAUSE 7.]

10. *Presidential Oath.* [SIMILAR TO ARTICLE II, SECTION I, CLAUSE 8.]

Article II. The Executive Department

The Confederate Constitution grants the President more powers than those exercised by that "elective monarch," the President of the United States. At only one minor point involving recess appointments (Article II, Section 2, clause 4) is executive power diminished. To the powers of the executive provided in the United States Constitution are added the right of cabinet ministers to sit in Congress (Article I, Section 6, clause 2); the item veto (Article I, Section 7, clause 2); the initiative in the budget (Article I, Section 9, clause 9); and an explicit power of removal (Article II, Section 2, clause 3).

The authors of this document obviously favored a President who could act independently and could exert leadership in Congress. They minimized any danger that the chief executive might exceed his powers by limiting him to a single six-year term. This restriction was also designed to take the presidential office out of politics. A President elected for a single non-renewable term was thought to be far less likely to court popularity and make himself a party leader than one working for reelection.

(Continued on p. 231)

Explanatory

Notes Article II, Section 1, clauses 3, 4, 5. In the presidential election of 1860, Abraham Lincoln won 180 of 303 electoral votes although he was the choice of only about 40% of the voters, nearly all of his support being in the free states. It is somewhat of a surprise, therefore, to find no change in a method of choosing the President that could result in such a victory for a minority, sectional candidate.

The only presidential election held under this Constitution took place in November, 1861. Jefferson Davis and Alexander H. Stephens were the unanimous choice of the 109 electors.

Section 2. Powers of the President

1. *Military Power; Executive Departments; Reprieves and Pardons.* [SIMILAR TO ARTICLE II, SECTION 2, CLAUSE 1, P. 118.]

2. *Treaties and Appointments.* [SIMILAR TO ARTICLE II, SECTION 2, CLAUSE 2.]

3. *Sole Power of Removal.* The principal officer in each of the executive departments, and all persons connected with the diplomatic service, may be removed from office at the pleasure of the President. All other civil officers of the executive departments may be removed at any time by the President, or other appointing power, when their services are unnecessary, or for dishonesty, incapacity, inefficiency, misconduct, or neglect of duty; and when so removed, the removal shall be reported to the Senate, together with the reasons therefor.

4. *Recess Appointments.* The President shall have power to fill all vacancies that may happen during the recess of the Senate, by granting commissions which shall expire at the end of their next session; but no person rejected by the Senate shall be reappointed to the same office during their ensuing recess.

Section 3. Presidential Duties

1. *Presidential Messages; Congressional Sessions; Executing Laws.* [SIMILAR TO ARTICLE II, SECTION 3, P. 120.]

Section 4. Impeachment.

1. *Removal of Executive Officers.* [SIMILAR TO ARTICLE II, SECTION 4, P. 120.]

The United States Constitution contains no provision for the removal of members of the executive department save by the cumbersome process of impeachment and trial. Did the President, then, have the power to remove subordinates, and, if so, were removals, like appointments, subject to approval by the Senate? These questions became a matter of heated congressional debate in June, 1789, little more than a month after Washington's inauguration as President. The particular question at issue concerned a bill to set up the State Department and give the President the right of removal without consulting the Senate. Congress passed the bill and it became a precedent. But the question was not closed, as was shown in 1867 when the Radical Republicans, as an incident in their struggle with President Andrew Johnson, pushed through the Tenure-of-Office Act, requiring Senate confirmation of removals.

The Confederate Constitution follows the earlier precedent in granting the executive full power of removal, subject only to informing the Senate of reasons for action. This has the virtue of tending to fix on the President clear responsibility for the acts of his subordinates.

Article III. JUDICIAL DEPARTMENT

Section *1.* FEDERAL COURTS

1. *Supreme and Lower Courts; Term and Salary of Judges.*
[SIMILAR TO ARTICLE III, SECTION I, P. 122.]

Section 2. JURISDICTION OF FEDERAL COURTS

1. *Kinds of Cases Tried in Federal Courts.* The judicial power shall extend to all cases [in Law and Equity] arising under this Constitution, the laws of the <u>Confederate</u> States, and treaties made or which shall be made under their authority; to all cases affecting ambassadors, other public ministers, and consuls; to all cases of admiralty and maritime jurisdiction; to controversies to which the <u>Confederate</u> States shall be a party; to controversies between two or more States; between a State and citizens of another State, <u>where the State is plaintiff</u> [between Citizens of different States]; between citizens [of the same State] claiming lands under grants of different States, and between a State or the citizens thereof, and foreign States, citizens, or subjects; <u>but no State shall be sued by a citizen or subject of any foreign State.</u>

2. *Original and Appellate Jurisdiction of the Supreme Court.*
[IDENTICAL WITH ARTICLE III, SECTION 2, CLAUSE 2, P. 124.]

3. *Jury Trial Guaranteed; Place of Trial.* [IDENTICAL WITH ARTICLE III, SECTION 2, CLAUSE 3.]

Section 3. TREASON

1. *Definition of Treason.* [SIMILAR TO ARTICLE III, SECTION 3, CLAUSE I, P. 124.]

2. *Punishment for Treason; How Limited.* [IDENTICAL WITH ARTICLE III, SECTION 3, CLAUSE 2.]

States' Rights Hamstring
the Confederate Judiciary

Nowhere was the preponderant influence of the forty-odd lawyers in the Montgomery Convention better revealed than in their treatment of the judicial department. Their definition of the organization and jurisdiction of the Confederate courts more scrupulously follows the U. S. Constitution than any other Article. The only changes are in Article III, Section 2, clause 1, where a perhaps superfluous phrase, "in Law and Equity," is omitted and the gist of Amendment XI (p. 142) is worked in. Not only is this Article III nearly identical with its model, but in Article VI, clause 3, the Fathers of the Confederacy made their Constitution "the supreme law of the land."

But when it came time to pass legislation actually setting up the judicial system, the Confederate Congress had second thoughts. District courts were organized in 1861, but no circuit courts, and no Supreme Court. Three days after his inauguration as permanent President in February, 1862, President Davis urged Congress to establish a Supreme Court. The matter was referred to a committee, and eventually the legislators postponed the matter without bringing it to a vote. In 1863 they debated the question again but again no action was taken, and thereafter it was not even seriously considered.

Why did the Confederate Congress flatly disobey the Constitution in this instance? The answer is simple: states' rights. Under the United States Constitution, one of the most potent forces making for the expansion of federal power and for curbing the sovereignty of the states had been judicial review by the Supreme Court. Confederate Congressmen feared that the Supreme Court might revert to the "poisonous doctrines" of John Marshall and use its appellate jurisdiction to overturn the decisions of state courts and to declare state laws unconstitutional. Better not to give any agency of the central government such immense power.

Article IV. INTERSTATE RELATIONS

Section 1. OFFICIAL ACTS

1. Reciprocal Recognition. [IDENTICAL WITH ARTICLE IV, SECTION 1, CLAUSE 1, P. 126.]

Section 2. MUTUAL DUTIES OF STATES

1. Exchange of Citizenship; Protection of Slavery. The citizens of each State shall be entitled to all the privileges and immunities of citizens in the several States, <u>and shall have the right of transit and sojourn in any State of this Confederacy, with their slaves and other property; and the right of property in said slaves shall not be thereby impaired.</u>

2. Extradition. [SIMILAR TO ARTICLE IV, SECTION 2, CLAUSE 2, P. 126.]

3. Fugitive Slaves, Apprentices, and Indentured Servants. [SIMILAR TO ARTICLE IV, SECTION 2, CLAUSE 3.]

"Tidying Up"

The Confederate Constitution clarified the wording, plugged loopholes, and improved the form of the one it replaced. We have already indicated how the first twelve amendments were worked into the document and the President explicitly granted the power of removal.

Its Article IV, dealing with interstate relations, contains further examples of this "tidying up" process. For instance, Article IV, Section 4, of the United States Constitution says that a state executive might ask for federal aid in suppressing domestic violence "when the Legislature cannot be convened." This is fuzzy. Who is to decide whether or not it is possible to call a legislature together? Changing this phrase to "when the legislature is not in session" in Article IV, Section 3, clause 4, of the Confederate document (next page) is much better. It is now perfectly clear whether it is up to the legislature or to the governor to take action. Also, action can be taken at once, without waiting to call the legislators together.

(Continued on p. 237)

Section 3. NEW STATES AND TERRITORIES

1. *Admission of New States.* Other States may be admitted into this Confederacy by a vote of two-thirds of the whole House of Representatives, and two-thirds of the Senate, the Senate voting by States; but no new State shall be formed or erected within the jurisdiction of any other State; nor any State be formed by the junction of two or more States, or parts of States, without the consent of the Legislatures of the States concerned as well as of the Congress.

2. *Control over Property and Lands.* The Congress shall have power to dispose of and make all needful rules and regulations concerning [respecting the Territory or] the property of the Confederate States, including the lands thereof [and nothing in this Constitution shall be so construed as to Prejudice any Claims of the United States, or of any particular State.]

3. *Acquisition and Government of New Territory; Protection of Slavery Therein.* The Confederate States may acquire new territory; and Congress shall have power to legislate and provide governments for the inhabitants of all territory belonging to the Confederate States, lying without the limits of the several States, and may permit them, at such times, and in such manner as it may by law provide, to form States to be admitted into the Confederacy. In all such territory, the institution of negro slavery, as it now exists in the Confederate States, shall be recognized and protected by Congress and by the territorial government; and the inhabitants of the several Confederate States and Territories shall have the right to take to such territory any slaves lawfully held by them in any of the States or Territories of the Confederate States.

4. *Guarantees against Invasion, Despotism, Domestic Violence.* The Confederate States shall guarantee to every State that now is or hereafter may become a member of this Confederacy, a republican form of government, and shall protect each of them against invasion; and on application of the legislature (or of the executive when the legislature is not in session), against domestic violence.

The United States Constitution nowhere grants the federal government the right to acquire new territory, an omission that embarrassed the strict constructionist Thomas Jefferson when he had the opportunity to purchase Louisiana in 1803. The Louisiana Purchase could be justified constitutionally by arguing that the United States as a nation state has an "inherent right" to annex land, or that Congress might vote to accept the Purchase under the right to appropriate money to "provide for the . . . general Welfare." Once accept either of these arguments, however, and there are few limits to federal power. Better not to invite such dangerous loose-construction arguments by making the grant of power explicit. So the Confederate government was given the right to "acquire new territory."

Many Southerners believed in the "manifest destiny" of the Confederacy to expand to the West and South. Robert Barnwell Rhett, a secessionist leader in South Carolina, told his fellow citizens that the territory of the Confederacy would stretch westward to the Pacific, "and down through Mexico to the other side of the Gulf, and over the isles of the sea."

Article IV contains two provisions that make explicit certain protections for slavery that the South had insisted upon in the long and bitter controversy with Abolitionists and Free Soilers of the North. Section 2, clause 1, guarantees the right to take slaves into any other state and Section 3, clause 3, guarantees a similar right in the territories.

Article V. THE AMENDING PROCESS

1. *How Amendments are Proposed and Ratified.* Upon the demand of any three States, legally assembled in their several conventions, the Congress shall summon a convention of all the States, to take into consideration such amendments to the Constitution as the said States shall concur in suggesting at the time when the said demand is made; and should any of the proposed amendments to the Constitution be agreed on by the said convention—voting by States—and the same be ratified by the legislatures of two-thirds of the several States, or by conventions in two-thirds thereof—as the one or the other mode of ratification may be proposed by the general convention—they shall thenceforward form a part of this Constitution. But no State shall, without its consent, be deprived of its equal representation in the Senate.

Easier Amendment

When the Montgomery Convention met in 1861, no amendment had been added to the Constitution of the United States for nearly sixty years. Yet during that time the federal government had assumed, through usage and judicial interpretation, important new powers such as the right to annex territory and to levy a protective tariff. The Fathers of the Confederacy intensely disliked this "backstairs" amendment through interpretation. Far better, they thought, to facilitate formal amendment than to read new powers into the constitution. Hence the new Article V made the process of change more easy. It requires only three states, instead of two-thirds of the states or of Congress, to require formal consideration of new amendments, and it reduces the proportion of states needed to ratify from three-quarters to two-thirds.

The Confederate Constitution also eliminated the right of Congress to propose amendments. This was held to be an invasion of state sovereignty, since Congress is an agency of the central government. Instead, changes might be proposed through a method described in the United States Constitution, but never yet used: the convening of a constitutional convention on the initiative of a certain proportion of the states. Similar conventions are used in many of the states today to consider methods of bringing government up to date, and it must be accounted a merit in the Confederate Constitution that the convention method is encouraged by making it mandatory when only three states request it.

Article VI. PROVISIONAL GOVERNMENT; SUPREME LAW; LIMITATIONS ON FEDERAL POWER

1. *Validity of Laws and Appointments of Provisional Government.* The Government established by this Constitution is the successor of the Provisional Government of the Confederate States of America, and all the laws passed by the latter shall continue in force until the same shall be repealed or modified; and all the officers appointed by the same shall remain in office until their successors are appointed and qualified or the offices abolished.

2. *Debts of Provisional Government.* All debts contracted and engagements entered into before the adoption of this Constitution, shall be as valid against the Confederate States under this Constitution as under the Provisional Government.

3. *The Supreme Law of the Land.* [SIMILAR TO ARTICLE VI, CLAUSE 2, P. 132.]

4. *Official Oath; No Religious Test.* [SIMILAR TO ARTICLE VI, CLAUSE 3.]

5. *People Retain Rights not Stated in Constitution.* The enumeration, in the Constitution, of certain rights, shall not be construed to deny or disparage others retained by the people of the several States.

6. *Retention of Undelegated Powers by People and States.* The powers not delegated to the Confederate States by the Constitution, nor prohibited by it to the States, are reserved to the States respectively, or to the people thereof.

States' Rights versus the Confederacy

Amendments IX and X of the United States Constitution, limiting the sphere of the central government to its delegated powers, were written into the Confederate Constitution as clauses 5 and 6 of Article VI. They are slightly altered to make it clear that "the people" of the Confederacy do not operate collectively, but only as citizens of their several states.

It is noteworthy that the Confederate Constitution nowhere mentions the right of secession. Such a clause was not thought necessary. Since each state in joining the Confederacy retained "its sovereign and independent character," it presumably had the right of withdrawal.

Extreme devotion to the principle of states' rights weakened the Confederacy, as Lincoln predicted in his First Inaugural Address that it would. The theory developed over the years to resist the government in Washington could just as well be used against the government in Richmond. Pleading the sacred cause of states' rights, Confederate governors organized their states to resist conscription laws, and courts refused to punish deserters from the army. Toward the end of the War Between the States Jefferson Davis complained that his great tasks had been "materially increased by the persistent interference by some of the State Authorities, Legislative, Executive, and Judicial, hindering the action of this government, obstructing the execution of its laws, denouncing its necessary policy, impairing its hold upon the confidence of the people, and dealing with it rather as if it were the public enemy than the Government which they themselves had established. . . ."

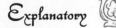

Explanatory

Notes— Article VI, clause 1. The Montgomery Convention set up a provisional government to act until the Constitution was put into effect. The convention elected a temporary President and Vice-President and constituted itself the temporary legislature.

Article VI, clause 3. Discussion of the importance of the inclusion of this important clause from the original Constitution is found on pp. 221 and 233.

Since the Confederate Congress could not at once pass all the laws necessary to run a government, it decreed that the laws of the United States would remain in effect until repealed or altered.

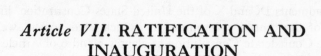

Article VII. RATIFICATION AND INAUGURATION

1. *Five States Needed to Ratify.* The ratification of the conventions of <u>five</u> States shall be sufficient for the establishment of this Constitution between the States so ratifying the same.

2. *First Elections; Interim Government.* <u>When five States shall have ratified this Constitution in the manner before specified, the Congress, under the provisional Constitution, shall prescribe the time for holding the election of President and Vice-President, and for the meeting of the Electoral College, and for counting the votes and inaugurating the President. They shall also prescribe the time for holding the first election of members of Congress under this Constitution, and the time for assembling the same. Until the assembling of such Congress, the Congress under the Provisional Constitution shall continue to exercise the legislative powers granted them; not extending beyond the time limited by the Constitution of the Provisional Government.</u>

3. *A Unanimous Convention.* <u>Adopted unanimously by the Congress of the Confederate States of South Carolina, Georgia, Florida, Alabama, Mississippi, Louisiana, and Texas, sitting in Convention at the capitol, in the city of Montgomery, Ala., on the Eleventh day of March, in the year Eighteen Hundred and Sixty-One.</u>

<u>Howell Cobb</u>
President of the Congress.

The South Divided

The seven states that joined the Confederacy in February, 1861, confidently expected the rest of the South to join them. Until after the attack on Fort Sumter, however, they were disappointed. The upper South was more devoted to the Union, and more disposed to compromise. Only three states—Virginia, Arkansas, and Missouri—elected conventions to consider secession, and in all of them the Unionists had a majority. On April 4 the Virginia Convention voted down secession by a vote of 85 to 45.

Lincoln's call for forces to suppress the Confederacy after the fall of Fort Sumter forced the states of the upper South to make a painful choice: would they obey Lincoln and assist in forcing their neighbors to submit, or would they help their sister states to resist? Virginia's answer to this question was given on April 24, when the same convention that had recently repudiated secession voted to put the state's military forces at the disposal of Jefferson Davis. Arkansas, Tennessee, and North Carolina followed the lead of the Old Dominion. The rest of the slave states stayed with the Union, after a struggle. In Missouri the governor's answer to Lincoln's call for troops was, "Your requisition is illegal, unconstitutional, revolutionary, inhuman, diabolical, and cannot be complied with." Only after a year of fighting was Missouri made safe for the Union. Kentucky attempted to remain neutral, but Federal troops overran most of the state by the end of 1861. In both Missouri and Kentucky secessionists set up provisional governments that were duly admitted to the Confederacy, but they had to operate in exile.

There was strong southern sympathy in Maryland, and the state anthem, "My Maryland," was written to persuade the state to join the Confederacy. Lincoln snuffed out secession, however, by occupying key points with troops and jailing Confederate sympathizers.

It is amazing that the Confederacy, with a total white population of about nine million against the twenty-two million in the North, held out for four years without even the wholehearted support of its own people. Not only did state governors refuse to cooperate fully with the Richmond government, but there were large areas where the people remained loyal to the Union, notably eastern Tennessee and trans-Appalachian Virginia. The latter region joined the Union as the state of West Virginia in 1863. Thus a part of a state seceded from a state.

Explanatory

Notes⌐ **Article VII, clause 1.** Ratification of the Confederate Constitution went speedily. It was generally done by the secessionist conventions which had remained sitting. Only one state, South Carolina, proposed amendments, all in the defense of states' rights and slavery.

243

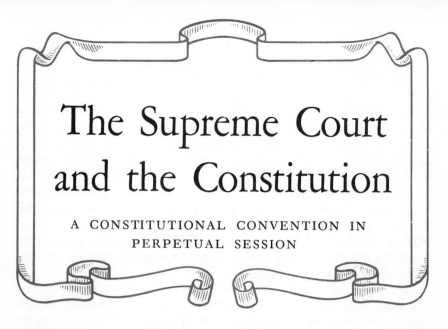

The Supreme Court
and the Constitution

A CONSTITUTIONAL CONVENTION IN
PERPETUAL SESSION

ECAUSE IT was so designed from the outset, the city of Washington is an "official" city, filled with great public buildings and monuments. Tourists visiting Washington soon discover that the magnificent building housing the Supreme Court yields little in grandeur to either the White House, or the Capitol, which house respectively the executive and legislative branches of the government. The contrast between this modern judicial palace of variegated marble and the basement room which was orginally provided for the justices in 1800 (see p. 171) symbolizes the fact that the Court has not only retained but enlarged upon the powers it had come to exert during the era of Chief Justice John Marshall.

Indeed it is not too much to say that no judicial body in the world enjoys such prestige as the Supreme Court of the United States, for in no other nation does the highest judicial court enjoy the great powers which American theory and practice assign to the Supreme Court.

Today the Court accepts only such cases as involve important questions of federal and state power and the rights of the individual. Its business is to state and clarify the law of the land. In a famous statement Justice Owen Roberts once made this process seem deceptively easy:

> The Constitution is the supreme law of the land and established by the people. All legislation must conform to the principles it lays down. When an act of Congress is appropriately challenged in the courts as not conforming to the constitutional mandate the judicial branch of the government has only one duty—to lay the article of

the Constitution beside the statute which is challenged and to decide whether the latter squares with the former.

This is an over-simplification. Many provisions of the Constitution no longer signify what they did when the document was written in 1787. Nearly two centuries of usage and of judicial interpretation have sometimes altered their meaning unrecognizably. And one of the principal agencies in changing the meaning of the words of the Constitution has been the Supreme Court itself. As Charles Evans Hughes once remarked (before he became a Supreme Court justice), "We are under a Constitution, but the Constitution is what the judges say it is." In fact the Supreme Court is like a constitutional convention in perpetual session, both guarding the principles laid down in the Constitution and adapting them to changing needs, circumstances, and aspirations.

It is important to realize that the Supreme Court is not omnipotent. There are large areas of political action where it rarely exercises jurisdiction, one of them being the whole field of foreign affairs, involving the great questions of peace and war, the treaty-making power, military strategy, and nuclear policy. Although a few cases involving the rights of individuals before military tribunals may reach the Court, the big matters of policy—involving decisions on which may hang the very existence of the United States—are not the business of the nine justices. Another great area of government normally outside the Court's jurisdiction is that which may be loosely termed the budget. The decisions as to exactly how federal funds shall be raised and how they shall be spent have immense impact on people's lives, yet seldom do cases involving fiscal policy come before the Supreme Court. The Court only occasionally interferes with the administrative business of government, and not at all with the ordinary processes of congressional lawmaking.

Even within those areas where the Supreme Court operates, it does so with a strong sense of self-restraint. Unlike some high state courts, it does not give advisory opinions to inform the legislature in advance whether or not it considers a proposed piece of legislation to be constitutional. The Court acts (with minor exceptions) on cases appealed from lower courts, and actually considers only a small proportion of these. In the cases it does accept it usually avoids laying down broad constitutional principles when a narrower interpretation will dispose of the case.

Even though much of the workings of government is outside its scope, and although it generally acts with discretion, the powers of the Court are still immense. They lie especially in two areas: (1) definition of the rights of individuals as opposed to the power of government, both state and federal, and (2) the apportionment of powers between the states and the federal government. Both of these areas involve the basic principles upon which this country was founded. The first is an obvious consequence of the theory expressed in the Declaration of Independence that governments exist for the protection of the individual. The second stems from the divided sovereignty inherent in the federal system as set up by the Constitution.

Cases pertaining to personal rights and the federal government generally involve application of the first eight amendments to the Constitution to modern situations. They turn on questions such as these: Does the right of freedom of speech in the First Amendment prevent Congress from making it a crime to advocate the forcible overthrow of the government of the United States? Does the right of the people to be secure against unreasonable searches prevent the F.B.I. from the use of wire tapping to get evidence against criminals? May a witness who "pleaded the Fifth Amendment" and refused to testify before the House Un-American Activities Committee be, for that reason, denied a commission in the Medical Corps of the United States Army?

The most important single grant of power to the federal judiciary since it was first established by the Judiciary Act of 1789 was the passage of the Fourteenth Amendment in 1868 (see pp. 146–149). The first clause of that amendment forbade any state to "deprive any person of life, liberty, or property, without due process of law, nor deny to any person within its jurisdiction the equal protection of the laws." This provision greatly expanded the already existing power of the Supreme Court to review the decisions of state courts, the laws passed by state legislatures, and the actions of state officials. The most important phrase here is "due process of law," which is also found in the Fifth Amendment where it restricts action by the federal government. The Supreme Court has always left the definition of this phrase in "convenient vagueness"; to define it too exactly would be to weaken its effectiveness. There are clearly, however, two types of due process—procedural and substantive.

"Procedural due process" involves the restraints imposed upon the police, courts, and jailers in order to protect the rights of individuals suspected or accused of misdoing. The phrase includes the rights spelled out in Amendments I–VIII of the Constitution plus other restraints such as the right to the writ of *habeas corpus*. In the federal Constitution these are restraints upon the federal government, but through the Fourteenth Amendment (as well as through most state constitutions), these restraints have been generally applied to the states. So the Supreme Court has dealt with questions such as these: Has a state health officer the right to inspect a home without a search warrant? May the conviction of a self-confessed murderer be voided because the state police did not furnish him with a lawyer before he admitted his guilt? May a drug peddler who swallowed his wares when arrested be convicted on evidence obtained by a stomach pump? May a Negro be convicted by an all-white jury in a district where Negroes have been denied the right to sit on juries?

"Substantive due process" is involved when the actual substance or content of a law is held to violate personal rights. Thus for many years the Supreme Court held that statutes designed to limit hours of work and to establish minimum wages were unconstitutional, on the ground that such laws deprived workers and employers of "freedom of contract" i.e., their freedom to bargain over terms of employment. Sometimes it is most difficult to assess whether personal rights are promoted or restrained by legislation. For instance, state laws against picketing may be held to violate due process on the ground that picketing is a normal means of expression in labor disputes and to forbid it is to deprive the workers of freedom of speech. But when picketing threatens violence, or is directed against individuals not immediately involved in a labor dispute, it destroys the rights of others and may constitutionally be forbidden.

In cases that concern federalism, the relationship between state and federal power, the Supreme Court has to steer a line between the "elastic clause" (Article I, Section 8, clause 18) and the "supreme law of the land" clause (Article VI, clause 2) on the one hand and Amendment X which reserves to the states or people all power not delegated to the federal government. Perhaps the most common area where there is conflict or overlap between state and federal power is that of interstate and intrastate commerce. Railroad employees are pretty clearly engaged in interstate commerce and taxi drivers in intrastate commerce, so the federal government regulates the terms of employment and qualifications of the former, and the states of the latter. But what of men driving buses between two railroad stations—are they subject to federal or state legislation or both?

Out of scores of decisions in particular cases, some of them seemingly petty, the Supreme Court is constantly defining and redefining, preserving and adapting the Constitution. Its task is one of great delicacy and difficulty and it is carried on in the full glare of public attention. "Every sentence that the justices write, every argument they offer, moves into as searching a spotlight as falls perhaps on any printed word except the Bible or Shakespeare. . . ." By the very nature of its business, the settlement of disputes, the Supreme Court is always involved in public controversy. Yet at the same time the justices are not responsible directly to the people. They gain their positions by appointment, not election, and once chosen they remain in office until they die or resign. Several justices have remained in office over thirty years. This situation leads to the charge that the judges are always behind the times, always in a position to oppose the will of the majority as expressed through elected officials.

Small wonder, then, that the Supreme Court has throughout its history been under almost constant attack and that sometimes its will has been openly flouted. On the eve of the War Between the States the Republican party, dominant in the northern states, refused to accept the Dred Scott decision as the final word on slavery (see p. 203). During the reconstruction period after the war congressional legislation first reduced the Court from nine members to six; then raised it back to nine again to make sure that the justices would "vote right." From the early 1880's for over a half century the Supreme Court was predominantly conservative and was repeatedly accused of protecting propertied interests, especially big business, at the expense of the "human rights" of the people at large. This period reached a climax between 1935 and 1937 with the conflict between Franklin D. Roosevelt and the "nine old men" who were hamstringing the New Deal. Recently the pendulum has swung the other way, and conservatives insist that the Court has destroyed states' rights in order to protect minority groups and has endangered the security of the United States by "coddling Communists."

As this continuous record of criticism and controversy suggests, the justices of the Supreme Court do not operate in a rarefied atmosphere, far above the hurly-burly of politics. Mr. Justice Holmes once wrote:

> In the ordinary and low sense which we attach to the word "partisan" and "politician," a judge of the Supreme Court should be neither. But in the higher sense, in the proper sense, he is not in my judgment fitted for the position unless he is a party man, a constitutional statesman. . . .

The fact is that judges are men with political opinions and are appointed by Presidents with political opinions. In all our history Democratic Presidents have appointed only one Supreme Court justice from the opposition party; Republican Presidents, like Federalists and Whigs before them, have behaved much the same way. So the Court gradually, sometimes very gradually, responds to the changing popular will. It acts in the long run as a kind of governing wheel, sometimes slowing down change, sometimes preserving an unpopular right against popular clamor, but operating constantly to insure that the old is not lost in the new, and that time-tried principles are adapted to changing conditions.

The following pages contain excerpts from the opinions in four Supreme Court cases which illustrate important aspects of the way the Supreme Court interprets the Constitution. *Munn v. Illinois* (1876) declared that when private property is "affected with a public interest" it must be prepared to submit to government regulation. *National Labor Relations Board v. Jones & Laughlin Steel Corporation* (1937) broke a famous judicial log jam and extended the regulatory power of the federal government by extending the definition of interstate commerce. *Youngstown Sheet & Tube Co. v. Sawyer* (1952) set bounds to the ever-increasing emergency powers of the President of the United States. *Brown v. Board of Education* (1954), the most controversial Supreme Court case since the Dred Scott decision nearly a century earlier, revealed both the use of the Fourteenth Amendment to overturn state legislation and the way the Court may change its mind with changing times. We have chosen these four cases among many others because they all have profoundly affected men's lives and because they have significantly shaped the frame of government today.

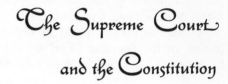

The Supreme Court
and the Constitution

❦

MUNN v. ILLINOIS
1877

Question at Issue. The question to be determined in this case is whether the general assembly of Illinois can, under the limitations upon the legislative powers of the States imposed by the Constitution of the United States, fix by law the maximum of charges for the storage of grain in warehouses at Chicago and other places in the State.

Constitutional Objections to Illinois Statute. It is claimed that such a law is repugnant—

1. To that part of sect. 8, art. I, of the Constitution of the United States which confers upon Congress the power "to regulate commerce with foreign nations and among the several States";

2. To that part of sect. 9 of the same article, which provides that "no preference shall be given by any regulation of commerce or revenue to the ports of one State over those of another"; and

3. To that part of amendment 14 which ordains that no State shall "deprive any person of life, liberty, or property, without due process of law, nor deny to any person within its jurisdiction the equal protection of the laws."

"Affected with a Public Interest"

Perhaps the most important single reason for the rapid development of agriculture in the Middle West and prairie regions after the War Between the States was the building of the railroads that transported staple crops over long distances in an area with few waterways. Yet at the same time the railroads benefited the farmer, they were guilty of many abuses. They charged more for "short hauls," where they had a monopoly, than for "long hauls," where they had competition. They conspired to keep up rates by "pooling" or by "gentlemen's agreements." They bribed legislatures to secure favorable state laws and evade fair taxation. Not surprisingly, the farmer developed a strong sense of grievance, not only against the railroads, but against bankers, middlemen, and warehouse companies, all of whom he regarded as conspiring to rob him.

In 1867 the first nation-wide farm organization, the Patrons of Husbandry, was founded. Generally known as the Grange, this began as a fraternal organization designed to promote sociability and improvement of agricultural practices. It grew like wildfire, gaining over a million members within half a dozen years. Becoming a political force, it pushed through state laws setting maximum rates for railroads and other semi-public agencies such as grain elevators and slaughter houses, with heavy fines for companies which failed to comply. These "Granger laws" were a decisive reversal of the Jeffersonian-Jacksonian tradition of *laissez faire*.

The railroads went to court to get the Granger laws declared unconstitutional. Railroad lawyers argued that once a state legislature had granted a railroad corporation a charter to do business, it had no more control over it. Any attempt to regulate its operations or to readjust the rates it could charge was a violation of the principle laid down by John Marshall in *Dartmouth College v. Woodward*—that to tamper with a corporation charter was to violate Article I, Section 10, clause 1 of the Constitution that forbids states to pass laws "impairing the Obligation of Contracts." It was further argued that railroads and warehouses were engaged in interstate commerce and were therefore beyond state control. Above all, counsel for the railroads argued that the recently passed Fourteenth Amendment made the Granger laws unconstitutional. A corporation was a legal person and the Fourteenth Amendment forbade any state to "deprive any person of life, liberty, or property, without due process of law." The Granger laws deprived corporations of "life," by interfering with their charters; of "liberty," by denying them the right to fix their own rates; and of "property," by cutting down on the prices they might charge.

The cases testing the constitutionality of the Granger laws were first argued in several state courts, starting as early as 1871. Finally a batch of them reached the Supreme Court together in 1875. *(Continued on p. 253)*

We will consider the last of these objections first. . . .

The Constitution contains no definition of the word "deprive," as used in the Fourteenth Amendment. To determine its signification, therefore, it is necessary to ascertain the effect which usage has given it, when employed in the same or a like connection.

Principles and Precedents. When one becomes a member of society, he necessarily parts with some rights or privileges which, as an individual not affected by his relations to others, he might retain. "A body politic," as aptly defined in the preamble of the Constitution of Massachusetts, "is a social compact by which the whole people covenants with each citizen, and each citizen with the whole people, that all shall be governed by certain laws for the common good." This does not confer power upon the whole people to control rights which are purely and exclusively private; but it does authorize the establishment of laws requiring each citizen to so conduct himself, and so use his own property, as not unnecessarily to injure another. This is the very essence of government, and has found expression in the maxim, *sic utere tuo ut alienum non laedas.* From this source come the police powers, which, as was said by Mr. Chief Justice Taney in the License Cases, 5 How. 583, "are nothing more or less than the powers of government inherent in every sovereignty, . . . that is to say, . . . the power to govern men and things." Under these powers the government regulates the conduct of its citizens one towards another, and the manner in which each shall use his own property, when such regulation becomes necessary for the public good. In their exercise it has been customary in England from time immemorial, and in this country from its first colonization, to regulate ferries, common carriers, hackmen, bakers, millers, wharfingers, innkeepers, &c., and in so doing to fix a maximum of charge to be made for services rendered, accommodations furnished, and articles sold. . . .

The Common Law. This brings us to inquire as to the principles upon which this power of regulation rests, in order that we may determine what is within and what without its operative effect. Looking, then, to the common law, from whence came the right which the Constitution protects, we find that when private property is "affected with a public interest, it ceases to be *juris privati* only." This was said by Lord Chief Justice Hale more than two hundred years ago, in his treaties *De Portibus Maris,* 1 Harg. Law Tracts, 78, and has been accepted without objection as an essential element in the law of property ever since.

The principal case, *Munn v. Illinois,* involved not railroad regulation as such, but a law passed by the Illinois legislature in 1871 fixing maximum rates for grain elevators and public warehouses—a similar form of enterprise. The opinion was delivered by Chief Justice Morrison R. Waite on March 1, 1877. Waite concentrated on the question of whether or not the rate-fixing legislation "deprived" the warehouse owners of rights within the meaning of the Fourteenth Amendment. After a long examination of precedents both English and American, the Chief Justice decided that "Property does indeed become clothed with a public interest when used in a manner to make it of public consequence, and affect the community at large." Since the grain elevator business in Chicago vitally affected the grain producers of seven or eight states, since the business was tightly held by a few companies and was practically a monopoly, it was surely one in which the public had an interest and therefore one which the Illinois legislature had a right to regulate.

Other parts of the *Munn v. Illinois* decision denied that the Illinois legislation was *ex post facto* or that it interfered with interstate commerce. Here Waite followed the theory of state "police power" developed by Marshall's successor as Chief Justice, Roger Brooke Taney (pronounced "tawny"). The police power has been defined as "the right of the State legislature to take such action as it saw fit, in the furtherance of the security, morality, and general welfare of the community, save only as it was prevented from exercising its discretion by very specific restrictions in the written Constitution." The doctrine of state police power weakened the sanctity of contracts preached by John Marshall in *Fletcher v. Peck* and *Dartmouth College v. Woodward* (see p. 193). It also permitted states to legislate within the sphere of interstate commerce, at least until Congress chose to do so. In 1837, for instance, the Supreme Court had supported

(Continued on p. 255)

Explanatory

Notes **Principles and Precedents.** *Sic utere tuo ut alienum non laedas* means, "Use what is yours in such a way that you do not harm others."

The Common Law. This opinion, with its references to English precedents and the principles of the common law, makes clear how great is the debt of American law to its English inheritance.

The common law, as applied to regulation, had its origins in the Middle Ages when wages, charges, and the cost of goods were supposed to be set by the principle of the "just price." The just price might be set by usage, by guild regulations, or by law. The basic ideas of *laissez faire,* that prices and costs should be set by supply and demand, and that business should be free of governmental control, did not develop until the eighteenth century.

When Private Property Must Submit to Public Regulation.
Property does become clothed with a public interest when used
in a manner to make it of public consequence, and affect the community at large. When, therefore, one devotes his property to a
use in which the public has an interest, he, in effect, grants to the
public an interest in that use, and must submit to be controlled by
the public for the common good, to the extent of the interest he has
thus created. He may withdraw his grant by discontinuing the use;
but, so long as he maintains the use, he must submit to the control. . . .

Warehouses are Common Carriers. From the same source
comes the power to regulate the charges of common carriers,
which was done in England as long ago as the third year of the
reign of William and Mary, and continued until within a comparatively recent period. . . .

Common carriers exercise a sort of public office, and have duties
to perform in which the public is interested. Their business is,
therefore, "affected with a public interest," within the meaning of
the doctrine which Lord Hale has so forcibly stated.

But we need not go further. Enough has already been said to
show that, when private property is devoted to a public use, it is
subject to public regulation. It remains only to ascertain whether
the warehouses of these plaintiffs in error, and the business which
is carried on there, come within the operation of this principle. . . .

In this connection it must also be borne in mind that, although in
1874 there were in Chicago fourteen warehouses adapted to this
particular business, and owned by about thirty persons, nine business firms controlled them. . . .

They stand . . . in the very "gateway of commerce" and take
toll of all who pass. Their business most certainly "tends to a common charge, and has become a thing of public interest and use."

a New York State law that sought to prevent ship owners from bringing in pauper immigrants from Europe; the act was held to be an enforcement of the state poor laws and not an interference with interstate commerce. So in *Munn v. Illinois* Chief Justice Waite admitted that the Illinois warehouse law affected interstate commerce, but held that the legislation was nevertheless within the power of the state, at least until Congress chose to act.

On the same day as the *Munn v. Illinois* decision, the Court upheld laws passed by four midwestern states fixing railroad rates.

The so-called "Granger cases" caused widespread controversy. The feeling against the railroad corporations and the fear of their immense power was so great that some lawyers and newspaper editors hailed the decisions as a great victory for the people. Critics of the decisions said that they were a threat to all property rights and a long step toward socialism.

The immediate impact of *Munn v. Illinois* and the other Granger cases was not great. The Granger laws proved unworkable and other factors forced the railroads to lower rates. Also the Supreme Court changed its mind. In the 1880's several extremely conservative justices joined the Court and their influence was soon felt in cases involving the same issues as the Granger cases. In *St. Louis & Pacific R.R. Co. v. Illinois* (1886), the Court flatly reversed the closing argument of *Munn v. Illinois* by holding that a state had no power to regulate railroad rates on shipments going from one state to another. In *Chicago, Milwaukee & St. Paul R.R. v. Minnesota* (1890), the Court held that the right of a state legislature to fix rates was not unlimited, and that it was for the courts to determine whether or not rates were "reasonable." (Continued on p. 257)

Explanatory

Notes Warehouses are Common Carriers. Common carriers are agencies engaged in public transportation, such as taxis or buses. They are peculiarly subject to government regulation, both because they are vital to society and because their business is by nature monopolistic.

Not ex post facto. It matters not in this case that these plaintiffs in error had built their warehouses and established their business before the regulations complained of were adopted. What they did was from the beginning subject to the power of the body politic to require them to conform to such regulations as might be established by the proper authorities for the common good. . . . The same principle applies to them that does to the proprietor of a hackney-carriage, and as to him it has never been supposed that he was exempt from regulating statutes or ordinances because he had purchased his horses and carriage and established his business before the statute or the ordinance was adopted.

Not Interference with Congressional Power over Interstate Commerce. . . . The warehouses . . . are situated and their business carried on exclusively within the limits of the State of Illinois. They are used as instruments by those engaged in State as well as those engaged in inter-state commerce. . . . Incidentally they may become connected with inter-State commerce, but not necessarily so. Their regulation is a thing of domestic concern and, certainly, until Congress acts in reference to their inter-State relations, the State may exercise all the powers of government over them, even though in so doing it may indirectly operate upon commerce outside its immediate jurisdiction. . . .

Judgment affirmed.

FIELD, S. J. delivered a dissenting opinion.

Even though its arguments were whittled down, *Munn v. Illinois* was nevertheless of monumental importance in the history of constitutional law. The basic principle, that private property rights—particularly those of a monopolistic nature—must ultimately be subject to regulation in the public interest was written into the law of the land. It provided the legal basis, especially, for state commissions controlling public utilities and for the great federal regulatory commissions, such as the Interstate Commerce Commission, the Securities Exchange Commission, and the Federal Communications Commission.

Explanatory

Notes Not *ex post facto.* The counsel for the warehouse owners argued
•   against the Illinois statute on the ground that it was passed after the
      warehouses were built and was therefore a violation of Article I, Section
      10, clause 2 of the Constitution that forbids states to pass *ex post facto*
      laws.
          "Field, S.J. delivered a dissenting opinion." The Court split 7–2 on
      the *Munn v. Illinois* decision. Justice Stephen J. Field's dissenting
      opinion gloomily foretold that the decision would destroy all rights
      of private property. Field was one of the leaders when the Court later
      employed the "due process" clauses of the Fifth and Fourteenth
      Amendments to curb both federal and state regulation of business.

NATIONAL LABOR RELATIONS BOARD v. JONES & LAUGHLIN STEEL CORPORATION

1937

Facts of the Case. In a proceeding under the National Labor Relations Act of 1935, the National Labor Relations Board found that the respondent, Jones & Laughlin Steel Corporation, had violated the Act by engaging in unfair labor practices affecting commerce. The proceeding was instituted by the Beaver Valley Lodge No. 200, affiliated with the Amalgamated Association of Iron, Steel and Tin Workers of America, a labor organization. The unfair labor practices charged were that the corporation was discriminating against members of the union with regard to hire and tenure of employment, and was coercing and intimidating its employees in order to interfere with their self-organization. The discriminatory and coercive action alleged was the discharge of certain employees.

Appeal to Supreme Court. The National Labor Relations Board, sustaining the charge, ordered the corporation to cease and desist from such discrimination and coercion, to offer reinstatement to ten of the employees named, to make good their losses in pay, and to post for thirty days notices that the corporation would not discharge or discriminate against members, or those desiring to become members, of the labor union. As the corporation failed to comply, the Board petitioned the Circuit Court of Appeals to enforce the order. The court denied the petition, holding that the order lay beyond the the range of federal power. We granted certiorari. . . .

Steel Corporation Arguments. Contesting the ruling of the Board, the respondent argues (1) that the Act is in reality a regulation of labor relations and not of interstate commerce; (2) that the Act can have no application to the respondent's relations with its production employees because they are not subject to regulation by the federal government; and (3) that the provisions of the Act violate Section 2 of Article III and the Fifth and Seventh Amendments of the Constitution of the United States.

The Court Reverses Itself

In the presidential election of 1936 Franklin Roosevelt was swept into office for a second time, by 523 electoral votes to eight. The voters also sent huge Democratic majorities to both houses of Congress. When Roosevelt delivered his Second Inaugural Address to a rain-soaked audience on January 20, 1937, he promised a continuation of New Deal legislation to better the lot of "one-third of a nation, ill-housed, ill-clad, ill-nourished." But standing directly in opposition to the President and Congress and the recently expressed will of the electorate stood the "nine old men" of the Supreme Court, a solid dike against change.

Several New Deal measures introduced new departures in governmental powers and methods. The National Recovery Act (N.R.A.) had set up a vast network of agencies staffed by both business and government, and these were granted power to fix prices and wages. The Agricultural Adjustment Act (A.A.A.) endeavored to raise the agricultural income by paying farmers to take acreage out of cultivation. The Tennessee Valley Authority (T.V.A.) planned the economy of a vast region extending over six states. It was not until 1935 that such legislation was reviewed by the Supreme Court. Then it fared badly. In that year and the next the Court held New Deal measures unconstitutional in seven out of nine major cases. N.R.A. was struck down in a unanimous decision, A.A.A. by a vote of 6 to 3. In some cases the vote was 5 to 4, meaning that legislation passed by great majorities in Congress and affecting the lives of many thousands of people was in effect upheld or vetoed by a single judge. As the Court was then composed, four extremely conservative judges—Van Devanter, Mc-Reynolds, Butler, and Sutherland—stood firmly opposed to legislation, state or federal, that involved interference with private property rights.

(Continued on p. 261)

Explanatory

Notes Appeal to Supreme Court. "We granted *certiorari*." By a writ of *certiorari* a superior court calls up for review the records of an inferior court.

Steel Corporation Arguments. The second argument centers on the idea that manufacturing is not interstate commerce. The third argument maintains that the federal judiciary has no jurisdiction in the case and that the corporation is being robbed of its rights without "due process of law," especially since it was held guilty by a regulatory board and not by a jury.

Scope of Jones & Laughlin Operations. . . . . (The Jones & Laughlin Steel Corporation) is organized under the laws of Pennsylvania and has its principal office at Pittsburgh. It is engaged in the business of manufacturing iron and steel in plants situated in Pittsburgh and nearby Aliquippa, Pennsylvania. It manufactures and distributes a widely diversified line of steel and pig iron, being the fourth largest producer of steel in the United States. With its subsidiaries—nineteen in number—it is a completely integrated enterprise, owning and operating ore, coal and limestone properties, lake and river transportation facilities and terminal railroads located at its manufacturing plants. It owns or controls mines in Michigan and Minnesota. It operates four ore steamships on the Great Lakes, used in the transportation of ore to its factories. It owns coal mines in Pennsylvania. It operates towboats and steam barges used in carrying coal to its factories. It owns limestone properties in various places in Pennsylvania and West Virginia. It owns the Monongahela connecting railroad which connects the plants of the Pittsburgh works and forms an interconnection with the Pennsylvania, New York Central and Baltimore and Ohio Railroad systems. It owns the Aliquippa and Southern Railroad Company which connects the Aliquippa works with the Pittsburgh and Lake Erie, part of the New York Central system. . . . It has sales offices in twenty cities in the United States and a wholly-owned subsidiary which is devoted exclusively to distributing its product in Canada. Approximately 75 per cent. of its product is shipped out of Pennsylvania.

Summarizing these operations, the Labor Board concluded that the works in Pittsburgh and Aliquippa "might be likened to the heart of a self-contained, highly-integrated body. They draw in the raw materials from Michigan, Minnesota, West Virginia, Pennsylvania in part through arteries and by means controlled by the respondent; they transform the materials and then pump them out to all parts of the nation through the vast mechanism which the respondent has elaborated." . . .

Three more liberal justices—Brandeis, Stone, and Cardozo—were disposed to give most New Deal legislation, but not all, the benefit of the doubt. Chief Justice Hughes and Justice Roberts were "swing men," whose weight went sometimes one way and sometimes another. The average age of the justices in 1937 was 72; seven had been chosen by Republican Presidents and two by Democrats. The composition of the Court might have been changed had any justices died or resigned, but for the first time since James Monroe's first term as President a whole presidential term went by without a single vacancy.

The anti-New Deal decisions of the Supreme Court were reinforced by about 1600 injunctions issued by federal district courts, forbidding federal officials to enforce New Deal laws. Thus the entire legislative program of the Roosevelt administration, past and future, was put in jeopardy by judges appointed in previous administrations and holding office for life.

At one time Roosevelt thought of proposing a constitutional amendment, either one granting Congress power to override Supreme Court decisions by a two-thirds vote, as it overrides presidential vetoes, or requiring a higher majority—say 6–3 or 7–2—to declare a federal law unconstitutional. But amendment was a slow process, and with little likelihood of success. Roosevelt wanted quicker action. On February 5, 1937, he sent a special message to Congress urging a law empowering him to appoint additional judges to the federal courts when incumbents over the age of 70 did not choose to retire. If passed, this would allow him to "pack" the Supreme Court with six new justices. This was ill advised. He had not adequately consulted leaders of his party, had not campaigned on the issue, and had failed to reckon on the widespread loyalty to the Supreme Court as an institution. Many who deplored the Supreme Court's recent decisions were wholly opposed to Roosevelt's scheme. A bitter fight began in Congress. Eventually, after nearly six months of debate, the Court bill failed to pass, even though the President had used every political resource in its support. It was a resounding defeat, and left permanent scars.

Yet Roosevelt always claimed he had lost the battle but won the campaign, because during the legislative battle the Supreme Court reversed itself. In a message to the Senate Judiciary Committee, Chief Justice Hughes had sharply criticized Roosevelt's "court-packing plan." He then helped to kill it by a strategic retreat. In three 5–4 decisions—involving a District of Columbia minimum wage law, the National Labor Relations Act, and the Social Security Act—the Court upheld the constitutionality of New Deal legislation. In every case Justices Roberts and Hughes joined the three liberal justices to create a pro-New Deal majority and overrule the four rockbound conservatives. The change of position has been called "the switch in time that save nine." It was followed by Justice Van

(Continued on p. 263)

Labor's Right to Organize. Thus, in its present application, the statute goes no further than to safeguard the right of employees to self-organization and to select representatives of their own choosing for collective bargaining or other mutual protection without restraint or coercion by their employer.

That is a fundamental right. Employees have as clear a right to organize and select their representatives for lawful purposes as the respondent has to organize its business and select its own officers and agents. Discrimination and coercion to prevent the free exercise of the right of employees to self-organization and representation is a proper subject for condemnation by competent legislative authority. Long ago we stated the reason for labor organizations. We said that they were organized out of the necessities of the situation; that a single employee was helpless in dealing with an employer; that he was dependent ordinarily on his daily wage for the maintenance of himself and family; that if the employer refused to pay him the wages that he thought fair, he was nevertheless unable to leave the employ and resist arbitrary and unfair treatment; that union was essential to give laborers opportunity to deal on an equality with their employers. . . .

Industrial Strife and Interstate Commerce. Giving full weight to respondent's contention with respect to a break in the complete continuity of the "stream of commerce" by reason of respondent's manufacturing operations, the fact remains that the stoppage of those operations by industrial strife would have a most serious effect upon interstate commerce. In view of respondent's far-flung activities, it is idle to say that the effect would be indirect or remote. It is obvious that it would be immediate and might be catastrophic. We are asked to shut our eyes to the plainest facts of our national life. . . . When industries organize themselves on a national scale, making their relation to interstate commerce the dominant factor in their activities, how can it be maintained that their industrial labor relations constitute a forbidden field into which Congress may not enter when it is necessary to protect interstate commerce from the paralyzing consequences of industrial war?

Devanter's announcement that he would resign, taking advantage of a recently passed law that after reaching the age of seventy federal judges could retire on full pay. This at last gave President Roosevelt a chance to fill a Supreme Court vacancy.

One of the three cases mentioned in the last paragraph, *National Labor Relations Board v. Jones & Laughlin Steel Corporation*, was of longtime importance. It concerned the question whether the N.L.R.B. had the right to reinstate, with back pay, ten employees in a steel manufacturing plant who had been discharged for labor union activity. Two basic questions were involved: Was the control of labor relations a proper subject of governmental power? Was steel manufacturing interstate commerce? In answer to the first question the Court followed *Nebbia v. New York* (1934) which upheld a New York law establishing minimum prices for milk. In this decision the Court extended the concept of business "affected with a public interest," and therefore subject to regulation, laid down in *Munn v. Illinois*. Usually this had been restricted to fixing rates for natural monopolies such as railroads, public utilities, and grain elevators. Now it applied to any business, or business activity, of wide public concern—the retail price of milk, as in the Nebbia case; or federal control of labor relations, as in *National Labor Relations Board v. Jones & Laughlin Steel Corporation*. *(Continued on p. 265)*

Explanatory Notes Labor's **Right to Organize.** Section 7a of the National Recovery Act (N.R.A.), passed in June, 1933, had guaranteed employees "the right to organize and bargain collectively through representatives of their own choosing . . . free from the interference, restraint, or coercion of employers of labor, or their agents. . . ." In May, 1935, the Court unanimously found N.R.A. unconstitutional as a whole, without questioning explicitly the validity of section 7a. In July, 1935, the National Labor Relations Act (also called the Wagner Act after its principal author) was passed, reasserting labor's right to organize and bargain collectively and setting up the National Labor Relations Board to regulate labor relations.

Experience has abundantly demonstrated that the recognition of the right of employees to self-organization and to have representatives of their own choosing for the purpose of collective bargaining is often an essential condition of industrial peace. Refusal to confer and negotiate has been one of the most prolific causes of strife. This is such an outstanding fact in the history of labor disturbances that it is a proper subject of judicial notice and requires no citation of instances.

Regulation of Steel Industry within Congressional Power over Interstate Commerce. The steel industry is one of the great basic industries of the United States, with ramifying activities affecting interstate commerce at every point. The Government aptly refers to the steel strike of 1919–1920 with its far-reaching consequences. The fact that there appears to have been no major disturbance in that industry in the more recent period did not dispose of the possibilities of future and like dangers to interstate commerce which Congress was entitled to foresee and to exercise its protective power to forestall. It is not necessary again to detail the facts as to respondent's enterprise. Instead of being beyond the pale, we think that it presents in a most striking way the close and intimate relation which a manufacturing industry may have to interstate commerce and we have no doubt that Congress had constitutional authority to safeguard the right of respondent's employees to self-organization and freedom in the choice of representatives for collective bargaining. . . .

Conclusion. Our conclusion is that the order of the Board was within its competency and that the Act is valid as here applied. The judgment of the Circuit Court of Appeals is reversed and the cause is remanded for further proceedings in conformity with this opinion.

Reversed.

[Justice McReynolds delivered a dissenting opinion, concurred in by Justices Van Devanter, Sutherland and Butler, covering the principal case and two others decided the same day.]

In three cases decided in 1935 and 1936 (*Schecter Poultry Co. v. United States, United States v. Butler,* and *Carter v. Carter Coal Co.*), the Supreme Court had maintained that those engaged in wholesale poultry business, in wheat farming, and in coal mining were only "indirectly" involved in interstate commerce and so not subject to federal regulation. But in *National Labor Relations Board v. Jones & Laughlin Steel Corporation,* the Court said that to believe that the steel industry was engaged in purely intrastate commerce was "to shut our eyes to the plainest facts of our national life." In words strongly reminiscent of *Gibbons v. Ogden,* the Court held that the steel industry was so profoundly affected by the national economy that its regulation fell within the congressional power over interstate commerce.

Explanatory

Notes Conclusion. ". . . the cause is remanded for further proceedings in conformity with this opinion." "Remanded" here means sent back to the federal district court for enforcement, and to the National Labor Relations Board to work out details, such as the amount of back pay due to the ten discharged employees. This majority opinion was written by Chief Justice Hughes.

YOUNGSTOWN SHEET & TUBE CO.
v. SAWYER

1952

Mr. Justice Black delivered the opinion of the Court.

The Issue. We are asked to decide whether the President was acting within his constitutional power when he issued an order directing the Secrtary of Commerce to take possession of and operate most of the Nation's steel mills. The mill owners argue that the President's order amounts to lawmaking, a legislative function which the Constitution has expressly confided to the Congress and not to the President. The Government's position is that the order was made on findings of the President that his action was necessary to avert a national catastrophe which would inevitably result from a stoppage of steel production, and that in meeting this grave emergency the President was acting within the aggregate of his constitutional powers as the Nation's Chief Executive and the Commander in Chief of the Armed Forces of the United States.

No Statute Authorizes Seizure. The President's power, if any, to issue the order must stem either from an act of Congress or from the Constitution itself. There is no statute that expressly authorizes the President to take possession of property as he did here. Nor is there any act of Congress to which our attention has been directed from which such a power can fairly be implied. Indeed, we do not understand the Government to rely on statutory authorization for this seizure. There are two statutes which do authorize the President to take both personal and real property under certain conditions. [The Selective Service Act of 1948; the Defense Production Act of 1950.] However, the Government admits that these conditions were not met and that the President's order was not rooted in either of the statutes. The Government refers to the seizure provisions of one of these statutes . . . as "much too cumbersome, involved, and time-consuming for the crisis which was at hand."

Curbing Presidential Power

The most notable fact of American constitutional development in the twentieth century has been the immense expansion of the duties and powers of the President. Partly this has stemmed from the influence of three commanding personalities, all of whom believed that the President should use his authority and influence to the full. Theodore Roosevelt maintained that it was not only the right but the duty of the President "to do anything that the needs of the Nation demanded unless such action was forbidden by the Constitution or the laws." Woodrow Wilson wrote, "The President is at liberty, both in law and in conscience, to be as big a man as he can." Franklin Roosevelt in his First Inaugural Address frankly told the country that he might feel forced to ask Congress for powers comparable to those he would be granted in wartime in order to meet the problems of the Great Depression.

But the principal reason for the great expansion of the Presidency has been the recurrent crises that the United States has had to face—the two World Wars, the Great Depression, the Korean War, the Cold War. In crisis there is often little time for sober debate, or the slow processes of congressional law-making. The government must sometimes act, and act quickly, and the responsibility for action usually falls on the President.

One of the principal areas where executive authority has increased has been control of the national economy. In modern warfare the production line may be as important as the battle line. Therefore once the country has gone to war, Congress has empowered the President to set up agencies to direct what goods should be produced, who should get them, what prices should be charged, and what wages should be paid. Woodrow Wilson demanded and received from Congress power to take over the entire railroad system of the country. Without congressional authorization Wilson ordered the seizure of a munitions company that refused to follow the directions of the War Labor Board, an agency set up by executive decree. In World War II Franklin Roosevelt ordered the federal government to take over firms whose activities were considered vital to the war effort, usually when labor disputes threatened to close them down.

(Continued on p. 269)

𝓔xplanatory

𝓝otes↻ "Mr. Justice Black. . . ." In cases where the Chief Justice dissents
from the majority of the Court, as he did in this case, the senior justice
among the majority may write the opinion or may assign it to others.
Mr. Justice Black chose to write the opinion.

Taft-Hartley Law. Moreover, the use of the seizure technique to solve labor disputes in order to prevent work stoppages was not only unauthorized by any congressional enactment; prior to this controversy, Congress had refused to adopt that method of settling labor disputes. When the Taft-Hartley Act was under consideration in 1947, Congress rejected an amendment which would have authorized such governmental seizures in cases of emergency. Apparently it was thought that the technique of seizure, like that of compulsory arbitration, would interfere with the process of collective bargaining. Consequently, the plan Congress adopted in that Act did not provide for seizure under any circumstances. . . .

Alleged Constitutional Basis for Seizure. It is clear that if the President had authority to issue the order he did, it must be found in some provisions of the Constitution. And it is not claimed that express constitutional language grants this power to the President. The contention is that presidential power should be implied from the aggregate of his powers under the Constitution. Particular reliance is placed on provisions in Article II which say that "the executive Power shall be vested in a President . . ."; that "he shall take Care that the Laws be faithfully executed"; and that he "shall be Commander in Chief of the Army and Navy of the United States."

President's Military Powers not Applicable. The order cannot properly be sustained as an exercise of the President's military power as Commander in Chief of the Armed Forces. The Government attempts to do so by citing a number of cases upholding broad powers in military commanders engaged in day-to-day fighting in a theater of war. Such cases need not concern us here. Even though "theater of war" be an expanding concept, we cannot with faithfulness to our constitutional system hold that the Commander in Chief of the Armed Forces has the ultimate power as such to take possession of private property in order to keep labor disputes from stopping production. This is a job for the nation's lawgivers, not for its military authorities.

Executive Powers not Applicable. Nor can the seizure order be sustained because of the several constitutional provisions that grant executive power to the President. In the framework of our Constitution, the President's power to see that the laws are faithfully executed refutes the idea that he is to be a lawmaker. The Constitution limits his functions in the law-making process to the recommending of laws he thinks wise and the vetoing of laws he

In every case mentioned above, the President justified his action by military necessity. But gnawing questions persist. If the President can take such drastic actions, always pleading an emergency, what bounds are there to his powers? And if these bounds are not defined, what happens to the basic idea behind the Constitution—that the powers of the federal government are limited? Such questions as these were strikingly presented to the country when on April 9, 1952, President Truman ordered federal seizure of the entire steel industry.

In 1952 the United States was carrying on a war in Korea and was also engaged in arming its N.A.T.O. allies in Europe. The country was in a state of partial mobilization. Under the Defense Production Act of 1950 President Truman had established a series of control boards under an Office of Defense Mobilization. Among these were a Wage Stabilization Board and an Office of Price Stabilization. At the end of the year 1951 the contracts between the United Steelworkers and the major steel companies had run out after months of fruitless bargaining, but the steelworkers stayed on the job at the President's request while the Wage Board considered their demand for higher pay. In March the Wage Board recom-

(Continued on p. 271)

Explanatory

Notes　Taft-Hartley Law. One of the strongest arguments against Truman's seizure of the steel mills was that he had not used machinery set up by the Taft-Hartley Act to settle strikes that threatened to disrupt the national economy. In particular, he had not used a section of the law that allowed the President to decree a "cooling off period," during which a strike would be forbidden for 80 days, giving management and labor more time to reach a settlement.

". . . the President . . . the President . . . a President . . . the President. . . ." Throughout this decision there is no mention of "Sawyer," against whom the case was brought. Ever since President Jefferson refused to obey a writ issued by Chief Justice Marshall ordering him to testify in the Burr conspiracy case, it was understood that a federal court could not issue a writ against the President in person. Hence the writ ordering the end of the steel plants seizure was directed not to Truman but to his agent—and an unwilling agent at that—Secretary of Commerce Sawyer. In this opinion, however, the legal technicality was ignored and the responsibility placed where it belongs —on the President.

thinks bad. And the Constitution is neither silent nor equivocal about who shall make laws which the President is to execute. The first section of the first article says that "All legislative Powers herein granted shall be vested in a Congress of the United States. . . ."

Executive Invasion of Legislative Power. The President's order does not direct that a congressional policy be executed in a manner prescribed by Congress—it directs that a presidential policy be executed in a manner prescribed by the President. The preamble of the order itself, like that of many statutes, sets out reasons why the President believes certain policies should be adopted, proclaims these policies as rules of conduct to be followed, and again, like a statute, authorizes a governmental official to promulgate additional rules and regulations consistent with the policy proclaimed and needed to carry that policy into execution. The power of Congress to adopt such public policies as those proclaimed by the order is beyond question. It can authorize the taking of private property for public use. It can make laws regulating the relationships between employers and employees, prescribing rules designed to settle labor disputes, and fixing wages and working conditions in certain fields of our economy. The Constitution does not subject this lawmaking power of Congress to presidential or military supervision or control.

Previous Executive Action does not Weaken Congressional Power. It is said that other Presidents without congressional authority have taken possession of private business enterprises in order to settle labor disputes. But even if this be true, Congress has not thereby lost its exclusive constitutional authority to make laws necessary and proper to carry out the powers vested by the Constitution "in the Government of the United States, or any Department or Officer thereof."

mended an increase in steelworkers' wages and other benefits, but the companies refused to accept the recommendation unless given permission to raise the price of steel immediately. The Office of Price Stabilization opposed this request. Truman supported the decisions of the wage and price administrators and without avail attempted to persuade the steel companies and workers to negotiate. With no prospect of a wage increase in sight the United Steelworkers announced that its 600,000 members would strike on April 9. Less than two hours before the walkout was to begin Truman directed his Secretary of Commerce, Charles B. Sawyer, to take over the steel mills and run them until further notice. In a radio message to the nation Truman justified his action as a necessary defense measure in the face of "Communist aggression and hostility."

Once the seizure was announced, the steelworkers called off the strike, and the steel companies applied to the courts to forbid the government to control their property. On April 29 a district judge in Washington, D. C., issued a writ of *mandamus* (see p. 165) against Secretary Sawyer ordering him to give up the powers he had assumed. But the Circuit Court of Appeals of the District of Columbia held up this injunction until the case should be referred to the Supreme Court. On May 3 the Supreme Court agreed to take the case and on June 2 it issued a 6–3 decision con- demning the seizure. President Truman immediately obeyed the Court, and the steelworkers went out on a strike that lasted for seven months. How seriously the strike affected the defense effort is still disputed.

(Continued on p. 273)

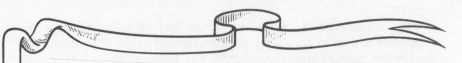

Conclusion. The Founders of this Nation entrusted the law-making power to the Congress alone in both good and bad times. It would do no good to recall the historical events, the fears of power and the hopes for freedom that lay behind their choice. Such a review would but confirm our holding that this seizure order cannot stand.

The judgment of the District Court is

Affirmed.

(Justices Frankfurter, Douglas, Jackson, Burton, and Clark delivered separate opinions concurring with the judgment of the Court.)

Mr. Chief Justice Vinson, with whom Mr. Justice Reed and Mr. Justice Minton join, dissenting. . . .

Justice Black's opinion in this case of *Youngstown Sheet and Tube Co. v. Sawyer* is one of the firmest statements limiting executive power ever issued by the Supreme Court. Not since *ex parte Milligan* (1866), which condemned President Lincoln's action in setting up military courts to try civilians suspected of disloyalty, had the Court stated so clearly that military emergencies do not justify the executive department in invading personal rights or in exerting authority that belongs to other branches of government. Black's opinion was based squarely on the principles of separation of powers (see p. 105). He stated that neither the military nor the executive powers of the President justified seizure of private property unless Congress passed a law specifically granting him that power.

Youngstown Sheet and Tube Co. v. Sawyer restored faith in the traditional restraints of constitutional government. According to Arthur Krock of the *New York Times*, "The decision was one of the most popular ever rendered by the Court because it could be explained to the people . . . that 'no man, including the President, is above the law,' and that private property rights are still sacred in the United States. . . ."

Explanatory

Notes "(Justices Frankfurter, Douglas, etc. . . .)" The effectiveness of Justice Black's opinion was weakened rather than strengthened by the separate opinions written by all five of the justices who joined him in declaring the steel industry seizure unconstitutional. Only one justice went as far as Black in saying that the President must never take over an industry without congressional authority.

"Mr. Chief Justice Vinson, . . . dissenting. . . ." Vinson's dissenting opinion cited many cases where Presidents had acted in crisis without constitutional authority, going back to Lincoln's declaration of a blockade against the Confederacy and the Emancipation Proclamation. The Chief Justice argued that the Founding Fathers "created a government subject to law but not left subject to inertia when vigor and initiative are required." He derided the six separate opinions of the majority of the Court; suggesting that the justices could not find a single argument that all could agree upon.

BROWN v. BOARD OF EDUCATION

1954

Four Cases, Same Issue. These cases come to us from the States of Kansas, South Carolina, Virginia, and Delaware. They are premised on different facts and different local conditions, but a common legal question justifies their consideration together in this consolidated opinion.

In each of the cases, minors of the Negro race, through their legal representatives, seek the aid of the courts in obtaining admission to the public schools of their community on a non-segregated basis. In each instance, they had been denied admission to schools attended by white children under laws requiring or permitting segregation according to race. This segregation was alleged to deprive the plaintiffs of the equal protection of the laws under the Fourteenth Amendment. In each of the cases other than the Delaware case, a three-judge federal district court denied relief to the plaintiffs on the so-called "separate but equal" doctrine announced by the Court in Plessy v. Ferguson. Under that doctrine equality of treatment is accorded when the races are provided substantially equal facilities, even though these facilities be separate. In the Delaware case, the Supreme Court of Delaware adhered to the doctrine, but ordered that the plaintiffs be admitted to the white schools because of their superiority to the Negro schools.

The plaintiffs contend that segregated schools are not "equal" and cannot be made "equal," and that hence they are deprived of the equal protection of the laws. Because of the obvious importance of the question presented, the Court took jurisdiction. Argument was heard in the 1952 term, and reargument was heard this Term on certain questions propounded by the Court. . . .

Separate Schools Are Unequal

On March 6, 1857, the Supreme Court, in the case of *Dred Scott v. Sanford,* ruled that it was the duty of Congress to protect slavery in all the territories of the United States and said that slaves, as "beings of an inferior race," were never intended to be citizens. On May 17, 1954, the Court, in *Brown v. Board of Education* (of Topeka, Kansas), found that to segregate Negro children in separate public schools was to deny their rights as citizens of the United States. During the century between these two momentous, controversial, and contrasting decisions, the Supreme Court pursued a rather erratic course.

An immediate consequence of the War Between the States was the passage of the Thirteenth, Fourteenth, and Fifteenth Amendments; these effectively overruled the Dred Scott decision by guaranteeing the Negroes their freedom, citizenship, and the vote (see pp. 146–149). Congress passed several laws putting these amendments into effect. In 1871 the "Ku Klux Act" imposed fines and imprisonment on those who deprived "any person or class of persons of the equal protection of the laws, or equal privileges and immunities under the laws." In 1875 the most extensive of several Civil Rights Acts forbade racial discrimination in public places such as

(Continued on p. 277)

Explanatory

Notes Four Cases, Same Issue. The specific case that gave this decision its name originally concerned Linda Ann Brown, an eight-year-old girl in Topeka, Kansas. Because Topeka schools were racially segregated, Linda was unable to attend an elementary school within easy walking distance of her home. Instead she had to cross a railroad yard and then take a bus to an all-Negro school twenty-one blocks away. In 1951 Linda's father, joined by twelve other parents, brought suit in a United States district court to forbid enforcement of a Kansas statute that allowed cities to maintain separate schools for Negro and white children. The full name of the case was *Brown et al.* (and others) *v. Board of Education of Topeka, et al.* The district court ruled against the Negro children, citing *Plessy v. Ferguson* as a precedent. Two other district courts decided the same way in similar cases in Virginia and South Carolina. In Delaware the highest court also followed *Plessy v. Ferguson,* but to support a totally different conclusion. The Delaware court ordered a county school board to admit Negro children to all-white schools because the separate schools were not equal but were distinctly inferior.

275

Application of "Separate but Equal" Principle. In the first cases in this Court construing the Fourteenth Amendment, decided shortly after its adoption, the Court interpreted it as proscribing all state-imposed discriminations against the Negro race. The doctrine of "separate but equal" did not make its appearance in this Court until 1896 in the case of Plessy v. Ferguson (U.S.) supra, involving not education but transportation. American courts have since labored with the doctrine for over half a century. In this Court, there have been six cases involving the "separate but equal" doctrine in the field of public education. . . .

Here . . . there are findings below that the Negro and white schools involved have been equalized, or are being equalized, with respect to buildings, curricula, qualifications and salaries of teachers, and other "tangible" factors. Our decision, therefore, cannot turn on merely a comparison of these tangible factors in the Negro and white schools involved in each of these cases. We must look instead to the effect of segregation itself on public education.

Importance of Education Today. In approaching this problem, we cannot turn the clock back to 1868 when the Amendment was adopted, or even to 1896 when Plessy v. Ferguson was written. We must consider public education in the light of its full development and its present place in American life throughout the Nation. Only in this way can it be determined if segregation in public schools deprives these plaintiffs of the equal protection of the laws.

Today, education is perhaps the most important function of state and local governments. Compulsory school attendance laws and the great expenditures for education both demonstrate our recognition of the importance of education to our democratic society. It is required in the performance of our most basic public responsibilities, even service in the armed forces. It is the very foundation of good citizenship. Today it is a principal instrument in awakening the child to cultural values, in preparing him for later professional training, and in helping him to adjust normally to his environment. In these days, it is doubtful that any child may reasonably be expected to succeed in life if he is denied the opportunity of an education. Such an opportunity, where the state has undertaken to provide it, is a right which must be made available to all on equal terms.

hotels and theatres, and public services such as railroads. But in the *Civil Rights Cases* of 1883 the Supreme Court ruled that such legislation was an over-extension of congressional power, that the Fourteenth Amendment did not interfere with the right of the states, through their police power, to regulate the private relations between individuals. In *Plessy v. Ferguson* (1896), the Court held that a Louisiana law decreeing separate railroad accommodations for Negroes and whites was a "reasonable" exercise of state police power. *Plessy v. Ferguson* became a binding precedent, and for many years the federal judiciary followed the so-called "separate but equal" doctrine it established—that mere segregation of public facilities for Negroes was no denial of equality. By forbidding Congress to legislate against discrimination and by supporting discriminatory state legislation, the Supreme Court reduced the effectiveness of the Fourteenth Amendment as protection for Negro equality almost to a nullity.

During the last half century the tide has turned, and the Supreme Court has exhibited an ever stronger inclination to defend Negro rights from discriminatory state legislation. In 1917 the Court declared that a Kentucky statute requiring white and colored people to live in separate sections of Louisville was a denial of "constitutional rights and privilege." In the 1930's the Court began to interpret the "separate but equal" doctrine of *Plessy v. Ferguson* in such a way as to protect Negro rights, by insisting that public facilities be in fact equal. Thus if a railroad refused Negroes the right to ride as passengers in Pullman cars, it had to provide separate Pullman service for them, even if this meant a whole car for a single person. This insistence on equal treatment was applied to education between 1938 and 1950, in four decisions that defended the right of Negroes to attend the graduate schools of state universities on terms of full equality with whites. In the opinion of the Supreme Court, separate graduate school facilities such as libraries and teachers could never be really equal, and segregation deprived the student of the opportunity "to engage in discussion and exchange views and in general to learn his profession."

In 1952 it was obvious that the Supreme Court was approaching the ultimate question: was segregation in and of itself a denial of equality? In 1952 it heard arguments in five cases all involving segregation of children in public schools. In 1953 it asked for further hearings. So it was not entirely a surprise when in 1954 Chief Justice Earl Warren, speaking for a unanimous Court, declared that to segregate Negro children in school was to refuse them the equal protection of the laws guaranteed by the Fourteenth Amendment. (Continued on p. 279)

Segregation is Inherently Unequal. We come then to the question presented: Does segregation of children in public schools solely on the basis of race, even though the physical facilities and other "tangible" factors may be equal, deprive the children of the minority group of equal educational opportunities? We believe that it does. . . . To separate them from others of similar age and qualifications solely because of their race generates a feeling of inferiority as to their status in the community that may affect their hearts and minds in a way unlikely ever to be undone. The effect of this separation on their educational opportunities was well stated by a finding in the Kansas case by a court which nevertheless felt compelled to rule against the Negro plaintiffs:

"Segregation of white and colored children in public schools has a detrimental effect upon the colored children. The impact is greater when it has the sanction of the law; for the policy of separating the races is usually interpreted as denoting the inferiority of the Negro group. A sense of inferiority affects the motivation of a child to learn. Segregation with the sanction of law, therefore, has a tendency to retard the educational and mental development of Negro children and to deprive them of some of the benefits they would receive in a racially integrated school system."

Whatever may have been the extent of psychological knowledge at the time of Plessy v. Ferguson, this finding is amply supported by modern authority.* Any language in Plessy v. Ferguson contrary to this finding is rejected.

We conclude that in the field of public education the doctrine of "separate but equal" has no place. Separate educational facilities are inherently unequal. Therefore, we hold that the plaintiffs and others similarly situated for whom the actions have been brought are, by reason of the segregation complained of, deprived of the equal protection of the laws guaranteed by the Fourteenth Amendment. . . .

* FOOTNOTE: K. B. Clark, Effect of Prejudice and Discrimination on Personality Development (Midcentury White House Conference on Children and Youth (1950); Witmer and Kotinsky, Personality in the Making (1952), c. VI; Deutscher and Chein, The Psychological Effects of Enforced Segregation: A Survey of Social Science Opinion, 26 J. Psychol. 259 (1948). . . .

There were surprising features, however, about the case of *Brown v. Board of Education*. The justices had recently disagreed violently over civil rights cases, but this decision was unanimous. Unanimity made the case infinitely more effective than if there had been even one dissenter. The influence of the decision was also strengthened by the fact that three of the justices who supported it were from the South. Another notable feature of *Brown v. Board of Education* was that it was clearly a case involving a relatively new concept of law—sociological jurisprudence. Until the twentieth century, lawyers and judges regarded the law as a closed system, based entirely on constitutions, statutes, ancient legal maxims, and the precedents of earlier cases. The task of courts was simply to declare which of these applied to a particular case. But according to the new principles of sociological jurisprudence, lawyers and judges must look at the facts of life, and the law itself must change to fit changing human needs. In *Brown v. Board of Education*, the justices heeded the testimony given before lower courts where social scientists had taken the witness stand and maintained under cross-examination that segregated schooling was psychologically harmful to children. The members of the Court also read, on their own, scholarly books and articles dealing with segregation— witness the footnote reproduced in part on the opposite page. In *Brown v. Board of Education* the Supreme Court in effect wrote a new law and based it partly on the findings of social scientists.

The desegregation decision illustrates the immense power the Supreme Court may wield, all the more because neither the President nor Congress would, if only for fear of political reprisals, have interfered so drastically with state control of education. *(Continued on p. 281)*

Explanatory Notes Footnote. This famous footnote, revealing that the justices had done their homework in the writings of modern social scientists, contained seven titles in all.

Enforcement Deferred. Because these are class actions, because of the wide applicability of this decision, and because of the great variety of local conditions, the formulation of decrees in these cases presents problems of considerable complexity. On reargument, the consideration of appropriate relief was necessarily subordinated to the primary question—the constitutionality of segregation in public education. We have now announced that such segregation is a denial of the equal protection of the laws. In order that we may have the full assistance of the parties in formulating decrees, the cases will be restored to the docket, and the parties are requested to present further argument on Questions 4 and 5 previously propounded by the Court for the reargument this Term. The Attorney General of the United States is again invited to participate. The Attorneys General of the states requiring or permitting segregation in public education will also be permitted to appear as *amici curiae* upon request to do so by September 15, 1954, and submission of briefs by October, 1954.

Brown v. Board of Education resembled the *Dred Scott Case* in that it stirred bitter sectional disagreement. In the North and West the decision was widely applauded as a giant step toward the equality preached by the Declaration of Independence and protected by the Constitution. The Voice of America trumpeted the news around the world as evidence that the United States was living up to its professed ideals. In the South *Brown v. Board of Education* was denounced as "judicial tyranny" and as a usurpation of "the most sacred right that is guaranteed our people, the right to educate our children in our own way in our own schools." Because their action was so certain to arouse antagonism and even violence, the Supreme Court took the unusual step of deferring its enforcement until it heard further discussion of how the decision could be best put into effect.

Explanatory

Notes Enforcement Deferred. "Because these are class actions, . . ." This means that the cases dealt with in this opinion did not apply merely to those involved in the suits, but to all in the same "class"— a similar situation. Thus when a school district was ordered to cease its discrimination against the children whose parents sued for relief, all other Negro children in the school district were given the same rights. This feature of *Brown v. Board of Education* was one reason for its immense influence.

". . . Questions 4 and 5 previously propounded by the Court. . . ." These are explained in the text of the next case.

". . . amici curiae. . . ." A Latin phrase meaning literally "friends of the court"; in practice it means people who suggest or state some aspect of law for the court's assistance.

BROWN v. BOARD OF EDUCATION, SECOND DECISION

1955

Racial Discrimination Unconstitutional. These cases were decided on May 17, 1954. The decision on that date, declaring the fundamental principle that racial discrimination in public education is unconstitutional, are incorporated herein for reference. All provisions of federal or of local law must yield to this principle. There remains . . . the manner in which relief is to be accorded.

Further Hearings on Enforcement. Because these cases arose under different local conditions their disposition will involve a variety of local problems, we requested further argument on the question of relief. In view of the nationwide importance of the decision, we invited the Attorney General of the United States and the Attorneys General of all states requiring or permitting racial discrimination in public education to present their views on this question. The parties, the United States, and the States of Florida, North Carolina, Arkansas, Oklahoma, Maryland, and Texas filed briefs and participated in the oral argument.

Some Compliance Already. These presentations were informative and helpful to the Court in its consideration of the complexities arising from the transition to a system of public education freed of racial discrimination. The presentations also demonstrated that substantial steps to eliminate racial discrimination in the public schools have already been taken, not only in some of the communities in which these cases arose, but in some of the states appearing as *amici curiae* as well. Substantial progress has been made in the District of Columbia and in the communities in Kansas and Delaware involved in this litigation. The defendants in the cases coming to us from South Carolina and Virginia are awaiting the decision of this Court concerning relief.

Enforcement Should be Flexible. Full implementation of these constitutional principles may require solution of varied local school problems. School authorities have the primary responsibility for elucidating, assessing, and solving these problems; courts will have to consider whether the action of school authorities constitutes good faith implementation of the governing constitutional principles. Because of their proximity to local conditions and the

"With All Deliberate Speed"

It was a peculiarity of the *Brown v. Board of Education* decision that it did not require immediate compliance. Realizing the immense difficulties that lay ahead, the Supreme Court allowed delay and asked for enlightenment about methods of enforcement. In October, 1954, therefore, the Court heard oral arguments and received written briefs from the parties and *amici curiae* mentioned in the second paragraph on the opposite page. The Court asked the lawyers who appeared before them to address themselves especially to two of five questions that it had submitted when the case was argued the previous year.

Both queries concerned methods of enforcing a decision that segregation in public schools was unconstitutional. One question asked whether: (a) the Supreme Court should immediately order that Negro children be admitted to schools of their choice, or (b) might the Court, using discretion under its equity powers, permit "gradual adjustment" to "a system not based on color distinctions." If, asked the other question, the Court should decide in favor of gradual enforcement, should it then: (a) issue detailed decrees, ordering compliance; (b) if so, on what specific terms; or should it (c) appoint a special master to hear evidence and issue decrees; or (d) send cases back to the courts whence they originated?

These questions were so arranged as to lead to the conclusion that enforcement of the desegregation decision should be gradual and that it should be the business of lower courts. The second decision of the Court in *Brown v. Board of Education* was therefore predictable. Communities were told to work toward desegregated public schools "with all deliberate speed" and lower courts were told to supervise the details.

(Continued on p. 285)

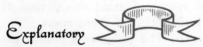

Explanatory

Notes Further Hearings on Enforcement. "Relief" here means "deliverance from hardship, burden, or grievance."

Some Compliance Already. ". . . Substantial progress has been made in the District of Columbia. . . ." On the day it delivered its opinion in *Brown v. Board of Education*, the Supreme Court in another unanimous decision, *Bolling v. Sharpe*, declared segregation in public schools in the District of Columbia to be unconstitutional. Since the District is under federal control, the Fourteenth Amendment did not apply here. Instead, segregated schooling was held to be an arbitrary deprivation of the liberty of Negro children and hence in violation of the due process clause of the Fifth Amendment.

possible need for further hearings, the courts which originally heard these cases can best perform this judicial appraisal. Accordingly, we believe it appropriate to remand the cases to these courts.

Equity. In fashioning and effectuating the decrees, the courts will be guided by equitable principles. Traditionally, equity has been characterized by a practical flexibility in shaping its remedies and by a facility for adjusting and reconciling public and private needs. These cases call for the exercise of these traditional attributes of equity power. . . . But it should go without saying that the vitality of these constitutional principles cannot be allowed to yield simply because of disagreement with them.

Extra Time may be Granted. While giving weight to these public and private considerations, the courts will require that the defendants make a prompt and reasonable start toward full compliance with our May 17, 1954, ruling. Once such a start has been made, the courts may find that additional time is necessary to carry out the ruling in an effective manner. The burden rests upon the defendants to establish that such time is necessary in the public interest and is consistent with good faith compliance at the earliest practicable date. To that end, the courts may consider problems related to administration, arising from the physical condition of the school plant, the school transportation system, personnel, revision of school districts and attendance areas into compact units to achieve a system of determining admission to the public schools on a nonracial basis, and revision of local laws and regulations which may be necessary in solving the foregoing problems. They will also consider the adequacy of any plans the defendants may propose to meet these problems and to effectuate a transition to a racially nondiscriminatory school system. During this period of transition, the courts will retain jurisdiction of these cases.

Cases Sent Back to Lower Courts. The judgments below, except that in the Delaware case, are accordingly reversed and remanded to the District Courts to take such proceedings and enter such orders and decrees consistent with this opinion as are necessary and proper to admit to public schools on a racially nondiscriminatory basis with all deliberate speed the parties to these cases. The judgment in the Delaware case—ordering the immediate admission of the plaintiffs to schools previously attended only by white children—is affirmed on the basis of the principles stated in our May 17, 1954, opinion, but the case is remanded to the Supreme Court of Delaware for such further proceedings as that court may deem necessary in light of this opinion.

The pattern of compliance with the desegregation decision has varied. In the four states that merely permitted it, and in the District of Columbia as well, segregation along racial lines has practically disappeared. In the northern "border states" (Missouri, Kentucky, West Virginia, Maryland, and Delaware), compliance with the Supreme Court's ruling has been widespread and in some districts close to complete. Massive resistance to the Court came, as was to be expected, from the states with the highest proportion of Negroes, but the degree and the form of their resistance have been various. In some states there was revival of the idea of nullification or of the right of a state to "interpose" its authority to protect its citizens. Some states actually threatened to close down the public schools in any district where a desegregation decree was issued and to subsidize private schools. One state has made it a crime to institute a desegregation suit in the state courts. There has also been violence, but fortunately it has been rare because southern leaders have set themselves firmly against it. In a "Declaration on Integration" signed by ninety-six southern Congressmen in 1956, *Brown v. Board of Education* was denounced as an "unwarranted exercise of power by the court, contrary to the Constitution . . . creating chaos and confusion in the states principally affected." The Congressmen pledged themselves "to use all lawful means to bring about a reversal of this decision . . . and to prevent the use of force in its implementation." Finally they appealed to Southerners "to scrupulously refrain from disorder and lawless acts."

Since 1956 the pace of desegregation by voluntary compliance with the principles of *Brown v. Board of Education* or by obedience to court decrees has slowed down. But progress has continued, sometimes in places that would have seemed impossible a few years ago. Atlanta, Georgia, for instance, started desegregation in 1961, and without disorder. All of which illustrates the basic fact that law must ultimately be an expression of the general will, and it can operate effectively only where the general will is willing to accept it.

Explanatory

Notes Equity. Article III, Section 2, clause 1 of the Constitution states that the power of the federal judiciary shall extend to cases "in Law and Equity." Equity is a legal concept that can be traced back to classical times. Aristotle defined it as "a better sort of justice, which corrects legal justice where the latter errs through being expressed in a universal form and not taking account of particular cases." As used here the term applies more particularly to usages developed in England in regard to cases where the common law did not operate or was held to work injustice. This concept of law allows courts considerable discretion in finding ways of enforcing their decisions so as not to work needless hardship.

Suggested Reading

1. The Declaration of Independence

* BECKER, CARL L., *The Declaration of Independence*. Knopf, 1942. A penetrating study in the history of ideas upon which Jefferson drew, as well as an illuminating analysis of the text of the Declaration.

BOYD, JULIAN, *The Declaration of Independence*. Princeton Univ. Press, 1945. An interesting study of the composition and revision of the text, and the process of adoption in the Congress.

DUMBAULD, EDWARD, *The Declaration of Independence and What It Means Today*. University of Oklahoma Press, 1950. A study of the political ideas of the Declaration and their applicability to 20th century problems and conditions.

* LATHAM, EARL (ed.), *The Declaration of Independence and the Constitution*. Heath, 1956 (rev. ed.). A useful collection of documents and papers comparing and contrasting the principles of the two documents. Part of the Amherst Series dealing with "Problems in American Civilization."

MONTROSS, LYNN, *The Reluctant Rebels: The Story of the Continental Congress, 1774–1789*. Harper and Bros., 1950. A lively account of the politics behind the Declaration of Independence, the Articles of Confederation, the Northwest Ordinance, and the Constitution.

2. The Articles of Confederation

* JENSEN, MERRILL, *The Articles of Confederation*. University of Wisconsin Press, 1948. A scholarly account of the drafting and adoption of the Articles by the Congress.

————, *The New Nation: A History of the United States during the Confederation, 1781–1789*. Knopf, 1950. A thorough, standard history of the period with careful attention to the virtues and shortcomings of the Articles. Jensen suggests that economic conditions during the Confederation period were rather more prosperous than many historians depict them.

MCLAUGHLIN, ANDREW C., *The Confederation and the Constitution, 1783–1789*. Harper and Bros., 1905. A pioneering work, well written, perceptive, and still useful.

3. The Northwest Ordinance

BARRETT, J. A., *Evolution of the Ordinance of 1787*. Putnam, 1891. A scholarly account of the way in which Congress handled the problem of the western lands between 1784 and 1787.

CRESSON, WILLIAM P., *James Monroe*. University of North Carolina Press, 1946. Monroe worked closely with Jefferson on the problem of the western lands in 1784. Later that year he made an adventuresome trip through much of the new territory. This book gives reliable accounts of both matters.

TATTER, HENRY, "State and Federal Land Policy during the Confederation Period," *Agricultural History*, IX, 176 pp., 1935. A useful study of the economic and political milieu out of which the Ordinance of 1787 emerged.

4. The Constitution of the United States

* BEARD, CHARLES A., *An Economic Interpretation of the Constitution of the United States*. Macmillan, 1913. A brilliant and highly controversial essay, arguing that the Constitution was drafted by men of wealth desirous not of establishing democracy but of protecting their property. For contrary views consult Latham, Earl (ed.), *The Declaration of Independence and the Constitution*, Heath, 1956 (rev. ed.), cited above.

BRANT, IRVING, *James Madison: Father of the Constitution*. Bobbs-Merrill, 1950. A painstaking, thoroughly documented study of Madison's work on the Constitution. This is volume three of Brant's six volume life of Madison.

BROWN, ROBERT E., *Middle-Class Democracy and the Revolution in Massachusetts, 1691–1780*. Cornell University Press, 1955. Using Massachusetts as his focal point, the author uses a great deal of primary material to prove that social and political institutions were more democratic than has been thought.

CORWIN, EDWARD S., *The Constitution and What It Means Today*. Princeton Univ. Press, 1958. A standard work, explaining the meaning of the Constitution clause by clause.

* ELKINS, STANLEY and MCCITRICK, ERIC, *The Founding Fathers, Young Men of the Revolution*. American Historical Association, 1962. This critical essay on the differing interpretations of the background of the Constitution shows how and why American historians have gone from almost blind worship of the Founding Fathers in the nineteenth century, then early in this century to a rather critical attitude, and recently to a more temperate view based on careful study of the available evidence.

KELLY, ALFRED H. and HARBISON, WINFRED A., *The American Constitution: Its Origins and Development*. Norton, 1955 (rev. ed.). A standard, thorough, and reliable textbook.

* SALBERG, W. U. (ed.), *The Federal Convention and the Formation of the Union*. Liberal Arts Press, 1958. A source book containing selections from Madison's notes on the convention, as well as the basic documents.

* VAN DOREN, CARL, *The Great Rehearsal*. Viking, 1948. A highly readable account of the making of the Constitution, written in the hope that it would provide a model for world government.

5. The Judiciary Act of 1789

STORY, JOSEPH, *Commentaries on the Constitution of the United States*. 2 vols., Little, Brown, 1891 (5th edition). The third part of this classic, first published in 1833, Justice Story (Supreme Court 1811–1845) deals with the history of American courts lying behind the Supreme Court and analyzes the role of the federal courts as established in the Constitution and the Judiciary Acts.

WARREN, CHARLES, "Judiciary Act of 1789," *Harvard Law Review*, XXXVII, 49 pp., 1923. A scholarly exposition of the nature and influence of the law.

6. John Marshall as Chief Justice

BEVERIDGE, ALBERT J., *The Life of John Marshall*. 4 vols., Houghton Mifflin, 1919. The third and fourth volumes of this standard work deal in great detail with Marshall's leadership of the Supreme Court and his controlling decisions.

CORWIN, EDWARD S., *John Marshall and the Constitution*. Yale University Press, 1936 (new edition). A scholarly essay on Marshall's constitutional decisions.

HAINES, CHARLES G., *The American Doctrine of Judicial Supremacy*. University of California Press, 1932. A study of the origins of the doctrine in the constitutional period, as well as its development in the hands of Marshall and later judges.

* SURRENCY, ERWIN C., *A John Marshall Reader*. Oceana, 1955. A useful collection of Marshall's writings, with helpful commentary.

WARREN, CHARLES, *The Supreme Court in United States History*. Little Brown, 1926. This two-volume work carries the history of the Supreme Court from its origins to 1918; it is especially useful in describing the difficulties of the Court during the Washington and Marshall administrations and the politics surrounding the Marshall decisions.

7. The Confederate Constitution

*DAVIS, JEFFERSON, *The Rise and Fall of the Confederate Government*. 2 vols., Thomas Yoseloff, 1938 (new edition). The President of the Confederacy, writing in his later years, deals authoritatively with the constitutional theory and principles of the Confederate Constitution.

OWSLEY, FRANK L., *States Rights in the Confederacy*. University of Chicago Press, 1931. A scholarly analysis of Confederate practice as compared with constitutional theory.

8. The Supreme Court and the Constitution

BLAUSTEIN, ALBERT and FERGUSON, CLARENCE, *Desegregation and the Law*. Rutgers University Press, 1957. A valuable analysis of the desegegration cases, with extensive quotations from the proceedings and decisions.

FRANK, JOHN P., *Marble Palace*. Knopf, 1958. This short book explains how the Court goes about its daily business.

FRANKFURTER, FELIX, *The Commerce Clause under Marshall, Taney, and Waite*. University of North Carolina Press, 1937. The author, now himself a Supreme Court justice, gives an incisive discussion of the problem of the "public interest" in constitutional law.

PRITCHETT, C. H., *The Roosevelt Court: A Study in Judicial Politics and Values, 1937–1947*. Macmillan, 1948. A scholarly and lively account of the Supreme Court in the New Deal era, helpful for understanding such landmark cases as those discussed in this chapter.

——————, *Civil Liberties and the Vinson Court*. University of Chicago Press, 1954. The Supreme Court in the period 1946–1953, including discussion of the steel seizure case.

SWISHER, CARL B., *The Supreme Court in Its Modern Role*. New York University Press, 1958. This work is especially valuable in explaining the pattern of Supreme Court decisions on different kinds of constitutional issues.

TRIMBLE, BRUCE R., *Chief Justice Waite, Defender of the Public Interest*. Princeton Univ. Press, 1938. A readable biography containing thoughtful analysis of the Munn case and others.

* ZIEGLER, BEN M. (ed.), *The Supreme Court and Desegregation*. Heath, 1958. An interesting collection of articles both favorable and unfavorable to the Supreme Court's handling of the segregation problem.

Appendix

At the close of both the terrible World Wars of the twentieth century, there were efforts to prevent future hostilities by the creation of international organizations. The League of Nations was created by the Treaty of Versailles in 1919. The man most responsible for founding it was President Woodrow Wilson; but he failed—partially through his errors of judgment—to persuade the Senate to ratify the Covenant of the League of Nations. This helped doom the League and can be regarded as one of the remote causes of World War II.

In April, 1945, near the close of World War II, representatives of the victorious powers met at San Francisco and wrote the Charter of the United Nations. This time the United States was not only a leader in creating the international Organization, but has also been its strongest supporter.

The United Nations is not a government, nor was it ever intended to be one. It is an international effort to establish something like a rule of law. One of the great questions, frequently asked in America since 1945, is whether membership in the United Nations limits the sovereignty of the United States. Of course the U.N. Charter is a treaty, and any treaty usually involves a voluntary limitation of a nation's freedom to act. The U.N. Charter is unusual in that it is a treaty that we have signed with most of the nations of the world for great but rather indefinite purposes, like maintaining peace and security, developing friendly relations among nations based on the principle of equal rights and self-determination of peoples, achieving international cooperation in solving economic, social, cultural and humanitarian problems, and promoting respect for human rights and fundamental freedoms.

The only body in the United Nations, however, which has the right to require action by its members is the Security Council, and under the Charter any one of the five permanent members of the Security Council (including the U.S.) may veto any proposed action. The General Assembly has only power to recommend action by member states, although such recommendations have of course strong moral influence.

In the light of the way the U.N. has developed, it is interesting to compare it with another organization whose members retained a rather large measure of independence of action—the United States under the Articles of Confederation.

There were three fatal weaknesses in the Articles of Confederation (see pp. 27–63):

1. Each of the thirteen states retained its "Sovereignty, freedom and independence," and every power not "expressly delegated" to the Confederation Congress.

2. The Confederation Congress had no power to tax, to regulate interstate or foreign commerce, or to control individual citizens of the thirteen states.

3. Each state, large and small, was represented equally in the Congress, and so Delaware with less than 60,000 inhabitants had the same influence as Virginia with more than 600,000. The large states were simply not going to be controlled by the vote of the small ones.

The same weaknesses appear in the U.N. Charter, but much enlarged:

1. The Second Article states the principles upon which the United Nations Organization is based. The very first principle is the "sovereign equality of all its members." While there are many fine-sounding phrases about what the member states ought to do, there is nowhere in the document even so much delegation of power as in the Articles of Confederation, which did indeed grant Congress exclusive power to declare war, make peace, run a postal system, deal with the Indians, and legislate for the western lands. The powers of the U.N. are less in degree and less clearly stated.

2. The U.N., like the Confederation, has no compulsory power to tax. The General Assembly assesses the Organization's expenses on the member states, but the only penalty for non-payment is that the state loses its vote in the General Assembly if its arrears amount to two years' assessments. There is a question as to whether the member states are obligated to pay assessments for peace-keeping operations, such as the maintenance by the U.N. of troops in the Gaza Strip and in the Congo. This question is now before the International Court of Justice for an advisory opinion. Several countries are substantially in default in payment of this latter type of assessments. The U.N. Organization includes an Economic and Social Council to promote prosperity and friendly relations, but it can only "investigate" and "recommend." It has no power over commerce, nor has the U.N. any more power to control individual citizens of member states than did the Confederation. Indeed, one of the principles on which it is based is, "Nothing in the present Charter shall authorize the United Nations to intervene in matters which are essentially within the domestic jurisdiction of any state. . . ."

3. In the U.N. General Assembly the equal representation of states is carried to the point of absurdity. Luxembourg with less than 350,000 inhabitants has the same vote as India with a population of over 400,-

ooo,ooo. As indicated above, the General Assembly may "discuss," "consider," and "make recommendations" which are technically not binding but actually have very strong persuasive force.

In some ways the U.N. has on paper more the appearance of a government than had the Articles of Confederation. According to the U.N. Charter the Security Council, in which the five great powers (U.S., U.K., France, China, and the U.S.S.R.) were given permanent seats, can be called into action at any time, and has the power to apply military or economic sanctions in order to preserve international peace and security. But any one of the permanent members was granted the power to veto action, and no permanent U.N. military force has yet been created. Similarly the U.N. Charter appears superior to the Articles in that it provides for a judiciary, the International Court of Justice. But the "World Court," as it is called, can act only if both parties to a dispute agree to submit their differences to it.

During the Confederation period the American union was plagued by interstate disputes over land claims that came to the verge of war (see pp. 65–67). But the Americans had fought together in the War of Independence; they spoke the same language, inherited the same tradition of English liberties, and they worshipped the same God. There were no such differences in language, custom, religious belief, and political practice as exist in the world today. As of 1962 it is impossible to see how an effective union on a world level, comparable to the union of the American states created at Philadelphia in 1787, can be achieved.

This is not to say that the U.N. is hopelessly weak. On the contrary, some of the defects of the Charter have been overcome. The General Assembly has on occasion proved to be much more than a debating society. In the "Uniting for Peace" resolution of 1950 the General Assembly provided a procedure whereby, in case of a Security Council veto, there can be called an immediate session of the General Assembly, which by a two-thirds vote, can take action to preserve the peace. Furthermore, the office of Secretary General has been greatly expanded in importance, especially during the term of office of the late Dag Hammarskjold, so that the Secretary General has some of the characteristics of a President or Prime Minister, with some freedom of action and room for personal initiative.

Furthermore, to say that the U.N. is not a government and that there is no immediate prospect that it will ever become one is neither to cast blame upon it, nor to brand it as useless. On the contrary, the U.N. performs vital services to humanity. It helps to promote prosperity and to relieve suffering. It has damped out small wars. It provides a world forum.

The most obvious good promoted by the United Nations has been accomplished through its many specialized agencies, such as the International Children's Fund (U.N.I.C.E.F.), the International Labor Organization (I.L.O.), the World Health Organization (W.H.O.), and the International Bank.

By activities as diverse as clearing swamps, preventing cholera epidemics, promoting better adoption laws, financing new industries, introducing new crops, and training administrators, the specialized agencies have made the world a better place to live in for scores of millions of people.

But the U.N. will ultimately be judged on whether or not it manages to preserve peace. The failure to bring about disarmament, especially in the field of nuclear weapons, and the continuing existence of the Cold War obscure the fact that the U.N. has had notable success in stopping bitter local wars, such as that between India and Pakistan over Kashmir, or that between the Arab States and Israel.

A great many Americans will always remember the September 1960 session of the General Assembly of the U.N. because of Khrushchev's pounding his shoe on his desk in protest over a speech by a Philippine delegate, and perhaps also because Fidel Castro harangued the assembly in a violent speech of three hours duration. More important than these unpleasant incidents, however, is the fact that the 1960 session, and other sessions too, have been attended by the leading statesmen of the member states. The 1960 session was attended not only by Khrushchev and Castro, but also by President Eisenhower, by Nehru of India, Macmillan of Great Britain, Tito of Yugoslavia, Diefenbaker of Canada, Nkrumah of Ghana, Menzies of Australia, and many others. These busy men did not come to New York to see Broadway. They came because the United Nations is the most important bridge of communication among the nations of the world.

But again, the point must be made—the United Nations is not a government, was not intended to be one, will not become one in the foreseeable future. Nor is political union the only possible road to permanent peace. There is not the remotest possibility, for instance, that the United States and Canada will ever go to war, and yet the two countries are bound together by nothing more than mutual good will and trust. War between Latin American states used to be a commonplace. Yet as of 1962 there had not been a war for over a generation. This prolonged period of peace has not been accompanied by the formation of a strong federation, but simply by better means of communication between diplomats and more willingness to discuss disputes before resorting to force. Yet it may be that at some time in the distant future the nations of the world, or perhaps only the free nations, will want to form a union. If they do, the United States Constitution may be a model because it has provided the world with its most durable and flexible combination of effective central government to keep the peace with effective local government responsive to local needs.